Of Vagabonds and Fel

CLASS : CULTURE

SERIES EDITORS
Amy Schrager Lang, Syracuse University, and Bill V. Mullen, Purdue University

Of Vagabonds and Fellow Travelers

AFRICAN DIASPORA LITERARY CULTURE
AND THE CULTURAL COLD WAR

Cedric R. Tolliver

University of Michigan Press
Ann Arbor

Published in the United States of America by
the University of Michigan Press
Manufactured in the United States of America
Printed on acid-free paper

First published October 2019

A CIP catalog record for this book is available from the British Library.

ISBN 978-0-472-07405-1 (hardcover : alk. paper)
ISBN 978-0-472-05405-3 (paper : alk. paper)
ISBN 978-0-472-12436-7 (ebook)

The University of Michigan Press gratefully acknowledges financial support
for the publication of this book from the Helen Tartar First Book Subvention Fund
of the American Comparative Literature Association.

Contents

Digital materials related to this title can be found on the Fulcrum platform
via the following citable URL https://doi.org/10.3998/mpub.9426664

Acknowledgments

Over the course of the journey that prepared me to write this book, I have accumulated more debts than I can ever hope to discharge. The origins of this project, my first book project, go way back to a time and place that seem like a lifetime ago now. As a high school student in the early 1990s in Macon, Georgia, I was introduced by friends to the Malcolm X Grassroots Movement, the Republic of New Afrika, and the Shrine of the Black Madonna bookstore in Atlanta, the beginning of my education in the black freedom struggle. This education was supplemented by a traditional, formal education at the hand of two exemplary public servants, my high school teachers, Ms. Marie Jones (English) and Mrs. Mary Whitfield (AP U.S. History). My world opened and shifted the day Ms. Jones shared with the class her recollection of being in New York when Fidel Castro made his first trip to the UN following the Cuban revolution, the trip when he left his midtown hotel to take up residency in Harlem's Hotel Theresa. That same year, with Mrs. Whitfield's help, I was able to attend the Princeton Model Congress, where I proposed a bill, summarily shot down, calling for curbs on the intelligence community to prevent COINTELPRO-type abuses on the black freedom struggle. These teachers and friends helped me both imagine and make my way out of central Georgia.

My first and pivotal stop after leaving home was at Sarah Lawrence College. Through the model and inspiration of great teachers and friends, I first began to imagine that I could make a place for myself in the academy. From Sarah Lawrence College, I want to thank my don Bella Brodzki, France Lorenstein, Chi Ogunyemi, Prema Samuels, Hélène Tissières, Komozi Woodward, and many lifelong friends, whom I don't get to see often enough but who remain in my thoughts.

After Sarah Lawrence College, I continued on to the Comparative Literature Department at the University of Pennsylvania, where I completed my doctoral work. The inspiration from amazing scholars and graduate school colleagues propelled me forward on this road. I would like to thank specifically the then chair of the Comparative Literature Department, Rita Copeland, and Joanne Dubil for their support through those years. I am immensely grateful for the support and guidance of those faculty members who served on my dissertation committee: Rita Barnard, Thadious Davis, David Kazanjian, and Lydie Moudileno. Of course, one does not make it through to the other side of grad school without the support of friends and colleagues, and I am grateful for those who made our time in Philly special: Esther Alarcon, Asma Al-Naser, Peter Gaffney, Kim Gallon, Chris Hunter, Jen Jahner, Edward Lybeer, Keith Poniewaz, Monica Popescu, Rebecca Sheehan, and Hervé Tchumkam.

As I was completing my dissertation I had the wonderful opportunity to spend a year at the Pennsylvania State University thanks to a fellowship from the Africana Research Center. My special thanks go to the center's then director, the late Lovalerie King, and the other scholars in the Comparative Literature and English Departments, who made my time in State College both productive and happy: Gabeba Baderoon, Jonathan Eburne, Caroline Eckhardt, Nergis Ertürk, Keith Gilyard, Eric Hayot, Aldon Nielsen, Shuang Shen, and Shirley Moody-Turner.

It is my great fortune over the past eight years to have had an intellectual home among excellent scholars and warm colleagues in the English Department at the University of Houston. Their example and support have inspired and encouraged me in ways impossible to quantify. I want to thank colleagues in my writing group who helped me work through multiple iterations of the various chapters and refine my thinking in these pages: Hosam Aboul-Ela, Margot Backus, and Karen Fang. In addition, I am thankful for my Americanist colleagues in the department who offered thoughtful suggestions at a critical stage when I was bringing the project to completion: Jason Berger, Sarah Ehlers, and Michael Snediker. I'd also like to thank colleagues who have offered me intellectual and institutional support at various points along the way: Ann Christensen, Maria Gonzalez, Elizabeth Gregory, Wyman Herendeen, Mat Johnson, J. Kastely, David Mazella, and Roberto Tejada. I am forever in a debt of gratitude to those of you who didn't hesitate to descend in the trenches with me when the time came. The front office staff and work study students of the English Department have provided constant support during the years I was writing this book. Thank you Carol Barr, George Barr, Fanisia Bundage, Judy Calvez, Andre Cobb, Kim Cooks, Julie Kofford, Rachel Weisz, and Kim Williams. For his willingness to read the manuscript and offer his comments, I am grateful to the inimitable historian of the African diaspora, Gerald Horne. Also, thank you to Jim Conyers and the African American Studies program for their support. I'd also like to acknowledge colleagues at other institutions, all of whom are model scholars of the African diaspora, that lent a hand of friendship and support along the way: Nicole Waligora-Davis, Ira Dworkin, Cheryl Higashida, Yogita Goyal, and Jennifer Wilks. Un grand merci à Hélène and Zawadi Tissières, it was great having you here in Texas when we first got here. Your friendship on this journey has been crucial in getting me this far.

Research for this project was made possible through the generous support of the former dean of the College of Liberal Arts and Social Science (CLASS), John Roberts, as well as from the Division of Research's New Faculty Grant and Small Grant programs.

While I was writing this project, I was able to spend a year at McGill University in Montreal, Canada as the Fulbright Research Chair in American Literature. For this incredibly enriching experience, I thank the local organizer of the program, Peter Gibian, and former chair of the English department, Allan Hepburn. I owe a special thanks to the wonderful colleagues at McGill who welcomed us and made our stay in Canada both pleasant and productive: Sandeep Banerjee, Katie Zien, Michelle Hartman, as well as the members of the Montreal African Studies Group. I am forever grateful to Monica Popescu, who has been a dear friend and colleague since our days back in Philadelphia. Thank you for being so generous with your time, support, and scholarly wisdom.

I was able to bring this project to completion with the help of a team of editors and assistants: Julia Brown, Laura Portwood-Stacer, Norman Rusin, and Rachel Weisz. Thank you all immensely for the time and energy you put into helping me improve the manuscript. Laura's keen developmental editing helped me cut through the fog of ideas floating around this manuscript.

I want to express my profound thanks to my editor at the University of Michigan Press, LeAnn Fields, for her belief in this project, support in getting it into print, and patience as I struggled to finish the book. I could not have had a better guide for my first time around the book publishing block. I'd also like to thank the editorial assistants at the University of Michigan Press, Sarah Dougherty and Anna Pohlod, for their help in the production process. I am immensely thankful to Bill Mullen and Amy Lang, the Class : Culture series editors, for their interest in including the project in their series. I could not imagine a more fitting home for this work. I'd like to especially acknowledge Bill Mullen for being a champion of my work and for helping me navigate the treacherous waters of doing scholarship on the left in the contemporary academy. Your support was invaluable. I am grateful to Pim Higginson and the anonymous reader for the press for their thoughtful comments; these were indispensable in getting the manuscript into shape.

I am glad to recognize the Research Committee of the American Comparative Literature Association for selecting my manuscript for the Helen Tartar First Book Subvention Award.

Writing this work would not have been possible without the support of family. I owe you more than I can ever hope to express. I'd like to thank my chosen family the Shaners, for all their support over the many years since we first met on a campus tour: Louann, Bob, Rob, and Jamie, my gratitude for all you've done and been to me and my family is immense. My Canadian family, the Kruidenier, Jean, and Leduc families provided love and support through the years, as we tried to manage writing books, maintaining dual tenure-track careers, and raising children. None of it would have been possible had you not been there to hold us up and keep things going. Thank you for opening your homes and hearts to us over long winter and summer vacations. Hopefully, the road we've been on so far turns toward north of the border sometime soon.

I owe everything and more to my Georgia family for their support and understanding over the years, which enabled me to pursue dreams that took me far away from home. I thank my momma and daddy, Gwendolyn and William Tolliver, my siblings, Tiffany and Joel, nephews, Tyrin, Jaden, and Bricen, as well as my grandmothers, Luvenia Tolliver and the late Lizzie Mae Redding, who shared in raising me and my siblings. I'd also like to thank my great aunt Barbara Rodgers, and my uncle and aunt, Steve and Melvinia, and my uncle Charles for their support in ways big and small over the years.

Finally, I want to thank *mes petits*, Éloïse and Marcel, for giving purpose and bringing joy to this journey. While writing this book brought me away from spending time with you more often than I would have liked, I hope one day you'll find inspiration in the lives and struggles it traces and be assured that another world is possible. The writing of this project and nearly every word in it has benefited from my ongoing conversation with a true *compagne de route* Julie-Françoise. I thank you for your willingness to travel with me on this road that has carried us to places we never could have imagined and some we definitely would not have chosen. Through it all you've made the journey not only possible but a pleasure and honor.

Portions of two chapters have been previously published and appear here in substantially revised form. Permission to reprint is gratefully acknowledged.

Sections of Chapter 1 appear in "Making Culture Capital: *Présence Afric-aine* and Diasporic Modernity in Post-World War II Paris" in *Paris, Capital of the Black Atlantic* (Johns Hopkins University Press, 2013).

Sections of Chapter 5 appear in "The Fragmented Heart of Blackness: the Congo Crisis in African American Culture and Politics" in *Neocolonial Fictions of the Global Cold War* (University of Iowa Press, 2019).

on this road that has carried us to places we never could have imagined and some we certainly would not have chosen. Through it all you've made the journey not only possible but a pleasure and honor.

Portions of two chapters have been previously published and appear here in substantially revised form. Permission to reproduce gratefully acknowledged. Sections of chapter 3 appear in *Making Cultural Capital: Presence, Place and Dignity in Black Lansing in Postwar World War II Flint*, in Don Mitchell et al., eds. (Minneapolis: University of Minnesota Press, 2012). Portions of chapter 5 appear in *The Fragmented Island of Blackness: the Congo Crisis in African American Culture and Politics*, in Nicole and *Framing of the Global Cold War* (Iowa: University of Iowa Press, 2011).

Introduction

Black (World) Reconstruction and the Cultural Cold War

In the late spring of 1948, Paul Robeson headlined a benefit concert in Dayton, Ohio, that raised a thousand dollars to support the great African American soprano Leontyne Price when she began her studies at the Juilliard School of Music that fall. Price would also receive financial assistance from Elizabeth (Wisner) Chisholm, a long-time white patron from her hometown of Laurel, Mississippi, whose family had ownership interest in the local timber industry.[1] Four years later in 1952, when Price was finishing up at Juilliard, the fortunes, and thus effectiveness, of Price's two artistic patrons would diverge starkly as a consequence of the cultural Cold War divide. By this time, Robeson had become a prime target of the anticommunist hysteria engulfing the nation, and his fundraising abilities had been significantly curtailed. In May of that year, he embarked on a two-month, fifteen-city fundraising concert tour to support several black leftist organizations with which he was affiliated. After the final accounting, the tour brought in only a few hundred dollars more than the one concert raised for Price's studies years earlier, largely a consequence of the official harassment that greeted the tour at every stop. By contrast, Chisholm was able to facilitate Price's international debut in a Parisian production of Virgil Thomson's opera *Four Saints in Three Acts*. The production's all-black cast was featured as a part of the Twentieth Century Masterpieces festival organized by the Congress of Cultural Freedom (CCF), the CIA's principal cultural front organization. Undoubtedly, Chisholm's efforts on Price's behalf were successful in large part because her brother, Frank G. Wisner, was the director of the Office of Policy Coordination (OPC), the CIA wing responsible for providing covert funding and guidance to cultural front organizations.[2]

Although Price's rise from humble roots in Mississippi to international stardom in Western art music was primarily understood in terms of the possibilities open to African Americans under American democracy, more importantly her career brings into focus the centrality of both race and culture to the Cold War struggle. Soon after her Parisian debut, Price was cast as Bess in the Everyman Opera company's revival of *Porgy and Bess*, which traveled the world for four years between 1952 and 1956. According to drama critic Charlotte Canning, "For various agencies and branches of the federal government—the President [Eisenhower][3] and his administration, the State Department, and the CIA to name only three—the production was an initial attempt at cultural diplomacy" (192). As part of this effort, *Porgy and Bess* and Price were utilized as weapons to both refute Soviet claims about the prevalence of American racial discrimination and to convince a wary public in the areas of the globe emerging out from under European colonial rule. To these regions, the United States had to assert its difference from their former rulers and to offer a more attractive alternative than the Soviet Union.

This sponsorship of African American artists and other political and cultural elites occurred in the context of the international struggle for hearts and minds, particularly for those in the decolonizing nations of Africa and Asia. Recent commentators have argued convincingly that the Soviet propaganda machine's use of American racism in the Cold War struggle gave civil rights activists the leverage they needed to wring concessions from various presidential administrations, starting with Harry S. Truman at the onset of the Cold War. One strategy the U.S. government deployed to counteract the negative attention the Soviet Union trained on the United States was to cultivate high-profile African Americans, whose very presence served to contradict Soviet claims. This strategy influenced the deployment of jazz as America's "stealth weapon" against the Soviet Union in State Department–sponsored tours, which according to Penny Von Eschen, "moved in a world of spies, espionage, and counterinsurgency" (*Satchmo* 2008, 28). Price started her professional career in the context of this strategy, and she and many others were enfolded into (often unknowingly) the covert patronage infrastructure that was being developed to support such work.

Of course, the understanding of the centrality of racism to the cultural, political, and economic development of the West did not originate with the Soviet Union, contrary to the claims of some of that era's most ardent Cold

Warriors. That critique had begun on the ships that brought the first en-slaved Africans to the New World. In the postwar period, that critique was continued by an array of African diaspora cultural producers, who located racism at the structural center of capitalist development. Those who con-tributed to this radical African diaspora intellectual tradition maintained that racism was a permanent feature of capitalist society; far from being an aberration, racism, in fact, had been essential to the production of the West's great wealth through the exploitation of black labor. Issuing from their own experiences and analysis of racialized exploitation, their racial and political consciousness developed independently of other forms of Euro-American radicalism, even if at times the two strains intersected and found common cause. The radical critiques of these cultural producers gave lie to the myths at the heart of the racial liberalism that formed the core message on the Western cultural front of the Cold War. At the same time, they also re-jected the economic reductionism of the Soviets, which failed to account for the mutual development of racism and capitalism and viewed racism as an epiphenomenon that would disappear after the dissolution of the capitalist mode of production.

African diaspora radicals of the postwar period launched a political-cultural movement that refused the ideological limits imposed by the East-West binary. The African diaspora writers and artists discussed in this book understood Western modernity as engendered through an always already racial capitalism, or that racial discrimination was central to the production of surplus value through economic exploitation. They refused to accept a version of freedom that did not account for both these phenomena in the creation of our world. In telling their story, this book reorients the cardinal points of the Cold War away from the East-West divide and shifts atten-tion to the North-South division of labor and the struggle for hearts and minds in Africa and Asia. Yet the structuring conditions of the Cold War intervened with great force on the activities and in the lives of African dias-pora cultural producers. As this book will show, the ideological and repres-sive state apparatuses of the United States mobilized to suppress radical black critique, and this suppression was integral to the nation's ascension to its status as global hegemon as European colonial powers crumbled in the face of concerted and organized anticolonial resistance. Condemned as fellow travelers of the communist regime yet resisting ideological enclosure on either side of the Cold War, African diaspora radicals became intellectual vagabonds whose very presence threatened the postwar reconstitution of the global order on the hierarchical foundation of racial capitalist production. *Of Vagabonds and Fellow Travelers* tells their story.

THE CULTURAL COLD WAR

At the end of World War II, with Europe facing widespread destruction and Japan crippled, the United States and the Soviet Union emerged as the two sole contenders for global superpower status. While the two countries had been allies in the fight against fascism during the war, within a year after the end of hostilities, cooperation had transformed into antagonism. Most histories of the period date the Cold War as beginning in the late winter, early spring of 1946. In February of that year, the diplomat George Kennan sent a long telegram from the American embassy in Moscow to the U.S. State Department outlining the reasons why peaceful coexistence with the Soviet Union was impossible. The next month, Winston Churchill followed Kennan's telegram with his "Iron Curtain" speech, given in President Truman's home state of Missouri. The following year American government leaders gave major speeches to sell the American people on the idea of a Cold War with the Soviet Union. President Truman made the initial sales pitch on March 12, 1947, in a speech to Congress requesting $400 million in assistance for Greece and Turkey. Casting in apocalyptic terms the threat posed by the spread of communism, Truman used the speech to outline his Truman Doctrine, which would ensure the world's peace in the face of this threat. This speech was followed by Secretary of State George Marshall's "Marshall Plan" speech, which he delivered during Harvard's commencement ceremonies on June 5, 1947. In between these two speeches, on May 8, 1947, Undersecretary of State Dean Acheson gave a speech to the Delta Council in Cleveland, Mississippi, ironically titled, given its location and audience, "The Requirements of Reconstruction." His speech sought to encourage Mississippi planters to support U.S. government aid to feed and clothe a war-devastated Europe.

Although less well-known than the other two speeches, Acheson's speech reflected a tacit understanding among U.S. government officials that postwar reconstruction would depend on the labor-power of black workers in both the US South and the Global South. Acknowledging that his audience appreciated and surely "derive[d] a certain satisfaction from the fact that the greatest affairs of state never get very far from the soil," Acheson argued that American reconstruction aid was destined to "free people who are seeking to preserve their independence and democratic institutions and human freedoms against totalitarian pressures" (Acheson 1947, 994). Acheson seems, however, to have thought little of the totalitarian pressures thwarting the democratic aspirations of the black workers whose labor transformed the Mississippi Delta's fertile, alluvial soil into the agricultural commodities on which the world's peace and prosperity would be rebuilt. Anders Stephanson has remarked that Acheson either "failed to see . . . or chose to ignore" that the majority black residents of this corner of Mississippi experienced as "totalitarian" "a Southern regime dedicated to apartheid and racial oppression" (Stephanson 2000, 82). Perhaps Acheson simply felt no need to state the obvious to his audience of planters, who were well aware that they extracted their economic and political standing in the world off the bent back of black labor. Explaining, or more to the point explaining away the precise nature of this standing and its consequent African American subjugation, became a major concern on the U.S. Cold War cultural front.

In *Of Vagabonds and Fellow Travelers* "the cultural front" refers specifically to those confrontations in the cultural realm between the US and the Soviet Union that paralleled and reinforced operations in the political, economic, and military spheres. In this sense, the cultural front has a military connotation as a battlefield where the two Cold War antagonists engaged one another. "Cultural front" is also used in this book as an adjective to describe those primarily cultural organizations that received covert funding and other support from the CIA while maintaining the façade of being exclusively devoted to cultural as opposed to political matters. Many readers will be familiar with the concept of "cultural front" as developed in Michael Denning's seminal *Cultural Front*. In that work, Denning deals specifically with "the sites and institutions, the networks and associations" radical artists built in and through the 1930s social movement animated by the historical bloc known as the Popular Front, which united a large cross-section of American society around "laborist social democracy, antifascism, and antilynching" (Denning 1996, 64, 4). While Denning's cultural front might be characterized as oppositional, the cultural front I describe is largely hegemonic and dedicated to the cause of anticommunism; it shares a similarity with the interwar cultural front in that it involved a cross-section of American society. This cross-section stretched from J. Edgar Hoover, the head of the nation's primary intelligence and law enforcement agency, to a vast network of civic organizations and private foundations such as the White Citizens' Councils and the Pioneer Fund, an organization that situated its funding of scientific racism research within the larger anticommunist crusade.

The largely antagonist cultural front I am describing has parallels with the cultural diplomacy or "soft power" strategy that developed in the years prior to World War II, largely within the context of President Franklin Roosevelt's Good Neighbor policy. Developed in the context of the rise of Nazi Germany, this policy sought to solidify U.S. influence, if not dominance, in the Western hemisphere and to thwart the aggressive spread of Nazi propaganda in the region, particularly among the German immigrant communities of South America. Good neighborliness was also meant to contrast with the period of political and military intervention, or the "gunboat diplomacy," that had characterized U.S. involvement in the region since at least 1898 and had purportedly come to a close with the end of the military occupation of Haiti in 1934. The Good Neighbor policy and cultural Cold War responded to two similar geopolitical realities. In both instances, there was the need to confront the aggression of a hostile nation-state, in the case of the Cold War the Soviet Union. Likewise, the success of the Good Neighbor policy and the cultural Cold War in potentially hostile regions depended on drawing a contrast to a prior method of engagement that relied heavily on force and military rule, such as European colonialism in Africa and Asia. Such an orientation relied heavily on cultural production and the language of mutual exchange, trading the might of the sword for the power of the pen.

Between the two policies, there were significant personnel overlaps as well. One of the most important figures linking the two moments of cultural diplomacy was Nelson Rockefeller. President Roosevelt recruited Rockefeller to serve as the coordinator of the Office of Commercial and Cultural Relations between the American republics, an office within the President's Council of National Defense. Later, Dwight D. Eisenhower appointed Rockefeller as a special assistant to the president, serving as the president's representative on the Operations Coordinating Board that oversaw the government's psychological warfare operations. A lesser-known figure, Mercer Cook, a professor of French and Romance Languages at Atlanta University and then Howard University, demonstrates the circulation of African diaspora intellectuals in these networks. In 1943, Cook left his post at Atlanta University to oversee the teaching of English teachers in Haiti. Part of an initiative spearheaded by Haitian president Elie Lescot, "a strong supporter of closer Haitian-U.S. relation," requiring English language instruction in

Haitian schools after the fourth grade, Cook was one of the four African Americans in the group of seven U.S. English teachers who helped launch the program "under the auspices of the Haitian government, the U.S. Department of State, the U.S. Office of Education and the Coordinator's Office" (Espinosa 1976, 310). In 1960, Cook served as the first director of the CCF's Africa Program before being appointed ambassador to Niger by President John F. Kennedy. The important point here is that such overlaps signal the importance of U.S. rule in the hemisphere serving as a model for later global dominance.

At the outset of the Cold War, the Soviet Union possessed a distinct advantage on the cultural front; they had benefited from several years of offensive operations without any sustained or effective counteroffensive from the West. George Kennan addressed this U.S. weakness in his Policy Planning Staff memo of 1948, which sought to warn government officials to the necessity "of creating a new government body devoted exclusively to covert operations" that would forcefully counter the Soviet offensive in the realm of political warfare (Wilford 2008, 26). As part of this offensive, the Soviet Union organized two major international peace conferences in the spring of 1949. A March conference at the Waldorf-Astoria in New York attracted high-profile American intellectuals like Albert Einstein and Lillian Hellman, while the roster of attendees at the April conference in Paris included, among others, Pablo Picasso and Frédéric Joliot-Curie. The prominent African American cultural icons W.E.B. Du Bois and Paul Robeson also attended the Paris conference; Robeson gave the impromptu speech there that was mischaracterized by the U.S. media and used to justify mobilizing the state's repressive forces against him. These conferences prompted a U.S. response that included a sizeable counterdemonstration in New York and a disappointingly attended International Day of Resistance to Dictatorship and War in Paris (Berghahn 2001, 129). Following the disappointment of the Parisian event, Kennan and the State Department and their CIA counterparts redoubled their efforts to counter apparent Soviet success on the continent and among European intellectuals.

These efforts set the agenda for a range of student, labor, and cultural organizations that received major financial backing from shell foundations set up by the CIA to covertly fund cultural front organizations. The CIA's principal front organization, the CCF, was instituted following the Congress of Cultural Freedom, the aim of which was to win Western intellectuals over to the cause of anticommunism. The congress was held in

June 1950 in Berlin, the front-line city of the Cold War. Among the mainly white and European intellectuals invited to present at the conference were two African Americans, the conservative columnist George Schuyler and Max Yergan, a former leftist and collaborator of both Robeson and Du Bois in the Council of African Affairs. Schuyler's and Yergan's presence at the conference signaled the evident concern with matters of race and the need to counter Soviet and Communist Party propaganda. Speaking on the subject "Negroes and Democracy in the U.S.," Yergan assured the assembled intellectuals with "quasi-legalistic" arguments that African Americans were making great strides in their quest to "be a part of the American nation" (Anthony 2006, 237). Reinforcing Yergan's message, Schuyler "circulated a report to delegates, complete with statistics, demonstrating that the situation of blacks in America never stopped improving . . . thanks to the capitalist system's constant ability to adapt to change" (Saunders 1999, 78). To the annoyance of conference organizers like Sidney Hook, French intellectuals like Jean-Paul Sartre and Maurice Merleau-Ponty pointed to the prevalence of racism in the United States as the reason behind their refusal to support the American-led, liberal anticommunist cause exemplified in the Berlin conference. If Yergan and Schuyler proved unable to make a convincing case about the ameliorating conditions of African Americans, their participation in the Berlin conference did lay the groundwork for the American Society of African Culture (AMSAC), the organization that served as both the CIA's vehicle to influence African Americans' domestic cultural activities and to incorporate African Americans into ideological and intelligence operations focused on the African continent. The origins of AMSAC, however, are to be found in the African American delegation to the First Congress of Negro Writers and Artists that francophone intellectuals associated with the journal *Présence Africaine* organized in Paris in September 1956, discussed in chapter 1.

THE U.S. COLD WAR STATE AND RACIAL LIBERALISM

From the very beginning, U.S. Cold War policy, specifically the policy of containment, was conceived in racial terms. In this regard, it is worth considering George Kennan's "The Sources of Soviet Conduct," which he published anonymously in the journal *Foreign Affairs* in July 1947. In this article, Kennan undertakes what he describes as the difficult task of a "psychological analysis," which aims to "trace the interaction" and "relative role of" ideology and circumstance in determining "official Soviet conduct" (Kennan 1947, 566). This conduct, in Kennan's analysis, turns on the "skepticism" Stalin and his followers supposedly carried with them from the "Russian-Asiatic world out of which they emerged." It is this skepticism that accounts for their utter inability to envision "the possibilities of permanent and peaceful coexistence of rival [political] forces" (568). By linking this "skepticism" to the "Russian-Asiatic world," Kennan frames containment as a strategy to confront a racialized other that shares neither a common worldview nor traditions. Kennan concludes this article with the suggestion that effective containment of this other depended on the United States' creating "among the peoples of the world generally the impression of a country which knows what it wants, [and] which is coping successfully with the problems of its internal life" (581). Although Kennan's reference is oblique, persistent and pervasive racial discrimination against African Americans was clearly the "internal" problem being closely scrutinized by the peoples of the world, particularly those large sections of the globe struggling against European colonialism. Kennan's observation on this matter reflected the policy rationale for enfolding domestic racial reform efforts within U.S. foreign policy objectives. Indeed, the legal historian Mary L. Dudziak argues that as "American foreign policy [sought] to promote democracy and to 'contain' communism," it was hindered by "the international focus on US racial problems . . . that [tarnished] the image of American democracy" (Dudziak 2000, 12). Faced with the intense scrutiny of decolonizing nations in Africa and Asia and the relentless pressure of the Soviet Union's anti-American propaganda, the United States realized that it was increasingly important to appear to be successfully managing race relations.

Within the past twenty years, the link between civil rights and the Cold War has been thoughtfully examined in groundbreaking historical work, such as Mary Dudziak's *Cold War Civil Rights*. A theoretical foundation for much of this work was legal scholar Derrick Bell's theory of interest-convergence.[4] In his seminal 1980 article "*Brown v. Board of Education* and the Interest-Convergence Dilemma," Bell theorized the connection between racial equality advances for African Americans and the self-interest of elite whites. As a consequence, he argued, achieving "racial justice—or its appearance" was only possible at those moments when it was "counted among the interests deemed important by the courts and by society's policymakers" (Bell 1980, 523). For Bell, the Supreme Court's landmark decision in *Brown v. Board of Education* was a case in point of such interest-convergence. Law-yers for both the NAACP and the federal government had argued that a decision stripping segregation of its constitutional authority would "provide immediate credibility to America's struggle with Communist countries to win the hearts and minds of emerging third world peoples" (524). The ap-parent victory in the *Brown* decision further encouraged establishment civil rights organizations to develop initiatives consistent with the government's anticommunist policies and to frame African American civil rights as part of the larger anticommunist struggle.

The crafting of civil rights movement strategy and policy to meet the U.S. government's needs in its propaganda battle with the Soviet Union was not without consequences. One such consequence was establishing "narrow boundaries [around] Cold War-era civil rights politics [that] kept discus-sions of broad-based social change, or a linking of race and class, off the agenda" (Dudziak 2000, 13). Although the Cold War exercised a determi-nant power over the shape of these boundaries, it should not obscure from view the material interests of those who benefited from these arrangements on both sides of the color line. In his critique of this overdetermining nar-rative about the Cold War, Preston Smith argues that black elites pursued strategies and policy, in this specific case postwar Chicago housing policy, that preserved and furthered their class interests (Smith 2012, xvi–xvii). Scaling Smith's insights to the level of Cold War policy brings into focus the benefits African American elites accrued, material and otherwise, from their willingness to dull the sting of Soviet criticism of domestic race relations and to legitimize militarization and global anticommunism as U.S. leader-ship of the free world.

As the dominant paradigm for addressing racial discrimination in this moment, racial liberalism provided ideological coherence to this conver-gence of interests between African Americans fighting for civil rights and the U.S. Cold War state. Underpinning the successful strategy in the *Brown* case, racial liberalism, according to legal scholar Lani Guinier, was developed to secure both legal victories in the courts and the sympathy of middle-class whites by insisting on "the damaging effects of segregation on black person-ality" (Guinier 2004, 95). Racial liberalism grew out of Gunnar Myrdal's *An American Dilemma* (1944), which argued that "discrimination stood in pro-found conflict with the most cherished ideals of the American polity" and that "the most effective way to solve [this] dilemma was to expose the moral gap between America's liberal precepts and racial practices and thereby in-spire the nation to take corrective action" (Horton 2005, 121, 125). Myrdal's framework placed the power to change racial conditions in the hands of middle-class and elite whites, acting out of a moral obligation to limit the psychological damage done to talented individuals like Edith Sampson and Ralph Bunche. Framing the fight against racial discrimination as a moral imperative effectively foreclosed the possibility of discussing the structural relationship between racialized economic exploitation and economic prosperity in the United States.

While racial liberalism fostered interest-convergences that allowed for juridical and legislative successes, it also occasioned a series of interest-divergences whose impact endures. Guinier argues that racial liberalism "intensified divergences between northern [white] elites and southern whites, . . . ignored the interest divergences between poor and middle-class blacks, and exacerbated the interest divergences between poor and working-class whites and blacks" (Guinier 2004, 102). *Of Vagabonds and Fellow Travelers* is most concerned with the consequences of this set of divergences in the realm of ideas. In the period from the Great Depression up to the Cold War, black radicalism and its emphasis on the primacy of the black working-class to the theory and realization of justice was "entangled" with a range of civil rights, left/labor, and anticolonial movements, imbuing any given political moment with a range of "different potential democratic futures" (Dawson 2013, 68). The most pernicious effect of interest-divergence, or what the political scientist Michael Dawson terms the "sundering" and eventual isolation of black radicalism,[5] was to "collapse these futures, as political cooperation between multiple movements ended and democratic futures faded from the imagination and were assigned to the realm of the 'impossible'" (69). By focusing on the Cold War and its operations within the realm of the ideas and the imagination, my book takes seriously the centrality of culture and ideology in reproducing and preserving the present order into the future. It both puts class struggle within culture and culture in the class struggle. *Of Vagabonds and Fellow Travelers* goes beyond simply recovering those ideas and voices silenced in the process of being rendered impossible and illuminates the function of that silencing in the production and maintenance of a racial capitalist order.

AFRICAN DIASPORA LITERARY CULTURE

Departing from racial liberalism's focus on the damaged black personality, African diaspora literary radicals trained their focus on the centrality of racial domination in the reproduction of class society. Such a focus threatened the established order, and it provoked a determined reaction from the defenders of that order. That reaction was realized in "the isolation of African-American radicals like Du Bois and Robeson, who denounced American racism as fundamental to American capitalism and demanded far-reaching changes in the country's polity and economy." This, Kenneth Janken argues, was part of a strategy to contain "potential fallout from such a politically expedient move" as "the Supreme Court's *Brown* school desegregation decision of 1954" (Janken 1998, 1090). The potential for fallout was particularly high given that just ten days after the Court's decision "Mississippi senator James Eastland stood before the Senate and accused the Court of pandering to Communism and its allies when it handed down the 'Black Monday' *Brown* decision" (Woods 2003, 54). Given congressional intransigence and the massive white resistance mobilized to defend the racist social order, establishment civil rights organizations were compelled to adopt strategies and policies that might garner liberal support. These pressures pushed organizations to take positions that ostensibly represented African American interests, but which actually served the ideological and material interests of a privileged few.

Developing an ideology that cast the narrow and material interests of the few as those of the many was a central problem of U.S. Cold War strategy both at home and abroad. At home, this strategy meant conflating the interests of the elite with those of the nation, while abroad the strategy involved aligning the interests of independent African and Asian countries with those of the United States. Even before World War II drew to a close, W.E.B. Du Bois set about exposing the gears of these ideological machinations. One of his first efforts was an article published in *Phylon* in late 1943. In this article, titled "Reconstruction, Seventy-five Years After," Du Bois drew a parallel between what the United States faced after the Civil War and what the world would encounter at the close of World War II. In the years immediately following the Civil War, the United States endeavored to establish the conditions for the full integration of formerly enslaved black workers into American democracy. Du Bois took this regional example and extrapolated it to the global level, suggesting that "no matter who wins this war, it is going to end with the question of the equal humanity of black, brown, yellow and white people, thrust firmly to the front." Under no illusions that the world's darker peoples would accept continuing to live under colonial rule (or segregation), Du Bois forcefully articulated the divergent paths postwar reconstruction might take: it would either be "a world where its people in mutual helpfulness and mutual respect can live and work" or "a world in the future as in the past, where white Europe and white America must rule 'niggers'" (212). The ideological problem confronting the United States as it ascended to dominance over the global order was to make the latter appear as the former.

Informed by his path-breaking analysis of the cost and consequences of the reversal of black Reconstruction in the United States, Du Bois launched himself into developing the insights from this work and using them as a frame for understanding the situation that would confront the world following the end of military hostilities in World War II. He fully fleshed out those insights in his *Color and Democracy: Colonies and Peace* (1945),[6] whose genesis can be traced to a series of lectures he gave during a visit to Haiti in the early fall of 1944. Du Bois decided to visit Haiti largely at the urging of Mercer Cook, a former colleague at Atlanta University who left his position there to oversee the training of English teachers in Haiti as part of a Good Neighbor policy initiative. During his visit to Haiti, Du Bois gave three lectures: "The Colonial Groups in the Postwar World"; "Democracy and Peace";[7] and "The Meaning of Education."[8] These lectures anticipated the critiques of U.S. dominance of the postwar world order, which deviated only so slightly from the pattern established by the European colonial powers, that *Color and Democracy* develops. They also argue for the critical importance of culture in reshaping the world according to a different, more democratic and peaceful pattern.

During World War II, it had been conceivable for Du Bois to seek U.S. government support for his travel to Haiti. With the onset of the Cold War, however, such support became unthinkable as Du Bois settled into his role as one of the government's fiercest critics. Indeed, Du Bois led the charge in pointing out the Truman administration's hypocrisy in having Acheson solicit the aid of Delta planters to preserve "democratic institutions and human freedom." If indeed, as Thomas Borstelmann suggests, "few democrats missed the irony" of Acheson's appeal to this particular audience, it is not insignificant that Du Bois is the only "democrat" he names (Borstelmann 2004, 70 note 115). In March 1947, when President Truman implored Congress for $400 million in aid for Greece and Turkey, Du Bois offered "scathing indictments" of the plan in the pages of the *Chicago Defender* and elsewhere, wondering how was it possible for the United States to "export democracy to Greece and not practice it in Mississippi?" (quoted in J. Rosenberg 2006,

177). The early years of the Cold War transformed Du Bois from democrat into communist foreign agent, in no small part because of his insistence on raising such questions. This transformation began with his ouster from the NAACP in 1948, followed by his arrest in 1951 on charges of being a foreign agent, and concluded with the revoking of his passport in 1952. Thus, Du Bois became the symbol of the Un-American.[9]

FELLOW TRAVELERS

In their fight against domestic oppression and imperialism, the African diaspora writers and intellectuals studied in *Of Vagabonds and Fellow Travelers* built alliances with the Euro-American left, and in many cases with the various national communist parties. Building on relationships forged in the interwar period but which began to fray in the lead-up to World War II, African diaspora writers maintained a complicated relationship with the predominantly white national communist parties. These complications arose particularly in light of the parties' shifting positions on race that were taken to support the foreign policy of the Soviet Union. For example, few in the African diaspora could stomach the parties' neutrality on Hitler that resulted from the Stalin-Hitler Pact, but when the Soviet Union joined the Allied fight against Germany, they resented even more the position adopted by these parties that protesting racial discrimination undermined the war effort. Yet even in the case of high-profile defections, such as that of Richard Wright, for example, these intellectuals continued to find value in Marxist analysis and its explanation of the determining forces of capitalist society. As a way to signal both their continued embrace of most elements of Marxist analysis and their distance from the institutions and sectarian positions of the communist left, I refer to the objects of my study as fellow travelers. The use of the term "fellow-traveler" is usually traced back to Leon Trotsky, who used it in *Literature and Revolution* to describe those writers and intellectuals who had an ambivalent relationship to the Bolshevik Revolution. This ambivalence manifested in their agreement with the tenets of socialism and their failure to embrace completely the program of the Communist Party. Trotsky summarized their art as "more or less organically connected with the Revolution," while not being exactly "of the Revolution" (Trostky 1960, 57). It didn't take long for the term to be used pejoratively to signal a lack of commitment to the Revolution.

The term "fellow traveler" had a particularly resonance in the United States, because in the immediate postwar period advocating for racial equality was associated with communism. Indeed, when President Truman established the loyalty boards to weed out communists in the government, interrogators sought to determine employees' position on racial equality as an indicator of their likelihood of being a communist. This widespread association meant that nearly all African Americans could be painted with the broad brush of fellow traveling, since few accepted their inferiority to white Americans. The association of racial equality with communist ideals set the stage for the racial liberals' long campaign of disassociation that made for strange bedfellows when they joined forces with arch-segregationists in the repression of African Americans on the left.

Yet despite the array of forces deployed in the effort to decouple racial equality from its association with communism during the early Cold War years, some African diaspora intellectuals did not completely eschew their affiliations with the communist left. To be sure, this affiliation was often fraught, particularly as they confronted Marxist orthodoxy that in practice gave precedence to class analysis and to the Euro-American working class as the revolutionary vanguard. Indeed, both within and without Communist Parties, African diaspora intellectuals began to offer up analysis that sought to show how class was articulated with race, as well as gender, to produce the exploitation that provides the foundation for the capitalist system. In this regard, one thinks of Claudia Jones's triple oppression thesis, which she first articulated in the context of a Communist Party debate about racial chauvinism in the late 1940s. *Of Vagabonds and Fellow Travelers* highlights this particular history of moving beyond orthodox Marxism through a reading of Aimé Césaire's *Une Lettre à Maurice Thorez*, which forcefully asserted that the struggles of colonial people and people of color were no mere "fragment" (Césaire 1956, 147) of metropolitan (European) workers' struggle against capitalism. While these pronouncements often signaled the distance taken from the communist orthodoxy, it did not preclude African diaspora intellectuals from traveling alongside their communist comrades when matters of black liberation were at stake. A telling example of this flexibility is the Martin Luther King, Jr.'s and the Southern Christian Leadership Conference's (SCLC) reluctance to give in to governmental pressure to remove known black communist Jack O'Dell from his position supporting fundraising and voter registration in the organization. The depth of their conviction is evident when one considers that at this moment the mere charge of fellow traveler or communist sympathizer often resulted in personal and professional ruin. The recuperation of the term "fellow traveler" serves to acknowledge African diaspora intellectuals' commitment to independence in a political and cultural climate that cast suspicion on all but absolute fealty.

VAGABONDS

Addressing racial discrimination as unrelated to economic exploitation came to operate as a kind of common sense during the Cold War. *Of Vagabonds and Fellow Travelers* recovers both those voices silenced in this process and their alternative ways of conceptualizing the problem of race in the constitution of Western society. The cultural Cold War ensured that alternative voices were marginalized and that those presenting alternatives suffered the consequences of being labeled subversive. Not entirely a negative operation devoted primarily to repression, the cultural Cold War built mechanisms for promoting those voices that did not pose a fundamental challenge to the reigning relations of production. In telling this particular story, *Of Vagabonds and Fellow Travelers* reorients the cardinal points of the Cold War away from the East-West divide and shifts attention toward the North-South division of labor and the struggle for hearts and minds in Africa and Asia. Importantly, *Of Vagabonds and Fellow Travelers* restores culture to a primary site of struggle, refusing the capitalist society imperative, intensified during the Cold War, of according culture an autonomous function removed from the materiality of social reproduction.

The necessity of attending to this materiality is the reason for this book's concern with those identified in the title as vagabonds. In the section of *Capital*, volume I, on "So-Called Primitive Accumulation," Marx reveals the point of departure of the capitalist mode of production, far from the idyllic genesis story represented in political economy, to be a story "written in the annals of mankind in letters of blood and fire" (Marx 1990, 875). In sixteenth-century England, this history "dragged [people] from their accustomed mode of life" and turned them "in massive quantities into beggars, robbers, and vagabonds," those "who could not immediately adapt themselves to the discipline of their condition" (896). It would be a mistake, however, to consign this process to the prehistory of capitalism, left behind once the capitalist mode of production has been established. The violence associated with the process undergoes a qualitative change and is integrated into the relations of production and constantly reproduced. According to Jason Read, "capitalist accumulation is . . . nothing other than a continuation of the modification of violence begun with 'bloody legislation' and the enclosure acts" (Read 2003, 29). This violence extends to all levels of capitalist society, including in the realm of the "superstructure" or the institutions of the state and the social consciousness of a given society, which certain forms of Marxist theory characterize as being dependent on society's economic "base."

Building on Marx's insights regarding the continuity and extension of this violence throughout capitalist society, I argue that this cadre of African diaspora intellectuals were not just communist fellow travelers but trod the road of radicalism as vagabonds who refused to adopt the discipline the United States and the Soviet Union sought to impose as the dominant Cold War superpowers. By refusing to operate within the ideological enclosures erected by these superpowers, they were as disruptive and threatening as those masterless men whom Marx describes as roaming the English countryside in the sixteenth century. As critical intellectuals, they challenged the reconstitution of the postwar global order according to the hierarchies of racial capitalist production. *Of Vagabonds and Fellow Travelers* reads the repression associated with the Cold War—blacklisting, red baiting, congressional subpoenas, passport revocations, and deportations—as fundamentally extensions of the violence deployed to discipline labor into adapting to the needs of capitalist accumulation.

Cold War repression followed a logic not unlike the legislation against vagabondage enacted at the end of the fifteenth and throughout the sixteenth centuries in western Europe. This legislation, according to Marx, "whipped, branded, and tortured [the agricultural folk] into accepting the discipline necessary for the system of wage-labour" (Marx 1990, 899). Functioning as the political complement to the enclosures that separated largely agricultural peoples from their means of subsistence, these laws created the necessary conditions for the emergence of the capitalist mode of production. Like the enclosures, Cold War anticommunism restricted the terrain of legitimate social action and knowledge. These restrictions imposed discipline not only at the point of production, but also in the social reproduction of workers, producing those subjectivities necessary for the mode of production. Thus, in the Soviet Union's spheres of influence, and reaching into the national Communist Parties, a discipline reigned that vigorously attacked any perceived deviations from Stalin's law of dialectical materialism. Although not nearly as dire in spaces under United States control, spectacular means were nevertheless employed to intimidate and silence intellectuals, artists, and activists who dared deviate from the liberal capitalist script. Lest all this be taken for hyperbole, the historian Martha Biondi reminds us that "Along with labor leaders, community activists, and politicians, Black artists, actors, poets, and painters were pressured during the 1950s to move away from radical affiliations, discourse, and worldviews. This pressure was not abstract; it was enacted in blacklisting, death threats, and congressional sub-poenas" (Biondi 2003, 175). In their refusal to adapt to Cold War discipline, the writers and intellectuals studied here became vagabonds, forced into a precarious existence subject to being imprisoned, deported or forced into exile, or denied the ability to earn a living or to travel.

Thinking and writing beyond the prescribed limits of this moment's ideological enclosures left African diaspora writers and intellectuals were vulnerable to the coercive power of the repressive and ideological state apparatuses, like the FBI and the CIA and its host of cultural front organizations. These organizations worked on multiple fronts to assure that the interests of Cold Warriors and African diaspora elites converged around the effort to rebut Soviet claims about U.S. racism. The FBI and CIA mobilized their repressive functions to ensure that those who failed to distance themselves from communist-affiliated organizations paid the price in surveillance, blacklisting, harassment, imprisonment, and deportation, among other consequences. As far as ideological operations are concerned, the CIA's vast network of front organizations directly, if covertly, supported work at both the individual and institutional level that could support the goal of anticommunism by offering a picture of American race relations that was at odds with Soviet depictions. This system of patronage assured that the U.S. government's position, or at the very least views that did not contradict that position, circulated in major publications and was represented at all the major conferences of the independence area. Through this combination of repressive and ideological operations, the U.S. government and African diaspora elites found common cause and assured that the dominant conversation was limited to expanding opportunities within the existing order. This alliance worked to make it unthinkable and beyond the limits of permissible discourse to insist that the foundations of that order rested on economic inequality and racial injustice.

Of Vagabonds and Fellow Travelers departs from the premise that a global, or at the very least not simply domestic, frame of reference is critical for understanding the developments in African diaspora literary culture in the

post–World War II period. Research for this project started from dissatis-
faction with criticism that dismissed as irrelevant, because inauthentic, the
literary production of African American writers once they located to spaces
beyond the United States. I simply wondered how the experience that the
writers themselves considered essential could be rendered so insignificant.
Pursuing this question revealed a deep web of engagement and intersection
linked to the Cold War emergence of the United States as a global superpower. What at the outset appeared to me as simply writers like Richard
Wright and James Baldwin escaping the indignities of American racism in
the smoke-filled cafés of Paris proved to be also embedded in the history of
global anticommunism and its intersection with the process of decolonization. Traces of theses cross-currents run through nearly every chapter of this
book to lesser or greater degrees.

The history traced in *Of Vagabonds and Fellow Travelers* covers the early Cold War period from the immediate postwar moment to the close of
the independence era in Africa, a time period that spans roughly the years
from 1947 to 1961. This period begins with the simultaneous selling of the
American people on the idea of a Cold War by the Truman administration
and the founding of the *Présence Africaine* journal in Paris by francophone
intellectuals (and the not unrelated declaration of independence in India).
Both these events marked the beginning of processes that in a certain sense
dramatically reordered the globe, but also in another sense failed to produce
a truly definitive break with the old order. My study closes around 1961 because it marks the closure of a period of optimism about the possibilities of
remaking the postwar global order that came with achieving independence
in much of Africa and the first inklings of a neocolonial future in the events
surrounding the untimely death of the Congo's Patrice Lumumba (along
with the unsettling circumstances of both Richard Wright's and Frantz
Fanon's deaths). This time period and the events and texts studied in this
book all demonstrate that cultural production was a dramatic, if often overlooked, site of struggle during the Cold War. Far from trivial, the matter of
winning hearts and minds was a crucial element to success on all the other
fronts on which this battle was fought.

Of Vagabonds and Fellow Travelers begins its critique of the cultural Cold
War and its conceptualization of the problem of reconstructing the postwar
global order with a consideration in chapter 1 of the First Congress of Black
Writers and Artists. This conference, organized by *Présence Africaine* in Paris in 1956, was billed as a "cultural" Bandung, which guaranteed that despite

the conveners' stated goal a strict division between politics and culture did not hold. Both the 1956 Parisian conference and the subsequent conference held in Rome in 1959 were extensions of the anticolonial aspirations that drove francophone intellectuals to found the *Présence Africaine* journal in 1947 in Paris. Their anticolonial struggles were drawn into the anticommunist orbit of two CIA-sponsored organizations, the American Society of African Culture (AMSAC), an African American cultural front organization that sent delegations to these conferences, and the Congress of Cultural Freedom (CCF), also headquartered in Paris, which sponsored conferences and journals of its own.

In chapter 2, I consider two mid-century Caribbean writers, George Lamming and Jacques Stephen Alexis, who both attended the First Congress of Black Writers and Artists. My reading of Lamming's *In the Castle of My Skin* and Alexis's *General Sun, My Brother* anchors these novels in the process through which "the Caribbean [became] an American sea," as C. L. R. James famously asserted. The discussion begins in the early twentieth century with the U.S.-led construction of the Panama Canal using Caribbean migrant workers—a significant percentage hailing from Lamming's native Barbados—who labored under Jim Crow conditions; it ends with the U.S. occupation of Trinidad during World War II. The chapter covers the expansion of U.S. sugar interests in the region and the nearly twenty-year occupation of Alexis's Haiti by the U.S. Marines. My analysis focuses on these novels' representation of the costs exacted on Caribbean societies by U.S. imperialism in the form of military occupation, regional labor migration, and land dispossession. While normally considered in their regional contexts, I read these novels as a warning to African and Asian countries of what U.S. global dominance would entail.

Chapter 3 takes up the chilling effect on African American artistic and intellectual circles of the repression of leftist artists during the height of anticommunist hysteria in the United States. Langston Hughes, for example, went to great lengths to publicly distance himself from his past association with communists. His writing for the black press, however, criticized the racist underpinnings of the Red Scare and drew the connections between domestic issues and foreign events for his readers. Alice Childress, who began her career in the artist circles of New York's black left, clearly appreciated the radical substance of Hughes's work for the black press. In this chapter, I analyze Hughes's work for the *Chicago Defender*, both his Simple stories and his regular column, alongside the play Childress developed based on Hughes's Simple character and her "A Conversation from Life" column, which she wrote for the black leftist newspaper *Freedom*. In these writings, Hughes and Childress created black working-class characters that situated a sophisticated critique of the Cold War in the bars and tenements of black urban America.

Perhaps the most famous black artist in the world at the time, Paul Robeson also embodies the figure of the intellectual vagabond disrupting and threatening Cold War racial liberalism. His ordeal is the subject of chapter 4. Like Du Bois, Robeson's passport was also revoked and he was prevented from traveling outside the United States; the State Department had deemed his criticism of U.S. foreign policy, militant antiracist activism, and unapologetic association with communists contrary to U.S. interests. This chapter considers the Cold War blacklisting of Robeson through a reading of *Here I Stand*, the autobiography/manifesto he wrote and published with the help of a longtime friend and collaborator, the leftist African American writer Lloyd Brown. My reading argues that Robeson's experience was partially the result of the convergence of interests of white and black liberals. Liberal anticommunists of both races benefited from detaching racism from the U.S. political economy and promoting racial discrimination as a moral issue on which American society was making visible progress. The consequences for the African American working class, however, were nothing less than tragic.

Chapter 5, the book's final chapter, concludes with an analysis of the reverberations throughout the African diaspora of Patrice Lumumba's assassination, and it makes the case for thinking about the global implications of African diaspora literary culture. In this chapter, I consider Aimé Césaire's *Une Saison à Congo* and the demonstrations at the United Nations against Lumumba's assassination. Such luminaries as LeRoi Jones and Maya Angelou, among others, participated in the demonstrations, while James Baldwin and Lorraine Hansberry used the reaction to the demonstrations to offer a critique of the ascendancy of racial liberalism. This chapter ends with a call for criticism attentive to the ways that African diaspora literary culture is implicated within and offers criticism of a racial capitalist order whose domestic and imperial manifestations are necessarily entangled.

CHAPTER I

Reorienting the Cardinal Points

Présence Africaine and the Centripetal Pull of the Cultural Cold War

Emerging out of the ashes of World War II, the United States set in motion its plans to achieve global hegemon status with the allocation by Congress of $284 million in interim aid for France in 1947, months before the Marshall Plan was approved.[1] This aid was meant to help France feed its population and rebuild its economy, measures crucial to checking the spread of communist influence, Moscow being the unique challenger to Washington's claim to superiority on the world stage. A diminished power, Paris clung desperately to its status as both world cultural capital and imperial capital of a far-flung colonial empire. As the historian Robert Gildea notes, "possession of the Empire served as the basis of the French claim to great power status, vis-à-vis Great Britain, the rival colonial power, and the United States, the dominant superpower" (Gildea 2002, 19). African diaspora writers and intellectuals gravitated to Paris in the years immediately following the war partly as a consequence of both empire and the city's position as the cultural capital of the world. In turn, the city proved to be a crucible where anticolonial writers and intellectuals worked on multiple fronts to bring about the demise of Paris as an imperial capital. They produced literature, founded a literary journal, and organized cultural conferences, establishing a cultural front in the struggle to end Western imperialism. Through this work these writers and intellectuals rewrote the era's grand narratives, challenging the binary logic of the Cold War by affirming the foundation of modernity in African diaspora labor.

Intellectual life for African diaspora writers in Paris, if not always encouraged, was at least tolerated to a degree that contrasted sharply with the suspicion, commercialism, and political domination that asphyxiated writers in the different parts of the African diaspora. Many came under increased pressure to choose sides in the Cold War as resources for creative and intellectual development became increasingly concentrated in the hands of the two superpowers. Those powers, of course, used those resources as a carrot to bring cultural workers into their respective camps. Intellectuals like Aimé Césaire and Alioune Diop, who initially traveled from the colonies to the metropole to complete their educations, experienced Paris as significantly less policed than the French colonial territories from which they hailed.[2] For his part, Richard Wright relocated to Paris from the United States partly out of his avowed need to escape the limits, aesthetic, political, and otherwise, that he felt restricted the purview of African American literature.[3] Despite their different origins and political circumstances, this group of African diaspora writers shared the conviction that culture could be used to both critique the existing order and imagine its transformation. And finally, from a purely professional standpoint, these African diaspora writers, like other writers residing there, could avail themselves of the extraordinary concentration of "literary resources" that made Paris "the capital of the literary world, the city endowed with the greatest literary prestige on earth" (Casanova 2004, 23–24). This prestige depended on such literary resources as neighborhood cafés; artistic and intellectual networks; sustaining relations with mentors, friends, and acquaintances; access to important journals and potential publishers; and general support for the "creative destruction" of received artistic traditions. In the immediate postwar period, these institutions provided a base of operation from which the struggle against both artistic obscurity and colonialism could be waged.

Just as the competing camps of the postwar world started to congeal, the anticolonial whirlwind challenged French colonial authority on numerous fronts. In Indochina, a coalition of Vietnamese communists and nationalists led by Ho Chi Minh launched an insurgency against the French colonialists at the end of 1946. Three months later in Madagascar, partly inspired by the example of Ho Chi Minh, whom Malagasy nationalists leaders had previously met in Paris in 1946, the Malagasy people rose up in an island-wide revolt against the French colonial administration.[4] The French military forces responded brutally, massacring at least the eighty-nine thousand people acknowledged officially. In North Africa, rumblings of discontent were being felt as the French Union floundered and the French failed to articulate a long-term vision and to establish dialogue with nationalist leaders about deteriorating social conditions. Developments in metropolitan France compounded colonial problems as "the political changes that followed the Resistance and the Liberation brought into question, at least in terms of principles," according to Bernard Mouralis, "the traditional relationship that the metropolis entertained with the colonial territories" (Mouralis 1992, 34). This confluence of forces significantly altered the Parisian scene, producing conditions favorable for launching a cultural assault against French colonialism.

Because of France's strategic importance, though, every move in this assault passed through the overarching filter of the Cold War. For key architects of the U.S. Cold War such as then undersecretary of state Dean Acheson, the situation in France was of grave concern, the political situation being such that "a Soviet takeover could occur at any moment" (Rioux 1987, 113). The specter of an alleged Soviet takeover preoccupied U.S. officials because it would supposedly facilitate Soviet penetration of all of Western Europe, Africa, the Mediterranean, and the Middle East. This would give the Soviets access to "the raw materials coming from Europe's Third World dependencies," for which there was growing U.S. need (Leffler 1992, 164). In addition to matters of strategic political and economic concern, France, considered by most as the intellectual center of the "Western" world, also figured prominently in the cultural Cold War. Given the prominence of the Parisian existentialists, Sartre, de Beauvoir, and company, who embraced Marxism and refused to denounce Stalin, Paris was, for cold warriors like Arthur Koestler, "the world capital of fellow travelers" (Saunders 1999, 70). The presence of this widely influential circle of "anti-American" intellectuals made the city a key theater in the battle for the hearts and minds of Europe. The Congress for Cultural Freedom, from its Parisian Secretariat and supported by a network of affiliated national organizations, assumed responsibility for carrying out this mission. With enormous resources at its disposal because of its status as the CIA's principal front operation in the cultural field, the CCF played a dominant role in Western intellectual production and had wide influence throughout the globe. Its presence loomed heavy over much of what those African diaspora writers and intellectuals that gathered in Paris under the banner of *Présence Africaine* sought to accomplish.

These writers and intellectuals did not simply benefit from those institutions already existing in Paris. Their particular situation and needs demanded that they create institutions that served their specific interests. One such institution was the journal *Présence Africaine*, founded in 1947.

The journal published critical essays, literature, book reviews, and notices for events and matters of interests concerning Africa and its diaspora. The first issues drew on work in French from writers such as Léopold Sédar Senghor, Jean-Paul Sartre, and Michel Leiris and in English from Richard Wright, Gwendolyn Brooks, and C. L. R. James. The journal placed culture at the center of the anticolonial and antiracist struggles of the day by taking the erasure or denigration of the African diaspora in dominant modes of representation as its primary concern and field of engagement. Accordingly, those who contributed to the journal situated the act of documenting the African diaspora presence within the larger struggles of the world's darker peoples to wrest authority over the direction of their lives from their erstwhile European masters. As the list of contributors suggests, on one hand the committed black Trotskyist James and on the other hand the Négritude poet and politician Senghor, the journal did not conceive of this struggle in terms consistent with the binaries the Cold War superpowers sought to impose on the globe.

Part of this struggle, found in the cultural work of Césaire, Diop, and Wright, involved the critique of the Eurocentric narratives of modernity's history, which fail to account for its constitution in and through African diaspora labor. In their critiques, they furthered the tradition of putting the African diaspora at the very foundation of the modern world that works such as W.E.B. Du Bois's *Black Reconstruction* (1935) and C.L.R. James's *Black Jacobins* (1938) initiated. Assessing the revolutionary significance of these scholars' contribution, the literary critic Aldon Nielsen contends:

> James and Du Bois both argue far more than the simple case that black people, whether in the New World or in Africa, have not in fact lived outside the horizon of Occidental modernity ... [they] trace the emergence of new, modern world-encompassing economies to the rupture of the Middle Passage and the monumental labors of black workers. (2005, 19)

These critics' work was akin to a "Copernican revolution" in both the reconceptualizing of the history of modernity and the reordering of the intellectual division of labor with African diaspora writers casting the people of the African diaspora as the subjects rather than the mere objects of history. In their work, they insisted that peoples of African descent contribute as equals and not as colonial subjects or second-class citizens in reconfiguring

the global order in the wake of World War II. Today, the work of these artists evokes "anti-imperialist nostalgia," which, according to Jennifer Wenzel,
"holds in mind hope for changes that have yet to be realized" and "acknowledges the past's vision of the future, while recognizing the distance and the
difference between that vision and the realities of the present" (Wenzel
2006, 7). This chapter argues that the marginalizing as vagabonds and dismissing as fellow traveler those African diaspora writers who gathered (and
were prevented from gathering) in postwar Paris was critical to producing a
present decidedly "distant and different" from the future imagined by those
cultural workers of the past who strove to realize a different role for the African diaspora in a reconstructed global order.

RAISING THE PEN:
THE ORIGINS OF *PRÉSENCE AFRICAINE*

Alioune Diop, the founder and director of *Présence Africaine*, was born on
January 10, 1910, in Saint-Louis, Senegal, a coastal city that was an important
commercial hub during the nineteenth century and the capital of the Federation of French West Africa from 1895 to 1902. Because the city was one of
the "four communes" of French colonial Africa, its inhabitants were eligible
for French citizenship as residents (Coats 1997, 207). Diop came from an
aristocratic Wolof family, the ethnicity to which more than 75 percent of
Saint-Louis's population belonged. As a young child he briefly attended a
provincial French school directed by his uncle, but his total incorporation
into the French colonial world began when he entered the Lycée Faidherbe
at the age of twelve. At Faidherbe, a prestigious school that trained "a significant proportion of the future government functionaries, not only of Senegal
but of all of Francophone Africa" (Coats 1997, 210), Diop was taught respect
for the European Enlightenment and appreciation for French civilization.[5]
He continued his studies in classical letters in Alger, another colonial capital,
before completing his studies in Paris. Remaining in Paris through the war
years, Diop was elected to the French Parliament in 1946 as a Section Française de l'Internationale Ouvrière (SFIO) senator; he held this post for two
years until he resigned to devote his energies to *Présence Africaine* (Frioux-
Salgas 2009, 5 note 1).

The *Présence Africaine* project first took root under the German occupation of Paris during World War II. The Vichy regime established the Foyer

des Etudiants Coloniaux to provide students from the colonies with a library and meeting space. Beginning in 1942, Alioune Diop "directed the cultural circle of the colonial students in Paris, which was frequented by nearly all of those who would go on to embrace politics in the setting of the future French Union" (entreprit d'animer le cercle culturel des étudiants coloniaux de Paris que fréquentaient presque tous ceux qui allaient embrasser la politique dans le cadre de la future Union française) (Städtler 1998).[6] Reprising a role similar to when he tutored younger students at the Lycée Faidherbe, Diop mentored the students in the foyer's orbit, some of whom later assisted him in launching *Présence Africaine*. One member of this group, Jacques Rabemananjara,[7] later reflected on the journal's genesis during the war:

> In Paris, under the German occupation. With the French defeat all of the Western values that we had been taught under colonization to attach ourselves to and that had effectively left their mark were collapsing. We, students from the overseas French territories. Not numerous in the Latin quarter, we enjoyed visiting one another.

> (A Paris sous l'occupation allemande. Avec la défaite de la France s'effondraient les valeurs occidentales auxquelles sous la colonisation on nous avait appris à nous attacher et qui, effectivement, nous ont tous marqués. Nous, les étudiants d'Outre-Mer. Pas nombreux au Quartier Latin, nous avons pris plaisir à nous fréquenter.) (Rabemananjara 1977, 17)][8]

Rabemananjara's account points to the centrality of culture ("Western values") to the apparatus of French colonial domination and indexes the space for critiquing that ideology opened by the French defeat. In addition, he draws attention to the bonds formed ("we enjoyed visiting") that enabled these students to survive the dislocations and deprivations provoked by the war. These bonds endured after the war, providing the glue that sustained this group in their cultural assault on French colonial subjugation and refusal to abide by the dichotomous Cold War worldview.

Scholars have devoted little attention to how colonial subjects in particular experienced the occupation. The historian Pap Ndiaye notes, "future works will have to illuminate the everyday life of Blacks during Occupation. But it is fairly clear that, for many, life continued with the usual difficulty" (Des travaux futurs devraient nous éclairer sur la vie quotidienne des Noirs pendant l'Occupation. Mais il est à peu près clair que, pour beaucoup, la vie continuait cahin-caha) (Ndiaye 2008, 156).[9] According to Rabemananjara, this experience was a crucible for the group's budding anticolonialism, which was inspired by and crossed with the larger population's resistance to Nazi occupation: "Anticolonialism was energized from and grew with the rise of hatred for Nazi domination" (L'anticolonialisme s'amorçait et croissait avec la montée de la haine contre la domination nazie) (Rabemananjara 1977, 17). In making the connection between colonialism and Nazism, Rabemananjara makes an argument advanced not only in the works of African diasporic intellectuals such as Aimé Césaire, but also intellectuals of the European tradition such as Hannah Arendt.[10] Likewise, there were deep connections between the anticolonial and antifascist struggle, with the former seemingly evolving organically out of the latter. Consider, for example, Vietnam, where, according to the militant African-American journalist William Worthy, Ho Chi Minh led the "anti-Japanese maquis and dealt with the anti-Nazi maquis" and where "the people of Vietnam still call Ho's Vietminh Party 'le maquis' and 'la résistance'" (Worthy 1954, 78). The *Présence Africaine* project then, as Alioune Diop conceived it, extended the antifascist attack on the racial mythology that underlay Nazism and that also served as the foundations of European colonial regimes.

ESTABLISHING A POLITICS OF CULTURE

While anticolonial resistance took the shape of armed struggle in various parts of the globe, *Présence Africaine* made the difficult and elusive concept of culture its primary concern. Rabemananjara captures a bit of the difficulty of this concept when he states that "of all human activities, culture is the one which knows no boundaries or limits; it is man's permanent face; it is also the base and the condition for man's change and flourishing" (de toutes les activités humaines, la culture est celle qui ne connait ni contours ni limites; c'est la face permanente de l'homme; c'en est aussi la base et la condition de changement et d'épanouissement) (Rabemananjara 1977, 18). His definition makes it difficult to establish culture's limits. On the other hand, it is precisely its all-encompassing quality that attracted Diop to culture as a field of operation, gaining in versatility what might be lost in precision. Indeed in a 1959 editorial titled "Notre politique de la culture," he declares "the traditional definition of culture proposed and imposed by the West to be neither sufficient nor healthy. And that a capital of cultural experience precious in Asia and in Africa risks being lost for humanity" (la définition traditionnelle de la culture telle que l'Occident la propose et impose n'est pas suffisante. Ni saine. Et qu'un capital d'expérience culturelle précieuse en Asie et en Afrique risqué d'être perdu pour l'humanité) ("Notre politique" 1959, 5). In this statement, Diop offers the capital, or wealth, of cultural experience in Asia and Africa as a challenge to the definition imposed by the West and thus as a source of resistance to European cultural imperialism. This capital, he continues, resides in "the *will* of the peoples [of Asia and Africa] who actualize its value in everyday life" (la *volonté* des peuples qui en actualisent la valeur à travers la vie de tous les jours) (5). Thus, Diop as editor gives voice to the cultural mission of *Présence Africaine*, which consists in creating the conditions for and reflecting on the efforts of the masses to realize the value of culture in the transformation of quotidian realities.

While others in the African diaspora took alternatives routes toward this transformation, Diop expressed ambivalence about embracing other more conventionally political orientations such as Pan-Africanism. Although *Présence Africaine* initially articulated a position that sought "to fuse black and European cultural values in a universal humanist civilization," as Salah Hassan usefully observes, "the global geopolitical reorganization leading to the end of empire" had its effects in the increasing dominance of "Pan-African nationalism and anticolonialism" in the journal's cultural politics after 1955 (Hassan 1999, 203, 204). According to Rabemananjara, however, for Diop "politics always took on the character of second-rank importance. Primacy remains the privilege of culture; politics is precisely only an aspect and a support of culture" (à ses yeux, la politique a toujours revêtu le caractère d'une instance de second rang. La primauté demeure l'apanage de la culture; le politique n'en est précisément qu'un aspect et un support) (Rabemananjara 1977, 19). Formulated this way, culture comes to mean something closer to a "whole way of life." While attractive, this approach has a disadvantage in that it ignores the complexity and robustness of the political field, flattening out all difference to questions of culture. In making this move, Diop runs up against a limitation similar to one that Terry Eagleton finds in *Kulturkritik* and modern-day culturalism, which "is a lack of interest in what lies, politically speaking, beyond culture: the state apparatus of violence and coercion" (Eagleton 2000, 43). The founders of *Présence Africaine*, however, were acutely aware of the French state's interest in their activities, and they sought alliances that might protect the journal from the worst abuses of the state's power of violence and coercion.

For members of the circle around Diop, such as the poet Paulin Joachim, there was a compelling and direct objective to their emphasis on culture. In an interview with the cultural critic Bennetta Jules-Rosette, he states:

> We were all in the small group around Alioune Diop, and we had a mission. Essentially, it was to implant African culture in European civilization, to affirm our presence. And in Paris in those years we wanted to launch an African cultural renewal aimed at the white world in which we had been immersed. We wanted to assert our culture and our presence in this world. (Jules-Rosette 1998, 80)

Joachim's complicated argument postulates that despite their total "immersion" in the white world, the intellectuals around Diop retained a culture that predated and was distinct from the one in which they were immersed. This argument allows for otherwise alienated intellectuals to produce culture imbued with the power to bind them to a native population from which their education had estranged them. This logical, if compromised, position makes sense within the context of the globe-altering realignment of forces that followed World War II. By staking such a position, those associated with *Présence Africaine* "asserted" and laid claim to a "presence" at the very center of the struggle of the world's darker peoples to carve out a place for themselves as equals within modernity.

PARIS: CULTURE CAPITAL OF THE WORLD

Diop's decision to found and base the journal *Présence Africaine* in Paris took advantage of both the city's established reputation and its new climate. "The Paris of 1947," as Mouralis points out, "was no longer that place of exile that it was for the Négritude writers during the 1930s but a place where the African writers belonged, because the city was, from then on, one of the theaters in which the political and cultural future of Africa was being prepared" (Mouralis 1992, 3). Thus, by virtue of locating its headquarters in Paris, Diop placed his journal in a prime position to play an eminent role in Africa's future. On a more pragmatic level, the "new journal, by establishing itself in Paris, escaped the risk of marginalization inherent in any attempt to have peripheral voices be heard" (Mouralis 1992, 4). In addition, post–World War II Paris occupied the position as the intellectual center of the Western world. Several journals cemented the city's reputation, among them Jean-Paul Sartre's *Les Temps Modernes* and Emmanuel Mounier's *Esprit*. With both Sartre and Mounier as members of its Committee of Patrons, *Présence Africaine* inevitably "found itself endowed with the status of those journals that bore witness to the renewal of ideas in the intellectual climate that followed the Liberation, . . . this status [being confirmed in] the circulation that was established . . . between the collaborators of those journals and *Présence africaine*" (Mouralis 1992, 4). Indeed, members of the Parisian intellectual elite embraced Diop and his journal with a remarkable amount of enthusiasm and through the journal extended their intellectual and political purview. Increasingly, these intellectuals, who were variously associated with the French left, adopted anticolonial stances. In fact, the commitment to anticolonial and antiracist causes was presented as an obstacle to their supporting the anticommunist liberalism of the Congress of Cultural Freedom. Their position led Sidney Hook, one of the most important figures in the cultural Cold War, to remark bitingly that "Sartre and Merleau-Ponty . . . were quite aware of French and American injustices to Negroes when they supported the Resistance to Hitler. But they can see no justice in the Western defense against Communist aggression because the Negroes have not yet won equality of treatment" (Hook 1950, 718). Thus, this example attests that this was not a unidirectional exchange with *Présence Africaine* alone benefiting from its association with the leaders of Parisian intellectual circles, but one with some amount of reciprocity in that French metropolitan intellectuals developed their anticolonial thought and positions through engagement with the journal.

Présence Africaine's close association with the most important French intellectuals and journals of the day did not, however, assure its ready acceptance by the French authorities. In the journal's formative days, those associated with it were keenly aware of the risks. Rabemananjara describes them as "conscious of the riskiness of the stakes. Of the immense hostility that the enterprise could not fail to provoke. From the side of Oudinot Street, where the Ministry of the Colonies is located. From the side of the great interests invested in our countries; they had no wish at all for the awakening of black consciousnesses" (conscients de la hardiesse de l'enjeu. De l'immense hostilité que l'entreprise ne manquerait pas de provoquer. Du côté de la rue

Oudinot, Ministère des Colonies. Du côté des grands intérêts investis dans nos pays: ils ne tenaient absolument pas au réveil des consciences noires) (Rabemananjara 1977, 20). While I was not able to gauge the extent to which *Présence Africaine* was perceived as a threat, colonial authorities and their metropolitan counterparts surely had a vested interest in controlling information. The suppression of journals such as *L'Étudiant d'Afrique noire*, the organ of the FEANF, an African students' federation, and the banning of books published by the editor and anticolonial activist François Maspero (the first publisher of Fanon's *Peau noir, masques blancs*), clearly indicate that the French authorities understood the centrality of the ideological struggle and the need to control the publishing industry in the fight to preserve their colonial empire.[11]

Cultivating close associations with leading French intellectuals provided *Présence Africaine* with a form of insurance against repression from the colonial authorities. As Christiane Diop, Alioune Diop's wife and collaborator on the journal, explained in an interview with Bennetta Jules-Rosette:

> [T]hey would have arrested us or stopped us from publishing. So we needed protection by great names—Gabriel Marcel, André Gide. They didn't dare touch us under the protection of these people. They helped us culturally, because we were regarded as subversive. That's very important. (Jules-Rosette 1998, 45)

While the extent of the monitoring to which *Présence Africaine* was subjected to remains obscure, it is nevertheless clear that the Ministry of the Colonies deployed a special secret police under the direction of the military to conduct surveillance on the activities of certain individuals from the Overseas Territories residing in France. Anecdotal evidence suggests that the police did indeed monitor Diop and his group. For example, Rabemananjara recalls that during the interrogation related to his suspected involvement in the 1947 revolt in Madagascar, "the chief of Security in Madagascar, the sinister Baron, held against me both my belonging to the Negro movement in Paris that advocated the emancipation of the colonies and my friendship with Alioune Diop, whom he qualified for the circumstance as a dangerous, fiercely anti-French man" (le chef de la Sûreté de Madagascar, le sinistre Baron, me faisait grief de mon appartenance au mouvement des Nègres de Paris qui préconisait l'émancipation des colonies et de mon amitié avec Alioune Diop qualifié pour la circonstance d'homme dangereux, farouchement anti-français) (Rabemananjara 1977, 27). It seems safe to assume that the stirrings of anticolonial revolt in Indochina, Madagascar and Algeria undoubtedly led the French colonial administration to closely watch the activities of colonial subjects residing within the metropole. In fact, since the interwar years the police and the colonial ministry had worked together to develop special brigades charged with monitoring the activities of colonial subjects residing in France, particularly in Paris.[12]

In launching *Présence Africaine*, Diop and his circle did not limit themselves to France and the francophone world; they consciously drew on influences beyond their immediate context, giving voice to the wider world of the African diaspora, particularly the anglophone section. Including Richard Wright in the Committee of Patrons was the primary means through which the journal initially achieved this goal. When Wright arrived in France in the late summer of 1947, he was probably the most famous black writer in the entire world at the time. Those at *Présence Africaine* surely understood that Wright's stature might be a source of additional protection. Associating with Wright, who had visited France a year earlier "with his wife and infant daughter as guests of the Cultural Relations Section of the French Foreign Ministry" (Campbell 1995, 6), likely reduced the anxieties that Diop and his circle had about reprisals from the Ministry of the Colonies. In establishing these associations, those affiliated with *Présence Africaine* demonstrated themselves to be astute readers of the political climate and painfully aware of the limits imposed on colonial subjects drawn to the "City of Light."

BLACK VOICES EMERGE:
THE LAUNCH OF *PRÉSENCE AFRICAINE*

The effects of the recent war were still palpable when the inaugural issue of *Présence Africaine* appeared in the winter of 1947. Mouralis notes that "it was an impressive volume of 196 pages which was, in itself, quite a feat in that postwar period when paper was a rare commodity" (Mouralis 1992, 3). Despite the wartime deprivations, the journal announced itself with great ambitions: "the first copy," according to Jules-Rosette, "was distributed simultaneously in Paris and Dakar in December of 1947" (1992, 17). This first issue reflected the multiple aims, audiences, and allegiances of which the journal was a product and which would define its subsequent issues. The first section consisted of what Jules-Rosette characterizes as "pithy confessionals" (1998, 38) by French intellectuals, among them Gide, Sartre, and Mounier, as well as a salutatory text by Diop. Confirming the journal's orientation toward the diaspora, the second section was devoted to poems, plays, and short stories by "an international crew of black writers—Léopold Senghor, Bernard B. Dadié, Birago Diop, Gwendolyn Brooks, and Richard Wright, among others" (Jules-Rosette 1998, 38). Reviews of works of art, books, and ideas as well as summaries of articles in other journals related to the black world made up the third and final section.

Alioune Diop's introduction, titled "Niam n'goura ou les raisons d'être de *Présence africaine*," set the tone for the journal, which over the course of its nearly seventy-year history has "[grown] into a larger publication enterprise, an intellectual group, and a cultural movement" (Jules-Rosette 1992, 17). First, Diop draws the title of his essay from a proverb of the Toucouleur people of West Africa, "Niam Ngoura Vana Niam M'Paya," which he translates in a footnote as meaning "Eating in order to live is not eating in order to get fat" ("Mange pour que tu vives" ce n'est pas "mange pour que tu engraisses") (Diop 1947, 185 (7)). Diop's use of this proverb is perhaps meant to invoke a French word/concept, "assimiler," which means literally "to take in." This verb connotes not only the process by which food is brought into the body but also the policy of assimilation, the governing principle of France's relation toward colonial subjects in its colonies (and with regard to immigrants today). In this context, Diop uses this proverb to indicate a program by which *Présence Africaine* accepts just enough European culture and civilization necessary to ensure its own and African culture's survival, but not enough to constitute total assimilation and the replacement of African culture with European culture. Along this line of thinking, overindulgence signifies Africans coming to identify completely with Europe, and thus rupturing their links to African culture.

Throughout the essay Diop figures European civilization as providing the necessary sustenance for a healthy existence within modernity. For example, Diop writes,

> In establishing this magazine, our first and principal aim is to make an appeal to the youth of Africa who has long hungered for intellectual *food*. Few echoes of intellectual life in Europe reach him. His adolescent ardour, abandoned to arid isolation, dooms him to cultural asphyxiation or sterilization. Our hope is that this magazine can constitute itself a window through which young Africa can look out upon the world. (emphasis added)

> (En fondant cet organe, nous avons songé d'abord et nous nous adressons princaplement à la jeunesse d'Afrique. Elle manque d'*aliment* intel-

lectuel. Peu d'échos lui parviennent de la vie de l'esprit en Europe. Livrée à son isolement desséchant et à sa fougue adolescente, elle court le risque de s'asphyxier ou de se stériliser, faute d'avoir une fenêtre sur le monde.) (Diop 1947, 1851–86 (8), emphasis added)

While he does not make the point explicitly, Diop calls attention to the control that colonial authorities exercised over the flow of information in and out of the colonies by reminding his readers that few echoes of intellectual life reach African youth. In a situation of colonial subjugation, controlling information was a crucial means of limiting Africans' experience and binding them to the uneven relations of capitalist modernity. For Diop then, *Présence Africaine* introduces the life-giving sustenance that would transform African youth, and more generally those from the overseas colonial territories, and enable them to participate as subjects of modernity, assuming responsibility for improving humanity: "one wishes for the transformation of these overseas men into brains and arms adapted to modern life and sharing the responsibility of thinking out and bettering the lot of mankind" (on souhaite la transformation de ces hommes d'outre-mer en cerveaux et bras adaptés à la vie moderne et partageant la responsabilité de penser et d'améliorer le sort du genre humain) (Diop 1947, 187 (9)). As Gary Wilder has recently argued about Césaire and Senghor, and which is also true of those associated with *Présence Africaine*, "they ... felt themselves to be implicated in and responsible for remaking the world and redeeming humanity" (Wilder 2015, 8). Clearly Diop expresses a highly problematic idea when he represents colonized subjects as somehow ill-adapted to the exigencies of modern life; a more generous reading, however, might understand his words as a subtle critique of modernity's international division of labor that conscripted the colonized to perform the menial tasks while leaving the thinking and directing to the colonizers.

In addition to its concerns with modernity, the first issue of *Présence Africaine* locates it within a larger African diaspora community. In his essay "The Uses of Diaspora," Brent Hayes Edwards notes that "at its outset, *Présence africaine* was not primarily conceived as a diasporic project, focusing on issues of connection and collaboration among peoples of African descent. It was more expressly conceived as an African incursion into modernity" (Edwards 2001a, 47). Even so, Edwards continues, "if *Présence africaine* did not initially aim to theorize black internationalism, it represents black internationalism *in practice*, particularly through its translations" (2001a, 48). The first issue, for example, contains an English translation by Thomas Diop and

Richard Wright of Alioune Diop's essay "Niam n'goura ou les raisons d'être de *Présence africaine*," as well as French translations of a poem by Gwendolyn Brooks, "The Ballad of Pearly May Lee," and Richard Wright's short story "Bright and Morning Star." It should be noted that Brooks's poem was from her first book of poetry, *A Street in Bronzeville* (1945), which Wright had encouraged Harper & Row to publish, and he probably played a similar role at *Présence Africaine*.

Yet beyond the translations, Diop's introductory essay suggests that he conceived the journal's mission, at least in part, as a diaspora project. In the essay, he uses the example of the diaspora to buttress his claim about the value of imparting knowledge of Africa to Europe. In a footnote Diop writes:

> The coloured writers of America have already demonstrated the productive power of their spiritual vitality and its necessity to the world. . . . In the near future we shall devote a special issue to coloured non-African writers.
>
> (déjà, les Africains expatriés en Amérique—et dont la plupart ont tout oublié des moeurs africaines—ont amplement prouvé que la vitalité spirituelle du nègre et sa puissance créatrice sont désormais nécessaires au monde. . . . Nous consacrerons un numéro spécial aux écrivains noirs non africains.) (1947, 190 (12))[13]

This quote would seem to suggest that even if *Présence Africaine* was not primarily conceived as a diaspora project, as Edwards argues, it nevertheless founded its claim to relevancy and its hope for success on an engagement with the diaspora. Diop clearly understood that the Cold War and the emergence of the United States as a global power necessitated moving the journal beyond an approach focused exclusively on the relations between Africans and the European colonial powers.

GATHERING UNDER THE SHADOW OF COLD WAR: *PRÉSENCE AFRICAINE*'S 1956 CONGRESS OF WRITERS AND ARTISTS

Print culture, however, was not the most conspicuous of *Présence Africaine*'s diaspora activities. In the ten-year period from 1956 to 1966, the group organized a series of international congresses that brought together leading artists, writers, and intellectuals to discuss and debate the critical issues facing Africa and its diaspora. While no doubt drawing on the heritage of the Pan-African conferences that W.E.B. Du Bois organized in the first half of the twentieth century, *Présence Africaine* sought to distinguish its efforts by according more attention to cultural matters than narrowly conceived political ones. The title of the first congress held in Paris in 1956, "Le Ier Congrès des Ecrivains et Artistes Noirs" (The First Congress of Black Writers and Artists), speaks to this effort at distinction. Representing the congress as the first of its kind, the title also defines the participants as men of culture, "Writers and Artists," and not politicians. In his opening remarks to the congress, Alioune Diop reinforced these claims about distinctiveness:

> Other congresses had taken place following the other war; they did not have the originality of being essentially cultural or of benefiting from the remarkable gathering of such a large number of talents having arrived at maturity, not only in the United States, the Antilles and in the grand and proud republic of Haiti, but also in the countries of black Africa.

> (D'autres Congrès avaient eu lieu, au lendemain de l'autre guerre; ils n'avaient l'originalité ni d'être essentiellement culturels ni de bénéficier du concours remarquable d'un si grand nombre de talents parvenus à maturité, non seulement aux Etats-Unis, aux Antilles et dans la grande et fière république d'Haïti, mais encore dans les pays d'Afrique Noire). (Diop 1956, 9)[14]

If on the one hand Diop distinguished the congress from the Pan-African congresses that followed World War I, on the other hand he explicitly linked the congress with the Bandung conference of the previous year. At that conference, leaders from Asia and Africa came together to declare the independence from or nonalignment with either of the two superpowers engaged in the Cold War. Standing before the crowd of participants and spectators assembled at the Sorbonne for the opening ceremony of the congress, Diop claimed that "if since the end of the war, the Bandung meeting constituted for non-European consciousnesses the most important event, [he] believed [himself] able to affirm that this first congress . . . will represent for our people the second [most important] event of this decade [the 1950s]" (Si depuis la fin de la guerre, la rencontre de Bandoeng constitue pour les consciences non européennes l'événement le plus important, je crois pouvoir affirmer que ce premier Congrès . . . représentera pour nos peuples le second événement de cette décade) (Diop 1956, 9). By drawing this link between the two events, Diop initiated the approach of thinking of the congress as a kind of cultural Bandung. Obviously, the Bandung connection implicitly asserted the nonaligned character of the Paris congress and indicated the hope, against the odds, that it could resist the centripetal pull of the Cold War.

What went unremarked in Diop's opening statement was the lack of gender diversity among those writers and artists representing the African diaspora. Indeed, it would seem that the invitations to present at the congress were distributed to "men of culture" not solely on the basis of their relationship to culture but their gender identities as well. Merve Fejzula has recently noted women's absence from active participation in the congress and the lack of scholarship on women's role in *Présence Africaine*, a history she argues not necessarily about "silence and absence" but "the gap between the evidence of their participation and its acknowledgment" (Fejzula 2016). Surprisingly, given his reputation as a sexist and the misogyny at the heart of the works that made him famous, Richard Wright was the first presenter to address this gender imbalance in his congress remarks. Not sure of how many had noticed, Wright brought to the attention of his confreres that there had been "no women functioning vitally and responsibly upon this platform helping to mold and mobilize our thoughts." Wright did not presume to know the cause of black women's absence from the platform, either "some hangover of influence from the past" or "perhaps . . . an oversight," but he was unequivocal in his statement that "Black men will not be free until their women are free" (Wright 1956, 348).

Indeed, in the official photo of the congress delegates in front of the Sorbonne, there is only one woman seated in the center front row, next to the congress chair, Dr. Jean Price-Mars, the Haitian scholar, activist, and diplomat. A *Présence Africaine* postcard of the photo identifies the woman as Mme. Price Mars. It is not surprising that Mrs. Price-Mars would assert her presence in this masculine space, if one considers the description of Mrs. Price-Mars in Katherine Dunham's autobiography of her time in Haiti, *Island Possessed*. According to Dunham, Mrs. Price-Mars departed from the typical behavior she had observed in middle and upper class Haitian homes where wives oversaw "the serving of the table, gravitating between kitchen or serving pantry and dining room, seldom sitting at table with the guests, seldom joining in after dinner discussions." By contrast,

Mrs. Price-Mars was "an ardent feminist, involved in women's suffrage, newspaper publication, and any measures likely to liberate Haitian women from the secondary role they had occupied since colonial times" (Dunham 1969, 23). Clearly, given the opportunity Mrs. Price-Mars might have articulated thoughts left to Wright to express in his remarks and thereby making her presence and those of other women at the congress larger than that captured in the photographic and documentary evidence surrounding the congress.

Bringing together black artists and writers from Europe, Africa, and the Americas, this congress and those that followed provided a structure for realizing cultural projects centered on the African diaspora. These congresses spurred black artists and writers to create those networks, associations, and groups necessary for challenging the Cold War's binary logic. These spaces not only asserted the African diaspora "presence" in modernity, but also legitimized those voices that dared argue that the African diaspora was part of "that dark and vast sea of human labor . . . on whose bent and broken backs rest today the founding stones of modern industry" (Du Bois 1935, 15). It was insights such as these that threatened to upend the era's dominant narratives and that challenged the foundation on which the postwar global order stood.

Présence Africaine opened its Ier Congrès Mondial des Ecrivains et Artistes Noirs in the Sorbonne's Descartes amphitheater on September 19, 1956, "one of those bright warm days," according to James Baldwin, "which one likes to think of as typical of the atmosphere of the intellectual capital of the Western world" (1998b, 143). If the weather outside was pleasant, inside the amphitheater the palpable Cold War tensions cast a pall over the proceedings. In his often referenced essay chronicling the events, Baldwin writes that "everyone was tense with the question of which direction the conference would take. Hanging in the air, as real as the heat from which we suffered, were the great specters of America and Russia, of the battle going on between them for the domination of the world" (1998b, 145). Unbeknownst to him at the time, Baldwin himself had been impressed into this battle in the very act of covering the conference for *Encounter*, where he first published his account.[15] The journal was sponsored by the Congress for Cultural Freedom, an organization whose ties to the CIA were established later.

Describing the opening day's proceedings, Baldwin counts Richard Wright among the "eight colored men" who sat "behind the table at the front of the hall" (1998b, 143), a place reserved for those intimately involved in organizing the congress. It is not without consequence that Wright would position himself alongside the likes of Alioune Diop, Léopold Senghor, Aimé Césaire, Jacques-Stephen Alexis, Dr. Jean Price-Mars, and the other co-organizers. Price-Mars had been an important figure in the intellectual resistance to the U.S. occupation of Haiti, and Césaire and Alexis were members of the French and Haitian Communist Parties, respectively. While on this historic morning Wright presented himself before the world in solidarity with his cocollaborators, he had recently sung a different tune before a very dissimilar audience at the U.S. embassy in Paris. In the months leading up to the congress, Wright apparently visited the embassy to document his distance from the congress organizers who, much to his apparent disapproval, had fallen under the sway of communists. Wright's biographer Hazel Rowley suggests that his visits to the U.S. embassy were acts of "self-protection" (Rowley 2001, 474). Indeed, he eked out a living as a writer in Paris, walking the tightrope between the hospitality of one imperialist nation, France, and the long reach of another nation, the United States, hell-bent on ruining any citizen, especially a black one, who dared not toe the anticommunist line. Wright's predicament highlights the fact that even Parisian self-exile did not protect him from the excesses of the Cold War. While Moscow's opportunism with regard to African American civil rights during World War II surely informed Wright's actions at the embassy, the precariousness of his Parisian existence no doubt loomed large in his mind. Wright's distancing himself from the organizers' supposed communism, therefore, should be seen as a shrewd attempt to appease the irrational powers of anticommunism, an attempt to preserve his hard-fought but far from secure freedom.

To the extent that the Cold War hung silently over the Paris congress, the conspicuous absence of W.E.B. Du Bois loudly interjected it as a subject for consideration. At this advanced stage of his career, Du Bois was without parallel in intellectual accomplishments in the black world, having been engaged as an activist and scholar for well over fifty years. His world stature notwithstanding, the United States government had successfully branded him a pariah. Ensnared in the McCarthy witch hunt, labeled a communist, and denied a passport, he had not been able to attend either the Paris congress or the previous year's Bandung conference. While barred from being physically present, Du Bois put pen to paper and addressed the congress via a telegram, which was read aloud during the opening session.[16] According to Baldwin's account, Du Bois's telegram explained the reason for his absence and accused "any American Negro traveling abroad today . . . of either not car[ing] about Negroes or say[ing] what the State Department wishes him to say." Baldwin considered Du Bois's communication as "extremely ill-considered" and as compromising "whatever effectiveness the five-man American delegation . . . might have hoped to have" (1998b, 146). History confirms, however, that Du Bois was justified in raising suspicions about the American delegation and its relationship to the U.S. Cold War project.

The American delegation was the nucleus out of which grew the CIA-sponsored cultural front organization, the American Society of African Culture. As a member of the conference executive committee, Richard Wright enlisted the help of Roy Wilkins, the executive director of the NAACP, in putting together an American delegation to attend the congress.[17] Wilkins, in turn, sought out John A. Davis, a political science professor at the City College of New York, who had briefly worked for the Department of State as a consultant to the director of personnel for a little less than a year between 1952–53.[18] Shortly after being dropped from the State Department's payroll following budget cuts, he received funding from well-connected whites to study foreign reactions to American racial problems. The support was channeled through the American Information Committee on Race and Caste, which also bankrolled the American delegation, covering the costs of first-class travel to Paris and providing a twenty dollar per diem in exchange for post-Congress reports (Wilford 2008, 201). Besides Davis, the other members of the delegation were Horace Mann Bond, president of Lincoln University, where Davis had worked prior to his appointment at CCNY; William Fontaine, a philosophy professor at the University of Pennsylvania, the lone philosopher of color to occupy a position at an Ivy League institution; Mercer Cook, French professor at Howard University, later appointed by President Kennedy as ambassador to Niger after having served as the director of the African Affairs Program at the Congress of Cultural Freedom, the CIA's principal cultural front organization; and James Ivy, the polyglot editor of the NAACP's magazine, *Crisis*, who succeeded Roy Wilkins as editor.

The historical evidence is not conclusive about how much members of the delegations knew about the source of their support and their function in the cultural Cold War. Horace Mann Bond's biographer, Wayne Urban, notes that "the record cannot definitively answer" the question of Bond's wittingness: "there is ample evidence for concluding that, if he did not know, he did not want to know" (Urban 1992, 163).[19] As for William Fontaine, he "almost certainly did not know of the society's tainted origins and cash flow and had nothing to do with AMSAC's finances," concludes his biographer, Bruce Kuklick (2008, 111). In what is the most comprehensive account of AMSAC's dealings to date, Hugh Wilford arrives at the verdict that "the organization was unusually conscientious about observing front group security protocols," suggesting that "far from being dupes of the CIA, AMSAC's African Americans were among the Agency's most effective secret agents" (Wilford 2008, 213). The 1956 conference was this group's entree into Cold War spy craft and they performed ably enough to open up the flow of funds that allowed AMSAC to become a major player in African diaspora literary and cultural affairs for nearly a decade. AMSAC enjoyed this position until 1967, when the sources of its funding were revealed in a series of articles published in the *New York Times*.

Of course, the prominence of AMSAC must be considered within the context of the larger cultural Cold War. Perhaps not as readily associated with the Cold War as its military, economic, and political aspects, the cultural field was an essential domain that provided "lateral support to the military-political and economic struggle that had set in after 1945" (Berghahn 2001, 91). Just as with the Pan-African and nonalignment movements and *Présence Africaine*'s diaspora project, cultural conferences provided the prime site for waging this aspect of the Cold War. As Berghahn notes, "congresses and countercongresses of artists and writers as well as youth festivals and counterfestivals became the most visible expression of this struggle" (2001, 129). The Soviet Union was at a distinct advantage in this arena, having benefited from several years of offensive operations without any sustained or effective counteroffensive from the West. In testament to this strength, the Soviet Union organized two major international peace conferences in the spring of 1949: one in March in New York, which drew the attendance of such famous intellectuals as Albert Einstein, Lillian Hellman, and Aaron Copland; while the likes of Pablo Picasso, Pietro Nenni, and Frédéric Joliot-Curie attended the other conference held a month later in Paris. The Paris conference is noteworthy not only because W.E.B. Du Bois, Paul Robeson, and Peter Blackman, a Barbadian member of the Great Britain Communist Party, attended, but also because Robeson gave the speech here that set in motion the blacklisting that is the subject of Chapter 4.[20] In response to these conferences, the United States increased its activity, beginning with a counterdemonstration with a sizeable audience in New York and a minimally successful International Day of Resistance to Dictatorship and War in Paris (Berghahn 2001, 129).

Recognizing the centrality of Europe in this cultural struggle, the Americans set about to organize a major event on the continent. They chose the "front-line city of the Cold War," Berlin, as the venue for the Congress of Cultural Freedom held in June of 1950. The congress featured speeches by a "hundred invited writers, artists, and scientists," "almost all [of whom] were liberals or social democrats, critical of capitalism and opposed to colonialism, imperialism, nationalism, racism, and dictatorship" (Coleman 1989, 18, 20), but also committed anticommunists. Among the group of primarily German and American participants were two African American cold warriors George Schuyler and Max Yergan. The events were capped with "a mass rally, attended by an estimated ten to fifteen thousand people, and the establishment of an 'International Committee for Cultural Freedom'" (Berghahn 2001, 130). Five years after the Berlin conference and a year prior to the *Présence Africaine* Paris congress, the Congress of Cultural Freedom started to rethink its strategy of focusing solely on Western Europe. Convening in 1955, the Milan congress devoted to "The Future of Freedom" had a stronger representation from Asia, the Middle East, Latin America, and Africa, and according to Berghahn, it dedicated "a full day ... to the problems of nationalism and colonialism" (2001, 140). This shift signaled the increasing importance in the Cold War of the Third World, which shortly thereafter would become the major theater of operation of this struggle.

VOICES FROM THE DIASPORA: CONGRESS TEXTS CONSIDERED

With a profound sense of the historical moment for the colonized and a keen awareness of the overarching Cold War filter through which their words were being processed, thirty-some delegates presented papers at *Présence Africaine's* congress. They addressed from very different angles the essential role of culture in shaping the conditions for the African diaspora's emergence as a subject in modernity. The organizers of the congress privileged culture as a prime site in the political struggles of anticolonialism and antiracism, to which they linked their destiny. For example, in the essay "Modern Culture and Our Destiny" ("La culture moderne et notre destin") that prefaces the reproduction in *Présence Africaine* of the speeches given at the congress, the organizers write that "culture becomes a formidable means of political action at the same time that it has the ambition and vocation to inspire politics" (la culture devient, en effet, pour la politique, un redoutable moyen d'action, en même temps qu'elle a l'ambition et la vocation d'inspirer la politique) ("Modern Culture and Our Destiny," 5).[21] Here, *Présence Africaine* makes two claims essential to its work: first, that culture work in and of itself is a form of politics; and secondly, that culture, while distinct from the political, exists as a resource for politics. These claims legitimate *Présence Africaine's* work in the cultural field while also establishing its relevancy to struggles in different domains. If the organizers tied their conception of culture to the aims of the conference, they did not censor contrary voices. In fact, one of the congress's principles encouraged different approaches because it was understood that "the number, the quality, and the variety of our talents must be the first affirmation of our presence in the world" (Le nombre, la qualité et la variété des talents devaient être une première affirmation de notre présence au monde) ("Modern Culture and Our Destiny," 3). Here again the organizers drew attention to the important work of simply affirming a presence. The critical import of this position is painfully evident against the backdrop of the undeniable fact that "our histories in [the] progress of modernity and modernism have generally been written as if black people had little to do with the subject other than be subject to it" (Nielsen 2005, 26). By presenting a number of voices, this conference allowed African diaspora writers to present themselves to the world as subjects of modernity. Indeed, many of those that presented papers at the conference played leading roles in the movements that determined the position of the African diaspora in the postwar global order.

While Diop was undoubtedly less well known than many of his collaborators on the organizing committee and many of those who addressed the congress, his contribution was crucial. Although not the congress president (this honor having been bestowed upon Dr. Price-Mars), Diop was unquestionably the driving force behind the congress. In fact, he closed his opening remarks with a slightly embarrassed acknowledgment of his role in bringing about the congress: "I will not finish this rapid evocation of our problems without expressing my joy to all those artists, thinkers, and writers who helped me to fulfill the wish that had inspired me to serve black culture for over fifteen obstinate years" (je n'achèverai pas cette rapide évocation de nos problèmes, sans exprimer ma joie à tous ceux, artistes, penseurs, écrivains qui m'ont aidé à combler le vœu qui m'inspira plus de quinze années d'obstination au service de la culture noire) (Diop 1956, 17). In addition to his organizing activities, Diop used his opening remarks to assess the situation facing those artists committed to realizing a future for African diaspora peoples free from colonialism and second-class citizenship and to make a critical intervention into the debates that he anticipated animating the conference over the following three days.

Of those debates, Diop's contribution to the one on the relationship between politics and culture ranks as the most relevant to the present discussion. James Baldwin writes that "in speaking of the relation between politics and culture [Diop] pointed out that the loss of vitality from which all Negro cultures were suffering was due to the fact that their political destinies were not in their hands" (1998b, 144). By putting the question of political independence at the forefront of the congress and relating it to culture, Diop articulated a position central to the anticolonial struggle. Although it was at odds with the Cold War orthodoxy emanating from the United States, Diop's position recognized that the nation-state was "the prime political form of modernity" and that "cultures are intrinsically incomplete, and need the supplement of the state to become truly themselves" (Eagleton 2000, 57, 59). Diop broached the subject in the context of his discussion of the "scandalous question of peoples without culture," "a myth created expressly by those truly responsible for colonization" (la scandaleuse question des peuples sans culture . . . les vrais responsables de la colonisation ont sciemment forgé ce mythe) (1956, 12). Here Diop makes a clear and poignant argument about the role of culture in politics, providing in this instance a stinging critique of the ideological justifications for colonization. Diop categorically refuses to accept that peoples without culture exist. Here, he articulates an anticolonial position that rips away the mythical foundation on which the edifice of colonization was built. Diop attributes the circulation of such a myth to "the often overlooked and all too natural link, which [he feels] obligated to invoke in order to remain loyal, between the political and the cultural" (ce que l'on perd de vue assez souvent, c'est le lien tout naturel et que je suis obligé d'évoquer pour être loyal, entre le politique et le culturel) (1956, 12). Although he does not say so explicitly, Diop associates the ignoring of the link between politics and culture to a particular Cold War politics. He demonstrates how culture both smooths over the fissures and antagonisms that are the ground of politics and how it can bring those same antagonisms into relief.

Highlighting the antagonisms at work within and directed against the

African diaspora gave *Présence Africaine* and those gathered at the congress their raison d'être. Looking across the contemporary political landscape, Diop saw the desperate and urgent need for cultural intervention:

> If political authority (the State) can exercise a deadly pressure on culture and if dictatorship has become more dangerous today than centuries ago, then it is certain that it is the responsibility of culture, for people's safety and equilibrium, to inspire politics, to think and animate it.

> (Si l'autorité politique [l'État] peut exercer sur la culture une pression mortelle, et si la dictature est devenue aujourd'hui plus dangereuse qu'il y a quelques siècles; alors il est certain qu'il appartient à la culture, pour le salut et l'équilibre des peuples, d'inspirer la politique, de la penser et animer.) (1956, 13)

Faced with this urgent reality and awesome responsibility, Diop both critiques the idea that "politicians alone could create works that fulfilled the people's aspirations" (les seuls hommes politiques comme tels puissent formuler ou créer des œuvres qui comblent l'attente totale des peuples) and outlines the unique role of writers and artists "to translate for the world the moral and artistic vitality of our compatriots and at the same time to communicate to them the sense and flavor of foreign works or world events" (de traduire pour le monde la vitalité morale et artistique de nos compatriotes, et en même temps de communiquer à ceux-ci le sens et la saveur des œuvres étrangères ou des événements mondiaux) (1956, 17). Thus, Diop's opening remarks not only reaffirm the centrality of culture in resolving the world's pressing political problems, but they also assign artists and writers a critical role in bringing about the much-needed transformation of the modern world.

The role of artists and intellectuals as political agents would be revisited in varying degrees throughout the remainder of the congress. The most forceful and penetrating treatment would close the second day of the congress, when Aimé Césaire gave his address, titled "Culture and Colonization," which, "wrung . . . the most violent reaction of joy" from the audience, according to Baldwin (1998b, 157). According to Horace Mann Bond, Césaire "read his paper with deep feeling and eloquence that was met by frequent interruptions from an audience evidently 'stacked' with communists" (Bond 1956). Not everyone in the crowd, however, reacted enthusiastically to his speech. Among the Americans, his "comments set off alarm bells" (Singh 2004, 174). In his text, Césaire assigns to artists and intellectuals the important, if limited, role of "proclaim[ing] the coming and prepar[ing] the way for those who hold the answer—the people, our peoples, freed from their shackles, our peoples and their creative genius finally freed from all that impedes it and renders it sterile" (d'annoncer la venue et de préparer la venue de celui qui détient la résponse: le peuple, nos peuples, libérés de leurs engraves, nos peoples et leur génie créateur enfin débarrassé de ce qui le contrarie ou le stérilise)—political oppression in the guise of colonialism (Césaire 1956a, 142 [205]). Césaire's insistence on the link between the political and the cultural did not accord with the sympathies of the American delegation, and they took exception to and raised their strident objection to his paper on other grounds in the evening debates that followed his speech.

In his speech, Césaire had dared suggest that "our American brothers themselves are, by force of racial discrimination, artificially placed at the heart of a great modern nation in a situation [that] is comprehensible only in reference to a colonialism, abolished to be sure, but one whose aftereffects still reverberate in the present" (Césaire 1956a, 127). Mercer Cook took Césaire's word as an indication that the conference conveners had misled them and that the delegates had not been invited to discuss culture but "pour discuter ce colonialisme et seulement ce colonialisme" (in order to discuss this colonialism and only this colonialism) (213). The leader of the American delegation, John A. Davis, twisted Césaire's words to peg him as a communist, insisting that "we [African Americans] do not look forward to any self-determination in the belt if this is what Mr. Césaire had in mind" (215).[22] The American delegates' reaction to Césaire betrayed their willingness, perhaps their mission given their sponsorship, to promote an American exceptionalism that removed the question of racism in the United States from the history of capitalist development in the New World. Far from parroting the communist line on racism, Césaire put forth the black radical analysis that despite its particularities the situation of African Americans "is linked to the fact that the United States . . . was a colonial territory that at a certain moment, like in the Caribbean, introduced black [labor] from Africa to meet the needs of the plantations" (est liée au fait que l'Amérique a été, au début de son histoire, un territories colonial; et qu'on y introduit, à un certain moment, comme dans les Antilles, come dans set hémisphère, pours les besoins des plantations, des noirs venus d'Afrique") (1956a, 222).[23]

Other delegates that addressed the congress took up similar questions, if not in the same polemical vein as Césaire. These delegates pursued a dialogue on the relationship between culture and politics and the political role of artists and writers, a conversation that *Présence Africaine* would have a pivotal role in animating over the course of the next ten years. While often discounted as not politically relevant or effective, these conversations form part of a rich history of trying to imagine a radically restructured modernity. Such a modernity would be shorn of the "nastiness," to quote Cedric Robinson quoting Peter Blackman,[24] a Paris conference attendee, referring to "the brutal degradations of life and the most acute violations of human destiny" (Robinson 2000, 308) that has defined the five-hundred-year experience of African diaspora labor under racial capitalism.

That modernity has been structured along the color line has been evident at least since Paris's reign as the "capital of modernity." In his historical-geographical study of nineteenth-century Paris, David Harvey argues that modernity was born in the "moments of creative destruction" (2003, 1) that were the rebellions of 1848 and the French government's response, which culminated in Louis Napoleon's coup d'état and Baron Haussmann's transformation of the city. If this confrontation between the forces of revolution and repression gave birth to modernity, then it had been conceived in Africa. It was on this continent that officers such as "Louis Cavaignac, a bourgeois republican general," acquired the training and savoir faire to "ruthlessly and brutally put down the revolt" of the revolutionary proletariat (Harvey 2003, 6).[25] A century later, at a moment when the Algerian people were once again engaged in armed struggled against the forces of French imperialism, African diaspora writers and intellectuals gathered in Paris to confront the reality of their moment. Farcically, the era's dominant narratives were denying anew the links between colonial conquest and modernity. This repetition was farcical in much the same way that Marx characterized Louis Bonaparte's rise to power following the crushing of the 1848 revolution as a "farce" (Marx 1852, 594) in *The Eighteenth Brumaire of Louis Bonaparte*. If in the case of Louis Bonaparte, according to Marx, "the class struggle in France ... made it possible for a grotesque mediocrity to play a hero's part," a limited understanding of the class struggle would try to assign the world's colonial people a subservient role in the drama unfolding in the theater of Cold War. A mere month after the close of the Parisian congress, Aimé Césaire announced to the French Communist Party and the world his and colonial people's refusal to play such a diminished role.

CÉSAIRE'S PARTING MISSIVE

Wright's relocation to Paris in 1947 apparently gave him the space to reflect on big questions like "the character of Western civilization and the place of racism within it" (Gilroy 1993, 154). If so, his firsthand observation of the process by which leaders from French colonies in West Africa and the "old" colonies of Guadeloupe, Martinique, Réunion, and Guyane sought to redefine the nature of their relationship to France surely enhanced his reflections. These leaders envisioned resolutely anticolonial transformations that departed from the colonial past but did not necessarily assume the independent nation-state as the realization of their aspirations.[26] If he did not know of him beforehand, Wright would have become familiar with one of the leaders of this fight through his work in support of the journal *Présence Africaine*, which was founded the same year he arrived in France: the poet and intellectual, recently become politician, Aimé Césaire.[27] The year prior to Wright's arrival, Césaire had led the fight in the Constituent Assembly to pass a departmentalization law, which would establish Martinique, Guadeloupe, and French Guyana as French departments. Among other demands, this strategy aimed to secure equal legal status for these former colonies within the French Union. According to Wilder, Césaire conceived of departmentalization as a first stage in a dynamic development "from formal legal liberty to economic emancipation and then to significant social reorganization within the Antilles" (Wilder 2015, 112). Césaire's support for this strategy derived at least in part from his seven-month sojourn in Haiti, which, he later recalled, had "conquered its liberty ... its independence," but "was more miserable than Martinique" (quoted in Wilder 2015, 187). Of course, Césaire visited Haiti only ten years after the end of the nearly twenty-year brutal U.S. occupation of Haiti. Considered within the context of Haiti's particularly tragic freedom and growing U.S. imperial encroachment throughout the region, as discussed in chapter 2, Césaire's push for departmentalization seems less reactionary in its moment than it has become in ours.

Already a poet and teacher with a considerable reputation, Césaire entered electoral politics amid the postwar militant activity and organizing that followed the fall of the Vichy regime on the island. In May 1945, he was elected the mayor of Fort-de-France on the Communist Federation of Martinique's (FCM) electoral ticket. Following that electoral success, Cés-

aire officially joined the French Communist Party (PCF) in July, just prior
to the Constituent Assembly's October elections. For a little more than a
decade, Césaire was a communist delegate in the French National Assembly,
where he fought opposition to the full implementation of the departmentalization law. In October 1956, the month following the First Congress of
Black Writers and Artists sponsored by *Présence Africaine* and the Society
of African Culture and a little more than a year after the FCM withdrew its
support for departmentalization, Césaire resigned from the PCF in his *Letter to Maurice Thorez*. In this letter, according to Wilder, Césaire "attempted
to think beyond departmentalization, based on a narrow concept of political assimilation, and orthodox communism, based on an abstract concept
of proletarian emancipation" (2015, 170). Recently, critics have argued that
Césaire's decision to join the PCF represents either an errant detour from
the "royal road" of Négritude or the consequence of his having "swallowed
his previous objections" to communism (Kemedjio 2010, 97; Miller 2010,
748). Césaire's decision to join the PCF in 1945, however, was not a radical
departure; it was consistent with the course of his intellectual development
over the ten-year period prior to his joining the party.

As is well known, Césaire entered the prestigious l'École normale supérieure (ENS) in the fall of 1935. Beginning in the early 1930s, the PCF
had successfully established a presence at ENS, centered around a Jeunesses
communistes cell of about thirty members.[28] Up to that point, as David Alliot argues, the dominant influence at ENS was socialist, with the notable
exception being Paul Nizan, who joined the Communist Party during his
studies there from 1924 to 1927 (Alliot 2013, 40). The connection between
Nizan, the PCF, and ENS are relevant to Césaire's political education and
commitment in light of an earlier statement, in which he formulated Négritude within the rhetoric of communism. Césaire made this statement in an
only recently discovered article, "Racial Consciousness and Social Revolution" ("Conscience raciale et révolution sociale"), published in *L'étudiant noir*,
no. 3, May–June 1935.[29] This article, as Christopher Miller notes, "begins
with an epigraph from Paul Nizan's *Les chiens de garde* (*The Watchdogs*) and
contains at least two direct quotations from Nizan" (744, 749 notes 3, 4).
Césaire was probably drawn to Nizan because, despite his party membership, his writing was "anything but propaganda for the PC." The party had
complained about the "insufficient economic analysis" in his critique of colonialism in *Aden Arabie* and the absence of "an apology for the new Marxist
culture" in his critique of capitalism in *Antoine Bloyé* (McCarthy 1985, 197).

For the young poet, Nizan offered a model of radical political alignment that did not require a sacrifice of aesthetic independence to the altar of party discipline.[30]

The intellectual circles he frequented at ENS were but one of the influences on Césaire's political education. An equally, if not more, important influence were the Caribbean intellectuals, with impressive radical pedigrees in their own right, with whom he associated during this period. First among these was Suzanne (Roussi) Césaire, a friend of his sister, who like Césaire was a member of the l'Association des étudiants martiniquais and frequenter of the Clamart Salon of Jane and Paulette Nardal (Sharpley-Whiting 2002, 80). She was, according to his biographer, "much more radical—in politics as in literature—than Aimé Césaire" (Alliot 2013, 28). After Suzanne Césaire, the most important figure in Césaire's political development and career was Pierre Aliker. Aliker was "from a family with a long history of republican and socialist values," who would become "engaged in nearly all anticolonial and antiracist struggles" (Alliot 2013, 29). In 1945, Aliker ran alongside Césaire on the Communist Federation's ticket in the Fort-de-France municipal elections, and he remained one of his closest and most trusted advisers. Indeed, just weeks following the publication of the *Letter to Maurice Thorez*, in which Césaire had argued that black people needed organizations "made for them, made by them, and adapted to ends that they alone can determine" (1956b, 148), Aliker formed the Comité Aimé Césaire. The Comité "circulated a call by Césaire for the people of Martinique to establish an autonomous political organization" (Wilder 2015, 173).[31] With Aliker and Aristide Maugée, his sister's husband, Césaire would found the Parti progressiste martiniquais (PPM) in March 1958, not two years after his public resignation from the PCF.

Césaire opens his *Letter to Maurice Thorez* with an acknowledgment of Khrushchev's recent revelation of Stalinism's horrors. In this context, he deplores the Stalinist bureaucracy's lamentable achievement of having transformed into a "nightmare what humanity has for so long cherished as a dream: socialism" (1956b, 146). He quickly moves on from these concerns to address his particular grievances as a member of the French Communist Party and person of color. Insisting on the distinction between these two terms, Césaire privileges the latter in the remainder of the essay, using the first-person plural possessive pronoun "our" ("notre") to assert the singularity of the black "situation in the world,"—its "problems," "history," and "culture"—"which cannot be confused with any other" (147). Césaire here takes aim at a seemingly widespread tendency in Western communist parties to reduce racism to an epiphenomenon of the class struggle and to position black people as a subordinate fragment or section within the working class. This practice led to what many perceived as communist opportunism: embracing black struggles when they benefited the party, and by extension Soviet objectives, but abandoning them when they did not. In the United States, this alleged opportunism was most egregiously demonstrated in the compromise with fascism in the Hitler-Stalin nonaggression pact and, when that policy was subsequently reversed, communist opposition to black struggles against racial discrimination in war industries because they were seen as undermining the war effort.

Not simply a matter of party-level political strategy, this wavering among Western communist parties represents a failure to appreciate the theoretical significance of Marx's words on the role of racism at capitalism's dawn[32] and its continued reproduction. Césaire's insistence on the singularity of black experience is grounded in this historical reality and its contemporary manifestation. If following Christopher Miller's suggestion we read "Racial Consciousness" and *Letter to Maurice Thorez* as interlocking "pieces of a puzzle," it should also be noted that Césaire makes a theoretical advance in *Letter* that goes beyond claiming that "blacks will be better revolutionaries if they are in true communication with their blackness" (Miller 2010, 747-8). In the twenty-one-year interval between the two pieces, Césaire ultimately arrives at the bold assertion that the revolutionary potential of the white working class has been effectively neutralized by its and its leaders' inability to grasp the racist nature of capitalist development. In a formulation echoing his "Poetry and Knowledge" speech discussed in chapter 2, Césaire calls for nothing short of a "veritable Copernican revolution" to overcome the theoretical blindness manifested in the European "habit of doing, . . . arranging, . . . and thinking for" black people (Césaire 1956b, 150). Instead, he affirms the validity of black radicalism on its own terms. Césaire was not renouncing his project's affiliation with Marxism, but radicalizing that tradition by returning to, in Marx's words, "the root of the matter." Readers of *Capital* will recall that Marx had asserted that "the conversion of Africa into a preserve for the commercial hunting of blackskins" was among those developments "characteriz[ing] the dawn of the era of capitalist production" (Marx 1990, 915). In insisting on the pre-eminence of the Euro-American working class as the revolutionary agent of history, orthodox communist parties had preceded from a fundamental misreading of Marx.[33] Ultimately, Césaire objects to the inability of French communists to grasp that black struggles—colonial peoples against colonialism and people of color against racism—are "more complex, or better yet, of a completely different nature than the fight of the French worker against French capitalism, and it cannot in any way be considered a part, a fragment, of that struggle" (Césaire 1956b, 147). Such intransigence, or failure of the political imagination, made reconciliation impossible and resulted in Césaire's resignation.

When he left the PCF, Césaire was not simply rejecting a Stalinist bureaucracy that had perpetuated working-class domination under the guise of its liberation. His resignation is incomprehensible without reference to the PCF's position on Algeria, which he had publicly distanced himself from in late January of 1956. In his letter, Césaire refers directly to the party's unpardonable vote in support of granting the government of Guy Mollet "special powers" to "govern by decree in Algeria, and . . . to take whatever measures they considered necessary for the restoration of order" and defeating the Algerian rebels (Rioux 1987, 266). Indeed, the actions of the party were such that Césaire could conclude that the offices of the PCF's colonial branch on rue St-Georges were "the perfect counterpart of the Ministry of Overseas France on rue Oudinot" (Césaire 1956b, 150). After leaving the PCF, Césaire continued to contribute his voice to the anticolonial currents reshaping the global order without having to consider the correct communist line.

CHAPTER 2

Setting the Cold War Stage
George Lamming, Jacques Stephen Alexis, and the Critique of U.S. Imperialism in the Caribbean

In the debate session that followed the opening session of the First Congress of Black Writers and Artists in Paris in 1956, the Haitian writer and political activist Jacques Stephen Alexis took the floor to propose a clarification of the meaning of culture being bandied about among the delegates. Alexis urged the congregants to look no further than their choice to confer the presidency of the congress on his fellow Haitian, the venerable Dr. Jean Price-Mars, as indicating a way forward from the morass. He reminded those assembled that at "a dark moment of our history—a moment when the land of Dessalines was once again occupied by foreign forces" Price-Mars alone "stood up and proclaimed: 'In this land, there exists a culture, a *national* culture; or better yet, cultures are tied to the history of nations'" ("Debats" 69). Alexis's position is slightly at odds with the conventional wisdom that the honor bestowed on Price-Mars reflected the fact that his *Ainsi parla l'oncle* (*So Spoke the Uncle*) and Haiti's Africanist intellectuals had been considered precursors to the Négritude movement (Dash 1981, 121). In making the more political connection, Alexis did more than just anchor culture in concrete historical and political experience; he put culture at the forefront of the struggle against imperialism. That Alexis's remarks immediately followed Richard Wright's repudiation of a message from W.E.B. Du Bois, read during the Congress's opening session and that accused the American attendees of being agents in the pay of the U.S. government, suggests the import of his message about Price-Mars's place at the conference.[1] In effect, he managed to establish a continuity between the nearly two-decades-long occupation of Haiti by the U.S. Marines and what U.S. assumption of leadership over of the global order would portend for the peoples of Africa and Asia. In drawing out the connection between the Good Neighbor policy that followed the occupation and the cultural Cold War, the last section of this chapter establishes that this continuity manifested in both policy and personnel.

Price-Mars took his stand during the very first years of the U.S. occupation, shortly after returning to Haiti from France, where he had filled a vacant ministerial position. The timing of the appointment by his cousin, President General Vilbrun G. Sam, meant that Price-Mars did not witness the landing of U.S. Marines on Haitian soil on July 28, 1915. He had been in Haiti the previous winter, however, and so might have been among the "shocked and angry" Haitians who learned that the U.S. Marines brazenly seized a half-million dollars from Haitian coffers in the middle of the afternoon of December 17, 1914, conveyed it to a waiting U.S. Navy ship, and transported it to the United States for deposit into the National City Bank in New York City (Plummer 1988, 210). When the United States occupied Haiti the following summer, it was an important step in securing its dominance over the Western hemisphere and providing valuable lessons and personnel for its later emergence as the dominant global superpower in the early Cold War period.

Mere months after his return to an occupied Haiti, Jean Price-Mars launched a program of cultural resistance to the forces of occupation. Begun in April of 1917, this program consisted of three lectures the primary goal of which was to shake the elite from its resigned acquiescence to the occupation. As his biographer Magdaline W. Shannon notes, Price-Mars joined forces with a group of like-minded friends in "a campaign to rejuvenate the elite through lectures and their new journal *L'Essor*, hoping to create in them a national moral conscience which would lead to action and resistance" (Shannon 1996, 40). To achieve this goal, Price-Mars sought to inculcate within the elite a sense of identification with and responsibility for the Haitian peasantry. The Haitian peasantry had taken the lead in the resistance to U.S. occupation, most notably in the form of the armed Cacos' revolt. They suffered accordingly. In the first months alone, the peasantry was the target of "systematic acts of violence" conducted by the occupying forces, which "burned countless villages to the ground, destroyed most Haitian fortresses, and killed hundreds of Haitians" (Renda 2001, 146). The widely different responses of the peasantry and the elites to the occupation provided Price-Mars with the occasion for his lectures, which sought to bridge the enormous distance between the two groups. Declaring himself "profoundly shocked by the state of disarray of the elite since the American occupation," Price-Mars called on the elites to rediscover the "simple dignity of its calling" by making "better use of its moral, social, and intellectual resources" as the representatives and leaders of the entire nation (Price-Mars 2001, ix, xii).[2] The ideas laid out in these lectures would later be refined and further elaborated in *So Spoke the Uncle*, published in 1928.

So Spoke the Uncle established Price-Mars's reputation as at the forefront of the intellectual resistance to the U.S. occupation of Haiti. According to the historian Matthew Smith, the text solidified the La Nouvelle Ronde nationalist movement and made a call for a "truly inclusive" cultural nationalism that was both "original and potent" (Smith 2009, 8–9). The text's impact, however, was not confined to Haiti. It also inspired a cultural renaissance in the African diaspora, garnering a receptive audience among the generation of black francophone artists associated with the Négritude movement. In fact, J. Michael Dash considers it "as much a founding text of Haitian *indigénisme* as it was of Parisian Négritude," which Leopold Sedar Senghor acknowledged in "baptiz[ing] Price-Mars the 'father of Négritude'" (Dash 2013, 220). In the preface to *So Spoke the Uncle*, Price-Mars made the text's most enduring argument: the Haitian elite "suffered fatally from *bovarysme collectif*," which manifested itself in "servile imitativeness for which the nation paid the price of foreign occupation" (Dash 2013, 221).

The costs exacted on Caribbean societies of this rendering are explored in the two midcentury Caribbean novels discussed in this chapter, George Lamming's *In the Castle of My Skin* and Alexis's *General Sun, My Brother*. That both these authors were invited to participate in the First Congress of Black Writers and Artists is probably the result of the positive critical reception of their respective novels. Their participation, like that of Jean Price-Mars, made sure that the history of American intervention in the Caribbean was never far from the surface of the conference's deliberations. In its exploration of this history, this chapter begins with U.S. construction of the Panama Canal and the Caribbean migrant workers—a significant percentage hailing from Lamming's native Barbados—who labored under Jim Crow conditions at the turn of the twentieth century to build the canal; it ends with the U.S. occupation of Trinidad, Barbados's neighboring island, during World War II. The analysis in this chapter focuses on these novels' representation of the expansion of U.S. commercial interests in the region and the nearly twenty-year occupation of Alexis's Haiti by the U.S. Marines. Brenda Gayle Plummer has recently argued that "it is not possible to write the history of African-American freedom struggles without careful examination of their intersection with Caribbean goals and aspirations" (Plummer 2013, 12). Much of the work in *Of Vagabonds and Fellow Travelers* involves examining this intersection at the crucial moment of the early Cold War years.

This chapter argues that to understand the forces confronting the African American freedom struggle, particularly in the twentieth century, requires taking stock of the means and ends of U.S. imperial might as it was exercised in the Caribbean. Thus, when considered in their early Cold War contexts, these novels offer a warning to the peoples of Africa and Asia about the potential consequences of U.S. global dominance and an admonishment to African American elites on the costs of aligning their civil rights goals with that imperial project. It is not surprising that these Caribbean novelists would be in a position to deliver that message given the impact on the region of the U.S. construction of the Panama Canal at the turn of the century. With its racist, two-tiered pay system and other discriminatory policies, the U.S.-controlled Panama Canal Zone (PCZ) appeared to postwar observers throughout Latin America, Africa, and Asia as "a pure case of U.S. overseas imperial policy, directly analogous to European colonial policies abroad" (Borstelmann 2001, 80). Those African diaspora intellectuals who dared challenge the narrative of American difference from its European allies were considered as threatening to the social order as vagabonds and branded with the taint of communist fellow traveler to neutralize the potential impact of their experience and message.

"THE BIGGEST AN' BEST CANAL IN THE WIDE WIDE WORLD"

That control of territory in the Caribbean was critical to realizing U.S. imperial ambitions had been evident to American officials since the late nineteenth century. One of the first brazen attempts to realize this occurred in 1891, when the "US Government empowered an admiral to aggressively demand from Haiti the Môle St. Nicolas, a promontory with a deep-water harbor" as "repayment [for Haitian president] Hyppolite's political debt" (Plummer 1988, 27). The Môle would serve the U.S. Navy as a coaling station and provide a base of control over the Windward Passage. The strategic importance of this eighty-kilometer-wide strait between Cuba and Haiti resided in the fact that it offered the shortest route between the transisthmian canal under discussion and the eastern seaboard ports of the United States.[3] While this initial attempt to force Haiti to cede sovereignty over part of its territory was unsuccessful, the opportunity to gain a U.S. foothold in the Caribbean would present itself before the close of the century.

This opportunity came in the Spanish-American War of 1898. With the resulting military occupation of Cuba and Elihu Root's Platt Amendment, this war established a pattern in terms of U.S. relations with the world's "darker nations" that would be repeated throughout the twentieth century. Securing the naval base at Guantánamo Bay as part of the terms of the Platt Amendment initiated a process that would eventually transform the Caribbean Sea into an American lake. This transformation accelerated in 1903 when the United States "invent[ed] . . . a new country (Panama) in order to facilitate construction of a US-controlled transisthmus canal" (Smith 2003, 15). The canal bridged the continental divide between the United States' Atlantic and Pacific coasts and facilitated access to U.S. possessions in the Philippines and Hawaii. The commercial and military ship traffic through the Panama Canal made U.S. control in the Caribbean practically a strategic necessity. As a consequence, the first half of the twentieth century saw U.S. military occupation, annexation, and leasing of land at strategic points throughout the region. At every stage of this process, black labor was engaged in the work of rendering Caribbean soil into capital for U.S. military and financial interests.

When the U.S. Isthmian Canal Commission began construction on the canal in 1904, it searched the globe in search of unskilled labor to do the indispensable pick-and-shovel work. It found an abundant source of workers in the peripheral regions of Southern Europe and the Caribbean, which provided the "vast contingent of Silver workers who shouldered the drudgery of the canal excavation" (Major 1993, 81). The relations of production established in the Canal Zone explicitly followed the logic of racial capitalism so that racial hierarchies determined economic policy. Indeed, according to Major, "the labour policy brought in by the canal régime discriminated expressly between the two sections of the canal work force, the Gold and Silver Rolls," with the basis of the duality being race (1993, 78).[4] West Indians made up more than half of the Silver Roll workforce. In the ten years from 1903–1913, the construction period on the canal, twenty thousand Barbadian men were hired as contract workers, while another twenty-five thousand men and women migrated without a labor contract to try their chances in Panama. Overall, nearly 25 percent of the working-age men in Barbados worked in Panama in this period (Putnam 2013, 26). For those who arrived in Panama under a labor contract, the conditions in Panama did not deviate from the centuries-long pattern of racialized exploitation of black workers. Some of those without labor contracts formed the reserve army of labor that canal engineer William Burr judged necessary "to provide the Commission with a ready pool of employables to inhibit any strike movement" (Major 1993, 83–84). The prevailing conditions in both the Caribbean and Panama clearly placed these workers in a relationship to capital reminiscent of those vagabonds who attended capitalism's launch. Pushed from their accustomed way of life on their island homes and drawn by the lure of plentiful work, these workers would struggle to realize their dreams as they negotiated the disciplinary demands of racial capitalism, the foundation stones of the U.S. empire-building project.

George Lamming excavates the impact of this project on his native Barbados in *In the Castle of My Skin*, published in 1953, shortly after he arrived in England as part of the Windrush generation. An autobiographical tale of a young boy's coming of age in a small Barbadian village, the novel meditates on the dislocations experienced by characters caught in the maelstrom between two empires, one in the final stages of its decline and the other on the brink of realizing its imperial ambitions. These dislocations are channeled primarily through the exilic male characters, who all emigrate to areas within the American sphere of influence, from the Panama Canal Zone to the mainland United States and finally to occupied Trinidad. The novel manages these imperial developments by reducing their scale so that the novel's representation of the village achieves a "symbolic quality applicable to Barbados, to Jamaica, and to all of the other islands," which, Lamming suggests, accounts for "why [the] book has remained in West Indian memory" (Lamming 1972, 8). Through considered attention to Caribbean village life, the novel develops, according to Simon Gikandi, its "powerful narrative critique of the psychology of colonialism" and evokes "a narrative of decolonization and liberation" (Gikandi 1992, 70, 72) for which it was rightly celebrated. In the novel, the moment of decolonization, however, is not completed, as throwing off the yoke of British colonialism happens within the context of the United States' emergence as first a hemispheric and then global power. The novel figures its ambivalence about the possibility of a liberated future and the persistence of colonialism in the symbolic transfer of ownership of land in the village from descendants of Creighton to Mr. Slime and his nominally black "self-help" societies.

The critical literature on *In the Castle of My Skin* has emphasized the novel's critique of the crippling effect of British colonialism and its afterlife on Caribbean people and society. For example, in one of the first book-length studies of Lamming's work, Sandra Pouchet Paquet remarks that "the novel marks Lamming's initial effort as an artist to describe and influence the inherited values that distort and inhibit social relations in a former British colony" (Paquet 1982, 27). While the novel exposes the British educational system as the primary vehicle for the transmission of those distorted values, it does recognize alternative sources of knowledge from outside this system, which are associated with the shoemaker and the narrator's childhood friend, Trumper. It is not insignificant to my argument in this chapter that this knowledge originates directly or indirectly through an encounter with the U.S. imperial presence. More recently, J. Dillon Brown argues that the novel's clear resonances with Caribbean anticolonial struggles need not obscure the fact "that such an overtly anticolonial project found expression through a willingly intertextual dialogue with forms readily identified as metropolitan" or the context of its metropolitan production, the novel having been written and published in London (Brown 2006, 13). While these complementary critical perspectives solidly locate the novel and the anglophone Caribbean within center-periphery relations of the British Empire, these perspectives crucially overlook how the novel also captures the fact of the Caribbean's relationship to a United States expanding from hemispheric to global power status. Writing several years after the publication of *In the Castle of My Skin*, Lamming feels compelled to acknowledge this relationship in *The Pleasures of Exile* (1960): "America is very much with us now: from Puerto Rico right down to Trinidad.... [W]e have always been mixed up in America's business" (154). My reading of the novel in this chapter emphasizes those moments that turn our attention to the consequences for the Caribbean of being caught in the drift of American capitalist and imperialist expansion.

The novel first raises the issue of the U.S. imperial project's impact on Caribbean village life through the loneliness of G., the protagonist. He attributes this loneliness to the fact that his extended family no longer resides in the village, a situation, he suggests, that has left him devoid of memory. Faced with this void, the protagonist finds a substitute in inquisitiveness, a characteristic displayed in the novel's opening dialogue, in which the protagonist queries his mother about the whereabouts of his maternal grandmother and uncle. G.'s mother reminds him that her mother "is now in the

[Panama] Canal Zone" and that "[her] brother went to America" years ago and "is probably dead for all we know" (Lamming 1953, 12). We know that G.'s grandmother is still alive because his mother suggests that he write her a letter, but this is the first and last time the narrative mentions her. In this brief mention and even quicker dispatch of these family members, the novel characterizes the effect of the American imperial project on the region's inhabitants as similar to a hurricane: it uproots and deposits them in U.S.-dominated space that places seemingly intractable barriers between them and their kinsmen. This opening passage also registers this space as one whose allure of prosperity carries with it the ever-present threat of mortal danger.

These migrant characters all play an important part in G.'s psychological preparation for his own migration beyond the restricted worlds of Creighton village. The most important migrant figure in the novel is the village elder Pa, who as a young man worked on the construction of the Panama Canal. His sojourn is clearly meant to recall those tens of thousands of Barbadian men and women who left their homes in search of work in Panama in the first decade of the twentieth century. Pa's time working in Panama establishes his claim on the honorific "great," a title usually reserved for those with a higher status in the imperial order, such as the village landlord (28) and even Queen Victoria herself (38). It is not through association with British imperial rule, however, that Pa achieves his status as a "great," but from the material rewards earned through his vital role in laying the infrastructural foundation for the United States' emergence as the successor to Great Britain as the globe's hegemon. Pa's memories are flooded by his time in Panama, "where with [his very] hands [he] help to build the canal, the biggest an' best canal in the wide wide world" (85). Construction of this canal facilitated commerce and communication between the Atlantic and Pacific coasts of the United States and accelerated the process of transforming the Caribbean Sea into an "American lake." This transformation was enabled by West Indians, primarily Barbadians, who supplied the vast majority of the labor during the construction phase, constituting more than two-thirds of the semiskilled and unskilled workers on the Silver Roll. These workers built and maintained the Panama Canal in the first couple of decades of the twentieth century.

With the money received in exchange for his labor in Panama, Pa achieved a level of "greatness" that forms the core of his reminiscences about his time as a migrant laborer. Speaking to Ma, he recalls, "we wus great in them days as you says. We know what it means to drive in coach an' buggie, an' whatever the Great do in the open air. . . . We was great alright" (85–86). For Barbadians of peasant origins like Pa, Panama provided a means to experience pleasures, such as circulating in horse-drawn carriages, customarily reserved for those occupying the social position of "Great" in the island's racially inflected social and economic hierarchy. Rhonda Frederick astutely observes that Pa's dissipated riches were not the source of his enduring "greatness" in the village, but his "dignity, achievement, and perspective," all of which "disrupts how Greatness and 'lowliness' have been defined" along conventionally racist lines of money and white-skin privilege that consign impoverished blacks to the "swineherd" (Frederick 2005, 98). Of course, what Pa's reminiscences downplay are the humiliations that inevitably resulted from the United States having exported Jim Crow social and economic arrangements to the Canal Zone. In this regard, Pa's memory finds an echo in U.S. attempts during the Cold War to convince the people of Africa and Asia that its racist and imperialist past did not compromise its position as the world's defender of freedom against the Soviet menace.

As its symbolic heart, Pa's experience connects the village not only to the jungles of Panama but also to the island of Cuba on the Caribbean's northern rim. If it is to Panama that Pa's memory takes him "back to every now an' again" (Lamming 1953, 85), the forces that brought him there to create those memories were set in motion at the turn of the nineteenth century when the United States entered into the Spanish-American War. The war proved to be, according to Major, "a watershed in the long campaign for an American canal" (1993, 25). At war's end, the United States seized Hawaii, acquired Guam and the Philippines, thereby increasing its stake in the Pacific, and established its first footholds in the Caribbean. With these war-won acquisitions the United States began in earnest to compete for status as an international power. The construction and control of an isthmian canal would prove pivotal, as it would dramatically expand the U.S. position as an imperial, military, and commercial power. The canal venture would enable the United States to "abridge the enormous distances between American interests in the Caribbean and the Pacific," "significantly enhance the capacity of the US Navy . . . to meet a threat in one ocean or the other," and expand "American mercantile potential through quicker access to the markets of Europe and Asia" (Major 1993, 24). With the securing of the naval base at Guantánamo Bay, Cuba, and taking possession of Puerto Rico, the United States established control over the northern approaches to the Caribbean and took the initial steps toward the transformation of the Caribbean Sea into an American lake, a process completed during World War II with the construction of a military base in occupied Trinidad, to which the narrator G. emigrates at the novel's close.[5]

The U.S. ascent to global power status transformed its smaller, Caribbean island neighbors to the south. The effects of this transformation were borne most heavily on the peasantry. Their ordeal and dramatically altered relationship to the land echoes those changes that produced the vagabonds who roamed the sixteenth-century English countryside. *In the Castle of My Skin* subtly captures these altered dynamics in the life history of the characters Ma and Pa, who otherwise represent "the archetypal peasant tradition of the island" (Brown 2006, 679). These characters occupy a revered place in the village largely because of their vagabond past, in which they departed from their native land to work on the U.S. Panama Canal construction project. The other characters in the novel understand their experience in positive terms, finding in it the origin of Ma and Pa's financial stability and pride. For example, when the village's head teacher visits Pa to inform him of the decision to place him in the Alms House, the teacher recalls the facts of his life:

> He had been comfortable some years ago, and although much of what he had earned in Panama had been spent in one way or another, he had never been dissolute. He never seemed to regret anything, not even his present poverty which seemed tolerable. . . . Everyone remarked his tidiness, and they often said that the old man was great once. He had money and he had also that air of dignity which they associated with the Great. (Lamming 1953, 252)

The teacher's framing of Pa's experience working on the Panama Canal emphasizes its beneficial effects, while it mutes the exploitation and racism black workers like Pa would have encountered. The teacher's recollection participates in what cultural critic Rhonda Frederick describes as the "Colón Men mythographies," that offer a corrective to "binaristic accounts that cast canal authorities as powerful oppressor and [black canal workers] as powerless and oppressed" (Frederick 2005, 10). The appellation for these men refers to Colón, the port city on Panama's Caribbean coast that was the destination for these migrant workers. Instead of a cautionary tale of woe, Pa's experience is triumphant insofar as it provides him not only with fleeting riches, but the more important and enduring "dignity." This quality, as the teacher notes, had typically been limited to the island's mostly white elite social strata. In that way, Pa's experience is not simply one of literal vagabondage that required him to physically move in search of work; it is also symbolically vagabond because it disrupts the ideological enclosure that is the island's racial and class hierarchy, which would limit both money and dignity as the exclusive preserve of the white minority. His presence, there-fore, reminds the village's black inhabitants that there was nothing either natural or immutable about their present poverty.

As a constant reminder of the arbitrariness of the current ideological enclosure, Pa influences how villagers understand their history and imagine the future portended by changes in the village. Considering the situation of the village young people, Ma offers that "'Tis a next Panama we need now for the young ones. . . .'Tis a next Panama we want, Pa, or there goin' to be bad times comin' this way" (Lamming 1953, 86). In this instance, Ma defies traditional understanding of the peasantry's romantic relationship to their native soil. She hopes for another large-scale imperial project whose demand for labor would provide relief from the economic deprivation that threatens to wreak havoc on the village island's youth. Her prognosis evinces a profound understanding of the island's place in the U.S. imperial project; if the "bad times" are to be avoided, the young people will have to follow in the footsteps of their village elders and link their destinies not to the declining British Empire but to its successor to the position of global hegemon, the United States.

The idea that the United States will offer a solution for the current gen-eration of villagers is first advanced by the not-so-subtly-named character, Mr. Slime. A former teacher at the village school, dismissed after his affair with the schoolmaster's wife is revealed, Mr. Slime concocts two village self-help projects, the Friendly Society and the Penny Bank. To villagers like Pa, Mr. Slime represents a Moses figure. Ma's religious lessons "'bout the man Moses [who] rise up . . . to take his people out of the land of Egypt" provides Pa with an interpretive frame to understand Mr. Slime's actions: "I remem-ber it good . . . an' I says to myself . . . p'raps Mr. Slime is another moses come to save his people" (77–78). Although the novel does not reference it here, a figure such as Pa might have encountered the philosophy and opinions of another black Moses figure, Marcus Garvey, while working in Panama. Gar-vey's Universal Negro Improvement Association (UNIA) and its message of black empowerment through economic self-help and cultural indepen-dence found a receptive audience in this region. According to Laura Putnam, "nowhere was grassroots Garveyism stronger than in the circum-Caribbean migratory sphere," where more than half of the 271 UNIA branches outside the United States were located (Putnam 2013, 16). Indeed, Panama, with its forty-seven branches, had the third largest number of UNIA branches in the world, behind only the United States and Cuba (James 1998, 366). While the strong UNIA presence in these particular locations reflects the fact that they were destinations for British Caribbean migrant workers, it is not merely coincidence that in these same locales migrants were subjected to U.S. forms of racial and economic practice. Indeed, it was Garvey's encounter with the exploitation of black workers in zones of the U.S. empire that caused his divergence from the path typical of the nationalist colonial intelligentsia. Having already traveled beyond his island to other parts of the colonial world before his trip to London, Garvey, according to Michelle Stephens, "had already begun to identify with the trials of a *globally* imagined black community" (Stephens 2005, 87). It is crucial to underscore that this imagined black community had been constituted through its relationship to an expansive U.S. capitalism with nascent global ambitions.

The novel's description of both Mr. Slime's program and Pa's response to it emphasize that the villagers' fortunes were intimately linked to the United States. Whereas those in Pa's generation had sought their fortunes in the U.S. Panama Canal project, Mr. Slime upholds the North American mainland as the land where the current generation will realize its dreams. While she recognizes the current generation's need for a "next Panama," Ma adopts a guarded position with regard to the ultimate outcome. She senses it will result in a repetition of the cycle of emigration followed by a wistful return to the island: "You'll go an' you'll come back an' they'll sit under the lamp-post an 'say night after night what an' what they use to do." Seduced by Mr. Slime's rhetoric and the promise of America, Pa disagrees with Ma, countering that "this time . . . 'twill be America, a lan' where . . . there be milk an' honey flowin'" and "where they say money flow faster than the flood" (Lamming 1953, 86). The reference to the flood that ravages the village at the opening of the novel suggests that Pa intuits the potentially destructive force of American capitalism in the lives of the villagers. Ma remains skeptical and cautions Pa against Mr. Slime's intoxicating influence: "He's get a chance to go to yuh head like rum to a next man's" (Lamming 1953, 87). Indeed, Ma's skepticism proves prescient, since at the novel's end it is revealed that Mr. Slime has betrayed the villagers' trust and used their money to buy up land from which he then evicts them.

The novel depicts the younger generation as unlike Ma and without the resources, spiritual or otherwise, to resist the siren call of U.S. capitalism. Despite some reservations about certain aspects of American society, the novel's young male characters perceive the United States as a land of unlimited opportunity. This perception of America is the subject of a discussion between two characters, Trumper and Blue Boy, as they make their way on an illicit visit to the house of the landlord, Mr. Creighton. Trumper, who intends to immigrate to America, arrives at this decision based solely on having heard others "say things good there." Blue Boy finds it a reasonable enough proposition given that Mr. Slime has called "it the promise land" and that others "who been an' come back" have recounted tales of "food in galore . . . [that] you don' have to cook . . . yuhself" (168–69). Lamming himself captures this vague but undeniable presence of the United States in the lives of Caribbean villagers in an introduction penned thirty years after the novel's initial publication. Reflecting on the role of America in the novel, Lamming writes:

> [T]he United States existed for us as a dream, a kingdom of material possibilities accessible to all. I had never visited the United States before writing In the Castle of My Skin; but America had often touched our lives with gifts that seemed spectacular at the time, and reminded us that this dream of unique luxury beyond our shores was true. (Lamming 1972, xl)

These references record the U.S. incursion into the Caribbean, its spectacular presence in the form of material possibilities having already been established with the Panama Canal construction project and the fleeting prosperity it produced. While perhaps not equal to England in terms of its grip on the imagination of the island's habitants, the impact of the "dream" of the United States is clearly felt in the novel. Both the association with Mr. Slime and the repetition of "dream" in Lamming's introduction are meant to suggest the yawning gap between the dream of the United States and the reality. For many black immigrants, the reality of racism marred their experience of this reputed land of luxury.

Despite some wariness with regard to American life, characters in the novel remain steadfast in their belief that emigration to the United States offers the best solution to the island's acute social and economic problems, a consequence of land ownership concentrated in the hands of a small elite. The mystifying language of Mr. Slime, however, prevents the villagers from understanding this root cause of the island's woes. For example, in the conversation with Ma in which Pa extols the United States as a promised land, he parrots demographic information gleaned from one of Mr. Slime's speeches encouraging migration: "He use a word call emigration . . . Says . . . 'Twus a high burning' shame to put on a piece o' land no more than a hundred an' something square miles . . . 'twus a shame . . . to keep two hundred thousand people on it" (86). Mr. Slime's "facts an' figures" conspicuously avoid the question of private property and the distribution of land; the problem becomes one of "natural" facts related to geography and demography and not economic and political policy. The situation in Barbados, however, was the direct consequence of land monopolization: "as late as 1929 . . . only 17,000 acres of the cultivable land was owned by smallholders (who number about 18,000), while some 90,000 acres were under the control of the small white oligarchy" (James 1998, 37). In the novel, the impact of this monopolization is represented in the fact the narrator G. and his childhood friend, Trumper, both escape the crushing political and economic realities of Barbados through migration. These characters' migration to U.S.-controlled spaces—Trumper to the mainland and G. to U.S.-occupied Trinidad—registers the fact of the Caribbean island's absorption into the U.S. imperial project, or the transformation of "the Caribbean Sea into an American lake."

These transformations did not simply take place in the abstract and distant world of geopolitics but were registered in the new worldview of the narrator G's childhood friend, Trumper. On the eve of G.'s departure from the island, Trumper returns to the village after a three-year sojourn in the United States.[6] The transformations Trumper has undergone are not immediately discernible, but G. notices changes in his voice and language. He remarks that although Trumper's accent has not changed, "his voice was deeper, and he spoke more slowly and with greater care" (281). It is clear that such changes are meant to show that he has matured over the past three years, and they also suggest a different relationship to language. His pace and attention when speaking indicate that he has come to appreciate the weight and power of words. Trumper complements his new appreciation for language with a new and expanded vocabulary. G. first notices this particular acquisition from abroad when Trumper comments that "one or two things change round this joint" (282), "joint" being American slang for place and referring to the village in this sentence. According to G., "one or two words had changed for [Trumper], and it was only when he used these words that one detected a change in the manner of speech" (282). Language here signifies a change in the way that Trumper both apprehends and carries himself in the world.

This new way of being in the world literally manifests itself in Trumper's adoption of a new uniform. His sartorial choices mark him as someone who has returned from abroad, as Trumper appears in the village clad in a zoot suit: "He wore a thin brown suit with a bright tie and suède shoes. The jacket was long and deep and the pants were very narrow at the bottom and unusually wide at the knees" (283). His choice of a zoot suit marks his affiliation with the resistance culture of Mexican American and African American youth in the urban areas of the United States during the 1930s and 1940s.[7] A similar culture of resistance was also present in neighboring occupied Trinidad. There the "saga boys" adopted the zoot suit as both an emblem of glamorous fashion and "an uncompromising gesture of refusal" to submit to the disciplines of "work, village, and family," which elites and the colonial establishment sought to impose on them (Neptune 2007, 122). Trumper, thus, adorns himself in a symbol of racialized youths' resistance to the military discipline and self-sacrifice that American patriotism demanded in support of the war effort in World War II. It was in the context of this effort that the United States secured its control over the "American lake" and its surrounding Caribbean territories, control that signaled America's supplanting of British dominance in the region and of Britain on the world stage.

Trumper's most remarkable change, however, is in his political consciousness and his newfound understanding of race as a determining structure in the world. After introducing this idea in a letter sent to G. from the United States, Trumper raises the subject again over drinks at a village bar. As a lead-in to the conversation about race, Trumper plays for G. a recording of Paul Robeson singing "Let My People Go," which he describes as his "favourite piece" by his "favourite singer," "one o' the greatest o' my people" (294–95). (The song's lyrics, which reference the biblical story of Moses in Egypt, recalls the figure of Moses that Pa used when describing Mr. Slime earlier in the novel.) The reference to "his people" confounds G., who asks him to be more specific. Trumper's response, "the Negro race," clarifies little for G., which comes as no surprise to Trumper, who locates his own political awakening to the reality of race in his experience in the United States.[8] J. Dillon Brown insightfully notes that the novel "casts suspicions" and questions the "rigidity and close-minded self-certainty" of Trumper's "somewhat monological understanding of the world" (Brown 2006, 98). The focus on Trumper, however, misses the point and ignores the novel's work to locate this "monological understanding" in his experience in the United States. Trumper came to know a rigid and self-assured racism there, which categorically denied black humanity ("There ain't no 'man' an there ain't no 'people.' Just nigger an' Negro" [Lamming 1953, 297–98].) and dispensed with any "subterfuge" in maintaining exclusively white spaces. Thus it is not necessarily Trumper who is the object of critique here, but the dangerous expansion of this ordering principle across the globe as the United States replaced Great Britain as the dominant world power.

Trumper clearly appreciates the material abundance available in the United States, evidenced in his new clothes and portable radio, items of "unique luxury" to use Lamming's term. But his most cherished acquisition is his newfound political consciousness. He lectures G.: "An' I didn't understan' it myself till I reach the States. If there be one thing I thank America for, she teach me who my race wus" (295). Trumper counters G.'s retort that there are black people on their island with the following explanation: "They suffer in a way we don't here. We can't understan' it here an' we never will. But their sufferin' teach them what we here won't ever know. The Race, our people" (296).[9] In Trumper's estimation, African Americans' lessons in suffering had made them "a different kind of creature" (299), which provided the Caribbean, in seeming contradiction to his previous statements, with an image of its future: "[Y]ou an' none o' you on this island is a Negro yet; but if they don't know, you goin' to know . . . [and] it frighten the life out o' me know what's goin' to happen" (297–98). Trumper's words provide clear evidence of his apprehension for the village, and the wider Caribbean, as a consequence of a shift in the imperial pecking order from Britain to the United States.

Whereas being a colony under British rule had shielded the island's inhabitants from a specific type of racial "suffering," the advent of U.S. dominance in the region foretold the end of this protection ("you goin' to know"). The novel underscores the significance of this lesson by having Trumper impart these words of wisdom and caution just prior to G.'s departure for occupied Trinidad. World War II–era military commanders clearly understood the U.S. occupation of Trinidad as the last stage in realizing the nineteenth-century U.S. naval strategist "[Alfred Thayer] Mahan's dream" of "the Caribbean [being] an American lake," where "ingress to that lake [was] controlled by United States defense forces as if it were an inland body" (McLean 1941 952). If the transformation from sea to lake increased Caribbean peoples' exposure to American race realities, the exploration of this history by Caribbean authors in the early Cold War period served as a har-binger to the world's darker nations of what U.S. global dominance might occasion, despite the official pronouncements from Washington about great strides toward racial progress.

The choice to have Paul Robeson's voice serve as the catalyst for this pivotal and timely conversation between G. and Trumper places the novel in a vagabond relation to official U.S. positions and alludes to signifies the theme of fellow traveling. According to Trumper, U.S. dominance in the re-gion would bring African Caribbeans, who are "not *yet* Negro," together with African-Americans as both vagabonds and fellow travelers in the struggle against racism and imperialism. The Robeson reference also marks the novel politically as vagabond and fellow traveling, because it upholds him as one of "the greatest o' [his] people" at a moment when he had become a communist pariah in the United States.[10]

Lamming's gesture in the novel should be considered in the context of Robeson's own relation to the Caribbean and its people. In November 1948, Robeson made a two-stop tour of the Caribbean, visiting Jamaica and Trinidad. During his Trinidadian stop, he held two enthusiastically received concerts in Port of Spain, where Lamming resided at the time. At the con-clusion of his West Indian tour, Robeson gave an interview emphasizing the links between the Caribbean and African American freedom struggles. His words resonate with the connections Trumper attempts to draw for G. in the novel: "The march of freedom by the Negroes of the West Indies is a matter of profound importance to Americans. The sound of their march-ing can be heard by the Negroes of our country, and their own marching time will be quickened by it" (quoted in Goodman 2013, 26). In February of the following year, just several months before Lamming himself arrived in England in 1950, Robeson started a triumphant four-month concert tour of the British Isles, interspersed with speaking engagements to radical and anticolonial organizations, many of them led by Caribbean and African ac-tivists residing in London.[11] During this tour, one of Lamming's Barbadian compatriots, the radical left-wing writer and activist Peter Blackman, served as a general aide to Robeson (Duberman 1989, 340). It was during this Eu-ropean trip in the early part of 1949 that Robeson attended, accompanied by Blackman, the World Congress of the Partisans of Peace, where he made the misquoted impromptu speech that spurred the anticommunist repression against him discussed in chapter 4.

If his touring engagements are any indication, Robeson did not abide any artificial separation between his various commitments, and he melded together his aesthetic, racial, and political concerns, treating them as of the same piece. In other words, when he spoke about the West Indian freedom struggle, it was linked to racial struggles in the United States, and both had to be understood in the context of the political struggles of the world's poor and dispossessed. For his part, Richard Wright was clearly anxious about any such conceptual intermingling when he penned his introduction to the 1954 publication by McGraw-Hill of the *In the Castle of My Skin*. He insists that "the magnetic symbol of Paul Robeson" is "shown here purely in racial and *not* political terms!" (vii, emphasis in the original). Wright's insistence here speaks more to his own anticommunist politics and his desire to foreclose any possibility of being associated with Robeson. The textual evidence suggests, however, that Lamming understood perfectly well Robeson's politics, and this approving reference to him in the novel shows Lamming actively resisting the ideological enclosures that would seek to define what was and was not acceptable for and from African diaspora people during the Cold War.

It did not take outsiders like Robeson or migrant workers returning home after stints in North America to render the villagers leery of the U.S. presence in the Caribbean. The construction of military bases and the subsequent American military occupation of Trinidad during World War II also contributed to their wariness. Upon graduating from the high school, which prepared boys to enter either "the civil service or an English university where they read for one of the professions, law or medicine" (219), G. accepts a post teaching English at a small boarding school in Trinidad. Just prior to his conversation with Trumper, G. discusses his impending departure for Trinidad with his mother, who gives him a stern lesson on the pitfalls awaiting him in Trinidad, a society she says has been turned upside-down and inside-out by Yankee occupation.

The novel registers the destabilizing effects of this occupation in distinctly gendered terms. Presenting him with information gathered from her conversations with Dave, a fellow villager who spent several years in the army stationed in Trinidad, G.'s mother cautions him to exercise prudence when choosing female companions. She paints a picture for him of an island overrun by decadence as a consequence of the occupation: "since the Americans been there you don't know who is who . . . [T]hey make the decent indecent and the indecent decent, an' now you don't know who is a lady an' who ain't. . . . Everything in a skirt ain't clean" (271). In this passage, G.'s mother focuses on how the American occupation has subverted the gender and sexual codes regulating women's behavior and has more explicitly commodified their sexuality as they engaged in sex work to satisfy a demand directly related to the occupation. Indeed, as Harvey Neptune argues, the entrance of thousands of American men associated with the occupation "stimulated a complex of conflicts and anxieties . . . around race, gender, and sexuality" (2007, 159) that threatened to unravel the social order in Trinidad. The maternal lesson G. receives emphasizes the sullying effects of too close an association with the Americans, an association that interrupts the heretofore stable metonymical relation between a "skirt" and propriety.

The unsettling of gender codes is an instance of a larger interpretive crisis provoked by the occupation. Considered in this light, the novel argues that American dominance in the region will demand a new set of critical tools to interpret a new world where things are no longer what they had been or would seem. By closing the novel with the image of the narrator setting off to a Trinidad turned upside-down by American military occupation, *In the Castle of My Skin* allegorizes the uncertain and shifting terrain that confronted the nations of the Global South as they entered a Cold War world of ascendant American imperial might. Occurring in the southernmost reaches of the Caribbean, the foray into Trinidad represented a last step in securing U.S. dominion in the region and set the stage for the extension of U.S. power over the globe following World War II. This power, however, had been put on full display nearly a quarter of century earlier, when the U.S. Marines occupied Haiti at the northern entrance to the Caribbean.

SECURING THE PASSAGE

For the Haitian writer Jacques Stephen Alexis, as with Lamming, the imperial might of the United States in the Caribbean was an inescapable reality. Similar to Lamming, Alexis also expressed sympathy with the majority black peasants of his native island in his novels and made their experience of the U.S. occupation of Haiti and its immediate aftermath the focus of his first novel. The peasantry's experience offered a powerful counterpoint to the triumphant Cold War discourse promoted by an ascendant U.S. global power eager to bury the unflattering tale of its rise to hemispheric power. As Alexis acknowledged in his comments during the debate session following the first day of the Parisian Congress of Black Writers and Artists, the mold for his cultural intervention against the forces of U.S. imperialism had been cast nearly forty years earlier by Jean Price-Mars in the struggle against the U.S. occupation of Haiti.

Jacques Stephen Alexis's description of the deleterious impact of U.S. power in the region, particularly on the peasantry, in *General Sun, My Brother* stands in stark contrast to the rosy hues in which Washington painted its intentions for the world in the Cold War period. The novel offers an acerbic critique of the Haitian elite that served as a middleman for U.S. business interests in the country and allied themselves with the occupation forces. In contrast, it only celebrates those members of the elite, like the character Pierre Roumel, who defied the expectations of their class and aligned with the Haitian masses in their resistance to the occupation. The focus of the novel, however, remains on the heroic role of the masses. In fact, the narrator's first intrusions into the narrative as a character is to render homage to those masses from whose ranks, "in spite of the Americans, the leeches—in spite of the Vincents, the chickenshits, and the police, a harvest of new workers, new Charlemagne Péraltes, new fighters will spring up" (Alexis 1955, 27). The mention of Péralte in this passage inscribes within the text the Cacos rebellion against the forced labor, or corvée system, imposed by occupation administrators "to carry out a massive road-building project intended to link disparate communities and thus facilitate military and police operations" (Renda 2001, 32). Indeed, Péralte's name is also synonymous with the occupation's brutality, since after he was assassinated the U.S. Marines circulated a picture of his dead body in an attempt to break the people's spirit of resistance. The brutality of the U.S. Marines in stamping out the Cacos rebellion and making a spectacle of Péralte provided a pattern for responding to challenges to the imperial order that emanated from those vagabonds who refused to submit to the discipline of their new condition. In adopting the Good Neighbor policy in the years after the end of the occupation and retooling it for the cultural Cold War, the U.S. government sought to turn the page on this refusal and the brutality used to enforce a new discipline.

It is difficult to divorce the initial publication of *Compère Général Soleil* (*General Sun, My Brother*) from its Cold War context. When the prestigious French editor Gallimard published his first novel in 1955 (a year before the First Congress of Black Writers and Artists), Alexis had been residing in Europe for almost a decade, thanks to a government-sponsored scholarship to study in France. In 1946, Alexis and other young leaders of the Haitian

Communist Party led demonstrations and organized strikes that brought down the government of Elie Lescot, who had ruled Haiti for five years following the end of Sténio Vincent's dictatorship in 1941. In a shrewd political move, the new military-backed government of Dumarsais Estimé, Lescot's successor, precipitated Alexis's vagabond existence by offering him and the other organizers scholarships to study abroad. These scholarships, according to the historian Matthew J. Smith, diffused "the potential threat" posed by "an organized left-wing party with some of the strongest personalities of 1946 in its membership" (Smith 2009, 127). Alexis's role as a prominent political and labor organizer undoubtedly brought him to the attention of those in Washington, who watched developments in Haiti with keen interest. Indeed, a branch of Hoover's FBI, the Special Intelligence Service (SIS), had monitored events in the region since 1940; at its height more than six hundred intelligence agents served in Latin America (Maxwell 2015, 197).[12] Originally deployed to counter Nazi influence in the region, most of these agents were called back in 1946. This departure, of course, did not signal the end of intelligence operations in the region. There was a shift in mission as intelligence organizations focused on monitoring left-wing movements and their potential ties to the Soviet Union, which was soon to be cast in its role as a grave threat to the American way of life.

General Sun, My Brother, however, does not take the demonstrations of 1946 and Alexis's role in them as its subject. Instead, it provides a fictional account of events surrounding the last five years of the U.S. occupation, from roughly 1929 to 1934, and the first several years immediately following the withdrawal of the U.S. Marines. It covers an eight-year period bookended on one end by the Cayes massacre (sometimes referred to as Marchaterre, the precise locality) of December 1929, when U.S. Marines opened fire on peasants during a demonstration, and on the other end the 1937 pogrom against Haitians working and residing on the Dominican side of the border between the two nations. The novel's focus on these years provides crucial insight into the shift in American policy in the region away from military intervention and occupation to one of Good Neighborliness and soft power and its consequences on Haiti's peasant majority and their intellectual allies.

General Sun, My Brother examines this shift mainly through the main character Hilarion Hilarius and his encounters and friendship with communist intellectuals. As Hilarion and his friends try to survive and mount opposition to Stenio Vincent's repressive rule over postoccupation Haiti, they all become vagabond figures, forced into a life on the run as they try to make a living and avoid arrest for their political activities. The novel's opening sets the scene for this pattern. After being sentenced to one month in prison for attempted theft, Hilarion becomes acquainted with another prisoner at Fort Dimanche prison, Pierre Roumel,[13] a communist intellectual. It turns out that Hilarion first met Roumel when he was a boy. Roumel was a former neighbor of the Sigord family for whom Hilarion worked as a *restavèk*, "those kids that parents are forced to place with rich people rather than simply abandoning them" (Alexis 1955, 34). The novel bounds Hilarion's memory of Roumel up with the U.S. occupation, since he recalls Pierre having "once given him some short pants" during "the time of the strikes against the Americans" and "the slaughter carried out by the occupying forces at Marchaterre" (35).

The narrator's mention of Marchaterre and the time of the strikes alludes to the demonstrations that rocked Haiti in the fall of 1929. The unrest began with students protesting a change in scholarship policy at the Haitian-U.S. agricultural college, but it soon attracted other workers and evolved into a general strike. In the course of the disturbance, "thousands of Haitians demonstrating against the occupation and its client government" confronted marines "in cities and towns around the country" (Renda 2001, 34). "The slaughter . . . at Marchaterre" refers specifically to a confrontation on December 6, 1929, when the marines turned the weapons on a crowd, killing twelve and wounding twenty-three. This narrative allusion associates Roumel's philanthropic gesture with the resistance to the occupation. Hilarion's hardships as a young boy, however, are linked directly to the deprivations of American capitalism and imperialism. The emphasis on this connection in the novel provides a stark example of the consequences of U.S. power and influence in the region for the region's black majority. Hilarion's tale thus serves as a warning to the people of Africa and Asia of what they might expect from the emergence of the United States as a global power: the enrichment of a tiny, collaborationist minority at the cost of the widespread immiseration of the vast majority of people. This unflinching picture constitutes the novel's intervention into the Cold War discourse and supports my book's claim about the necessity of excavating the history of American intervention in the Caribbean as a precursor to its conduct as a global power.

When Hilarion joined the ranks of the *restavèks* in the Sigord household, he entered a world made possible by the Haitian elite's complicity with U.S.-led capitalist accumulation. The novel provides scant details on his specific experience with the Sigords, and instead speaks in general terms about the general state of *restavèks*. As a lot, they were "badly fed and housed," took "their blows, cr[ied]—and then learn[ed] not to cry," "wore rags and went bare-headed under the tropical sun," and were often victims of sexual assault (34–35). The narrator, however, does reveal critical information about the source of the Sigords' wealth and status: "The Sigords really liked the Americans. Mr. Sigord was a lawyer for HASCO and also a sworn follower of Borno. In addition, he was a member of the Council of State and he swore that only the Americans could save the country" (35). Mr. Sigord's work for the Haitian American Sugar Company (HASCO) and fidelity to Louis Borno, the client-president who ruled Haiti for eight years (1922–1930) under the American occupation, aligns him with elite contempt for the Haitian peasantry. That HASCO[14] exists in the novel as a metonym for the misery inflicted on Haitian peasants becomes clear when one considers that "thousands of peasants were driven from their lands to build the HASCO plantations and sugar refineries," and thousands more displaced to make way for the railroad that connected the Port-au-Prince refinery to the city's wharf (Kaussen 2008, 42; also Robinson 1996, 266).[15] Additionally, the repetition of "swore" in the novel to describe Mr. Sigord's relationship to Borno[16] and the Americans is meant to underscore his quasi-religious devotion to the gods of American capitalism and their local intercessor. Even when Hilarion finally escapes from the Sigords' clutches, he is still subject to the deprivations that American economic exploitation and military domination inflicted on the country's peasant majority.

Although the novel focuses on the impact of the American occupation on Hilarion's life, it figures in the presentation of other characters as well. For example, the occupation forms a central part of the narrative of the life of Claire-Heureuse, Hilarion's wife. Orphaned at an early age, Claire-Heureuse was reared by her godmother, Erica Jordan, who could afford to take her in because of her inheritance from a grandfather she never met. Joseph "Boss" Jordan, Erica's grandfather, was a small businessman and "an ardent nationalist," undone by the American occupation. The narrator informs us that he "died of a stroke one evening when an American Marine [entered his store] and treated him in an insolent manner" (82). The novel's emphasis on Joseph Jordan's frailty serves as an indictment of petty-bourgeois nationalists, who, lacking class consciousness, insisted on distancing themselves from the peasant majority. Clearly, this critique speaks directly to its contemporary moment and the decolonization struggles being waged in the context of the Cold War. In this representation, Alexis makes a poignant observation on the limits of nationalist struggles removed from the realities of the peasant and working-class majority among the world's darker peoples.

Despite the relative comfort of being Erica Jordan's goddaughter, Claire-Heureuse still remains of peasant origins, and like most peasants she is not able to avoid the brute realities of the occupation. While Erica Jordan regarded Claire-Heureuse as a daughter, she also considered her a servant and "sent Claire-Heureuse to sell things in the street, something she would never have considered for her [biological] daughter" (82). In her work as street vendor, Claire-Heureuse witnesses a scene that becomes a lasting memory of the occupation and an indelible image of the occupiers' glee in dehumanizing the Haitian masses:

> [D]runken Marines getting ready to burn a sheaf of dollar bills, a green splotch on the street. There was a bony woman with a diaphanous baby begging them to give her something. They had her dance, crawl on all fours, meow, bark, and whinny before they would give her one of the bills they were about to burn. Claire-Heureuse could see the woman picking up a bill with her mouth, tears flowing from shame and deprivation. Claire-Heureuse heard once more the hiccups, the laughter, the jibes and saw the red flame licking the green bills. (166)

Through this memory, the novel exposes the gendered nature of the occupation, which exposed women to particular forms of humiliation and violence. This representation of gendered violence underscores that the occupation was unrestrained in its assault on the Haitian peasantry. In this way, the novel seems to take direct aim at pretensions that American involvement in the world benefited and improved the lot of the most vulnerable. Instead, it shows the exercise of American power as taking a certain sadistic pleasure in acts of degradation, especially with regard to black women. The memory of this degradation undoubtedly informs Claire-Heureuse's later decision to become a vagabond alongside Hilarion and make the arduous journey to the sugar cane fields of the Dominican Republic.

The gendered violence of the occupation is the focus of the novel's only extended representation of a Haitian of Syrian descent. At the point in the novel when President Vincent faces a crisis that threatens his presidency, he negotiates to have three American warships bring U.S. Marines in for reinforcements. When the marines arrive they overrun the commercial zone, turning it into a war zone. In describing this round of imperialist violence, the novel introduces Habib Nahra, the son of immigrants, who is depicted as unlike most Syrians in his apparent knowledge of and love for his new country and its people. Sharing a lunch table with Hilarion and his fellow workers, Habib recounts the story of how he was beaten and given a black eye by three drunken marines, who entered his small fabric shop pursuing a young peasant woman attempting to elude their clutches. When Habib "stepped between them to protect her, the satyrs" beat him and ransacked his store (187). Through Habib's story the novel addresses the sexual violence committed against Haitian women, which, according to Mary Renda, "characterized the occupation from the beginning, but came to light following the use of the corvée and the resurgence of the Cacos rebellion" around 1918 (2001, 163). The inclusion of Habib's experience in *General Sun, My Brother* seems meant to underscore how the brutality of the occupation produced fellow travelers among those seemingly most removed from the Haitian peasantry and their resistance. It also furthers the assault on the Cold War narrative that the United States had and would act on the global stage to benefit the people of Africa and Asia.

To emphasize the point about the consequences of U.S. actions abroad, the novel is careful to demonstrate that the end of military occupation does not occasion a change in the circumstances of the majority of Haitians. The absence of the military changes little with regard to American influence and power over the fabric of their daily lives. For example, when Hilarion leaves prison, Pierre Roumel's mother finds him a job working at a factory making handbags, shoes, and hats from raffia and sisal. Initially described as a "modest" factory, the narrator later characterizes its owner, Mrs. Borkmann, as one of the "dishonest big industrialists . . . supported by the Americans" (161). This connection to the Americans helps explain Mrs. Borkmann's callousness when she fires Hilarion for defending a fellow worker accused of stealing sisal that Mrs. Borkmann had misplaced. Displaying the results of his rudimentary political education at the hands of Roumel and his friend Jean-Michel, a communist medical student character loosely based on Alexis, Hilarion boldly declares to Mrs. Borkmann that the true "crime" in this instance was "to steal the sweat of the brow from a poor worker" (123)! Although Jean-Michel helps him find a job at a small woodworking workshop, Hilarion only manages to support a simple life for himself and Claire-Heureuse, who maintains a small shop selling basic household goods like soap, sugar, and soda to local residents. A string of unfortunate events, however, highlights the precariousness of this meager existence. Their house is demolished to prevent a fire from spreading on their street, the workshop where Hilarion works is forced to close because of unfair competition, and Hilarion goes into hiding to evade being arrested for his political work. While the fire might be considered an accident, the novel draws a direct connection between Hilarion and Claire-Heureuse's plight and the continuing effects of U.S. domination in Haiti. When the couple decides to join the army of Haitians toiling in the sugar cane plantations of the Dominican Republic, this ostensible escape exposes them to even more of the brutal reality of the American imperial machine's operation in the region.

The novel first registers the wide-ranging footprint of this machine in the narrative of a return migrant, François Crispin or Franscuelo. Crispin pays a visit to Hilarion, arriving from the Dominican Republic with a letter from Hilarion's cousin Josaphat. Years earlier, Josaphat had fled to the Dominican Republic to escape arrest for the murder of an army officer that he discovers attempting to rape his sister. Over Haitian rum and Dominican cigars, Franscuelo recounts the tale of his ten years of peripatetic living and working around the Caribbean basin, an area completely enfolded into the imperial and economic machine of the United States. Significantly, Crispin's journey begins in the sugar cane fields of Cuba, the first foothold of U.S. imperialism in the Caribbean, dating back to the Spanish-American War of 1898. Franscuelo relates that he initially left Haiti "on a coastal sailboat that transported workers to the sugarcane plantations in Cuba at the time when the Bonnefil brothers were getting rich by dumping loads of Haitian workers, like *bwa debèn* on the shores of Cuba" (126). Franscuelo uses the Kreyòl word literally meaning "ebony wood," which was also used to refer to slaves in both French and Kreyòl.

The word also alludes to two classic texts of black literary radicalism. The most obvious allusion is to the poem and poetry collection *Bois-d'ébène*, published by Alexis's literary and political mentor Jacques Roumain in 1945. But it also makes a less evident reference to George Padmore's *The Life and Struggles of Negro Toilers* (1931). In that text, Padmore writes of the "Black Ivory Trade," which developed in the first two decades of the twentieth century and was stimulated by:

the General Sugar Company, the largest American concern in Cuba, [which] used to pay 25 dollars for every Haitian delivered on its reserva-

tions. During the boom years of the sugar industry trading in Negroes
became so profitable that steamship companies operating between Haiti
and Cuba made fortunes in the transportation of these black slaves. (67)

In Cuba, these Haitians worked primarily as cane cutters and were a significant contingent of the immigrant workers drawn by the interwar sugar
boom to eastern Cuba, where "US-owned sugar companies . . . invested
heavily and dominated the geographic and economic landscape" (Lipman
2009, 26).[17] It bears repeating here that eastern Cuba was (and remains)
strategically important in military terms to the U.S. imperial project. The
U.S. naval base at Guantánamo Bay assures U.S. control over the Windward Passage and the direct shipping lanes from the Panama Canal to the
east coast of the United States.

Given eastern Cuba's strategic importance to the United States' military
and economic interests in the region, it is significant that Franscuelo's tale
positions it as a space of workers' class consciousness and power. In a moment of doubt about his friend Jean-Michel's ideas about the reality and
possibility of class struggle, which seem "like distant dreams," Hilarion finds
support for them in Franscuelo's tale of labor unrest in Cuba. In that not-
so-distant time and place, "workers had refused to work, had begun a *heul-
ga* . . . several times in Santiago, Pilar del Río, and Matanzas" (eastern Cuban
towns), which had been organized by "men who had come from Oriente,
Havana, or Camagüey . . . the 'Reds'" (161). After working in Cuba for several
years, Franscuelo traveled throughout Central America[18] (travel that recalls
Garvey's) before eventually landing in the Dominican Republic, where he
meets Josaphat while working in a sugar refinery in Macorís. At each of his
stops as an itinerant worker around the Caribbean basin, Franscuelo would
have worked in American-controlled industries. The novel's description of
Franscuelo's experience underscores the penetration of American capitalism
in the region and cements the link between this American presence and the
racialized exploitation that he and Josaphat, and eventually Hilarion and
Claire-Heureuse, experience in the Dominican Republic.

While laboring under the relations of production imposed by American
capital in the Caribbean brings Fransculeo and Josaphat together, it is the
xenophobic discrimination Haitians living and working in the Dominican
Republic face that cements their bond. Josaphat comes to Franscuelo's defense in a fight against Dominican soldiers, "Trujillista rabble" (127), who
enter a café one Saturday evening and begin insulting Haitian workers. This

fight, of course, foreshadows the xenophobic tensions that rise to a bloody pitch at the novel's end. The novel insists, however, that the actions of Trujillo and his rabble cannot be reduced to mere atavistic nationalism or racism. These actions can only be properly understood within the context of the racialized hierarchies structuring the region's economy, which the novel describes as dominated by American capital.

In his tale of dangerous and exhausting work on sugar cane plantations and refineries, Franscuelo describes an industry whose international workforce is stratified along lines of national origin. Puerto Rican, Cuban, and Jamaican watchmen enforce unrelenting discipline on Haitian and Dominican workers whose labor produces the surplus value that the American owners of the plantations and refineries extract as profit (128). This description of the conditions in the Dominican Republic reinforces a connection maintained throughout the novel that ties the misery of the Haitian peasantry to American imperialism and capitalism. In drawing this connection, Alexis offers the pre–Cold War history of the United States in the Caribbean to readers as a powerful rebuke of American pretensions during the Cold War to be the true supporters of a liberated Africa and Asia.

Alexis's political commitment to recovering the shameful past of American domination in the Caribbean determines the representation in *General Sun, My Brother* of the events surrounding the 1937 massacre of Haitians living and working in the Dominican Republic. The third and final section of the novel covers Hilarion and Claire-Heureuse's sojourn to the Dominican town of Macorís, "a city with horizons" that exists "under the boot heel of Trujillista fascism and the Yankee imperialism of the surrounding sugar refineries" (225). The novel immediately discredits the idea of the massacre being motivated by some elemental "racial" difference between Haitians and Dominicans. The novel suggests that working side by side in the region's sugar industry had transfigured Haitians and Dominicans alike and those workers had transformed the region into a "strange," hybrid space where "the two national cultures mingled" (218). The novel emphasizes this mingling in an episode that highlights the somatic similarity between the two peoples. In this episode, the owner of the pharmacy, a Trujillo supporter, inquires whether Josaphat and Hilarion are Haitian as he serves them and then asks, in Spanish, "what they were doing in the Dominican Republic and why they had not stayed in their own country" (219). In contrast to the murderous bigotry of Trujillo and his supporters, the novel finds the seeds of a brighter future in the new, nonnational subjectivities being produced by the workers in their work together in the sugar cane fields. The labor organizer Paco Torres gestures toward that future when, in his last words before being shot to death, he urges his fellow sugarcane workers: "Sugarcane workers should never be divided. . . . As Dominicans and Haitians united, we shall force the Americans of the company to give us bread for our children" (236). Through Torres's words, the novel makes the case that the American own-ers of the refineries stood to benefit from the divisions between Haitians and Dominicans and that these divisions were aimed at breaking not only the present but also the future power of the worker's movement. In this way, Alexis places the massacre squarely within the context of continued American domination in the region, even under the guise of so-called "good neighbor" relations.

The novel clearly argues for the need to understand the massacre within the context of a direct challenge from workers to American imperialism and capitalism. In the weeks before the massacre and following the assassination of Torres, Haitian and Dominican workers participate in a strike for better wages. Of course, the novel locates this strike in a continuum with those earlier strikes in Cuba mentioned by Franscuelo. The Dominican strikes are represented in the novel as part of a country-wide wave of labor un-rest threatening both Trujillo's dictatorship and American profits. Knowl-edge of this unrest is introduced into the narrative by Doménica Betances, a Dominican communist painter who befriends Haitian sugar cane workers despite her class and nationality, in her warning to Hilarion of imminent danger. She alerts him that "strikes are breaking out all over, so the Jackal [Trujillo] must have decided to take some action" (253). Before the slaughter commences, Trujillo's soldiers come up with a scheme for separating Do-minicans from Haitians by having the workers pronounce "perejil," with any perceived difficulty pronouncing the "r" marking one as Haitian. In its fo-cus on this preparatory act of dividing Haitians and Dominicans, the novel insists on the massacre being understood as a method to break the unity that had empowered sugar cane workers to demand thirty cents a day in exchange for their backbreaking work.

In *General Sun, My Brother*, the 1937 massacre of Haitians working and living in the Dominican Republic provides a stinging indictment of the eco-nomic plunder and support for Trujillo's murderous dictatorship that the United States maintained under the guise of being a "Good Neighbor" in its relations with countries in the Caribbean and Latin America. *Of Vagabonds and Fellow Travelers* turns to the history of these relations, because many of the strategies the United States deployed to win hearts and minds in Africa and Asia in the cultural Cold War were developed in the context of pre–Cold War relations with its southern neighbors in the Western hemisphere. This history is mobilized to support the book's larger claim about the critical insight to be gleaned from reorienting the cardinal points of the Cold War away from the East-West divide and towards the North-South division of labor.

UNCLE SAM'S NEIGHBORHOOD: THE AFRICAN DIASPORA AND THE GOOD NEIGHBOR POLICY IN HAITI

With the withdrawal of the U.S. Marines from Haiti in 1934, President Franklin D. Roosevelt established his Good Neighbor policy to guide U.S. relations with its neighbors in Latin America and the Caribbean. This policy orientation represented something of a departure for Roosevelt, who as a younger man had played a bit part in the Haitian occupation as President Wilson's assistant secretary of the navy. After a tour of the island in 1917, Roosevelt praised and recommended for a Medal of Honor Major Smedley Butler, the commander of the Haitian Gendarmerie. Under Butler's leadership, the Gendarmerie brutally suppressed the Cacos rebellion, the Haitian peasantry's resistance to the occupation, and oversaw the corvée or forced labor system on the island. After more than three decades of armed intervention in the region, Roosevelt's Good Neighbor policy shifted course, instituting a policy of cultural suasion rather than military occupation as a more effective means of creating a stable environment for U.S. economic and political interests in the region. On the island of Hispaniola specifically, this new era of "good neighbor" relations propped up the dictatorial rule of Rafael Trujillo in the Dominican Republic and Sténio Vincent in Haiti. Long-standing ties to both of these regimes undoubtedly influenced the Roosevelt administration's refusal to support an inter-American committee to investigate the 1937 massacre of Haitians living and working in the Dominican Republic.

With an executive order in 1940 creating the Office for Coordination of Commercial and Cultural Relations between the American Republics, Roosevelt accelerated implementation of his Good Neighbor policy. The new agency was directed by Nelson Rockefeller, whom Roosevelt appointed to the position of coordinator of inter-American affairs (CIAA). The office and the coordinator premised their work on the idea that small outlays of funds to support cultural exchange programs and travel grants for Latin

American cultural figures to visit the United States would produce large returns in greater acceptance of U.S. military and economic presence in the region. In 1940, this mission took on greater urgency as Nazi and fascist advances in Europe raised concerns about European colonies in the Caribbean, particularly because of their proximity to the Panama Canal and the busy shipping trade routes from the Canal to the United States. In addition to the Caribbean, U.S. government officials looked warily at the spread of Nazism among German immigrants in South American countries like Chile and Argentina. As the official concern over the proximity of European Caribbean colonies to Panama Canal trade routes demonstrates, the Good Neighbor policy developed in such a way that "culture, security, and economics (to say nothing of domestic politics) were all bound inseparably together" (Pike 1995, 253). This combination of culture, security, and economic concerns was the CIAA's particular legacy to the Office of Policy Coordination, the main conduit for the CIA's covert funding of various organizations as part of the cultural Cold War. Indeed, the legacy was not limited to methods but also included personnel. As Hugh Wilford notes, "Rockefeller had pioneered many of the CIA's characteristic methods of psychological warfare while serving as [CIAA] during World War II" (Wilford 2008, 107). The Cold War enhanced Rockefeller's methods, as seen in the proliferation of cultural exchange programs such as government-sponsored cultural festivals, art exhibitions, jazz band tours, and scholar and student exchanges.

The scholarly exchanges organized in the context of the Good Neighbor policy brought to the fore the problem of racial discrimination, which during the Cold War would be considered the Achilles heel of the United States. In general, these exchanges made a positive impression on Latin American visitors to the United States. The one aspect that marred otherwise positive experiences, however, was the racial discrimination they witnessed. For example, the State Department historian J. Manuel Espinosa reports (in language that recalls Kennan's words in his "Long Telegram") that after his 1943 visit the Brazilian scholar Hernane Tavares de Sá commented that "the Negro problem [was] 'the most acute and difficult of all the domestic problems' to be solved in the United States" (Espinosa 1976, 286). The problem of racial discrimination in the United States persisted through the Good Neighbor policy and into the postwar cultural Cold War and threatened to undermine the U.S. foreign policy goal of winning hearts and minds among its southern neighbors and later among the newly independent countries of Africa and Asia.

These exchanges did not only operate in one direction, and with regard to Haiti they involved the visits of African Americans on educational and cultural missions. These postoccupation, good-neighbor missions to Haiti were channeled through several organizations operating on the ground in Haiti and charged with fostering a new spirit of neighborliness.[19] These organizations addressed a range of technical and cultural issues ranging from public health to English instruction in secondary schools. In addition to support from both the Haitian and American governments, these initiatives received funds from philanthropic organizations such as the Rockefeller Foundation and the Carnegie Corporation.[20]

Given Haiti's perceived status as the "blackest" of the independent nations in Latin America and the Caribbean, it is no surprise that African Americans played an important role in fostering connections between the two countries under Roosevelt's Good Neighbor policy. For example, Alain Locke took a leave of absence from Howard University to spend four months in Haiti under the auspices of the Inter-American Artistic & Intellectual Relations Committee and in collaboration with Maurice Dartigue, the Haitian minister of public instruction. Locke spent the months of April through July of 1943 in Haiti, giving a series of lectures. One of those lectures, "Race, Culture, and Democracy," was given in the presence of President Elie Lescot and subsequently reprinted in the March 1944 issue of *Cahiers d'Haiti*, which had yet to be founded at the time of his visit. Locke's Howard colleagues Rayford Logan and E. Franklin Frazier also visited Haiti around this time. Jean Price-Mars recorded the impact of these visits in an article published in the October 1943 issue of *Cahiers d'Haiti*: "Port-au-Prince has recently had the opportunity to appreciate the refinement of several of Howard's professors when Rayford Logan, Franklin Frazier, and Alain Locke demonstrated their intrinsic value with high quality research presentations" (Price-Mars 1943, 15).

These presentations were followed by the longer and more involved mission of the African American cultural critic and language professor Mercer Cook. In the fall of 1943, Cook left his position as professor of French at Atlanta University, where he had been a friend and collaborator of W.E.B. Du Bois on the journal *Phylon*, to supervise the training of English teachers in Haiti. In light of his success obtaining foundation support for his work, it is unsurprising that Mercer Cook was tapped for this mission. In the past, Cook had been the recipient of two Rockefeller grants, one in 1934 from the General Education Board to study in France and another in 1942 to study in Havana, Cuba; in 1937, he also received a Rosenwald Foundation grant, which funded his study in France, Martinique, and Guadeloupe. J. Michael Dash situates Cook's appointment in the context of the Good Neighbor policy, writing that "the need to reinforce good relations between Haiti and the United States was felt by Roosevelt, who set up a project in 1943 to train English teachers in Haiti under the direction of Mercer Cook" (1997, 74). An article published in *Cahiers d'Haiti* announcing Cook's arrival, however, suggests that it was "in accordance with a plan established by the Department of Public Instruction and in cooperation with the American government [that] Cook was designated supervisor" of the project, replacing James Forsythe, who had returned to the United States at the end of July ("Mercer Cook" 1943, 6). With his wife, Vashti Smith Cook, who worked as the secretary of the English teaching project, and their young son, Mercer Cook Jr., Mercer Cook participated in the elite cultural life of Port-au-Prince during their almost two-year sojourn in Haiti's capital.[21]

The following year, sometime in the early part of 1944, another African American couple, Max Bond and his wife Ruth Clement Bond, joined the Cooks in Haiti. Max Bond was the older brother of Horace Mann Bond, the educator and college president, whom Mercer Cook would later work with in AMSAC, the CIA-front organization discussed in chapter 1, while Ruth Clement's brother, Rufus, was the long-standing president of Atlanta University, where Cook had worked before coming to Haiti. Max Bond arrived in Haiti to direct the educational mission of the Inter-American Educational Foundation. According to an interview with Ruth Clement Bond, Max Bond "was director of the education program in a team of six or seven people, two of whom were women, sent out for the US Government's Good Neighbor Policy in Latin America, which Nelson Rockefeller headed up. They taught languages, science, homemaking in some of the schools" (Bond 1992, 1). For a while it seems Cook's teaching project was subsumed under Bond's mission, but by November 1944 the relationship had ended. Cook wrote to W. E. B. Du Bois, describing the situation: "finding it impossible to work under Bond, we resigned, much to his delight. The Washington office sent down an official who arranged for us to stay on until July. Now we are working more or less independently as we did last year" (Cook 1945).[22] At the end of that school year, the Cooks left Haiti for Washington, D.C., where Mercer Cook was set to begin an appointment as professor of romance languages at Howard University in the fall of 1945.[23] Three years after his return, Mercer Cook published a report on his work in Haiti, "Education in Haiti," through the U.S. Office of Education. In the report's introduction, Cook explicitly links the need for a second comprehensive account in English of education in Haiti to the student strikes that Jacques Stephen Alexis played a major role in organizing: "The student strike of January 7, 1946, which resulted in the overthrow of the Lescot regime, parallels that of 1929 [when a student strike precipitated the fall of Borno's client government] and therefore marks a convenient point at which to take stock" (1948, v). Cook's service on this project, first sponsored by the U.S. Office of Education and later by the Office of Inter-American Affairs as part of a larger program of cultural cooperation pursued under the auspices of the U.S. Department of State, clearly prepared him for later assuming leadership positions in both AMSAC and the Congress of Cultural Freedom. His record of government service provides yet another example of the continuity between the methods and personnel of the U.S. Good Neighbor policy and its cultural Cold War initiatives.

In addition to the African Americans working in an official government capacity to support the Good Neighbor policy, two African diaspora intellectuals, W.E.B. Du Bois and Aimé Césaire, also traveled to postoccupation Haiti. During their visits, they both presented work speculating on the role of culture and black and colonial peoples in the reconstruction of the world order following World War II. In their Haitian lectures, Du Bois and Césaire anticipated and critiqued the establishment of a postwar world order on the colonial foundations of the past. *Of Vagabonds and Fellow Travelers* argues that these lectures present germs of the anticolonial critique that matured in the postwar period and put these intellectuals in a vagabond relation to the ideological enclosures of the Cold War period. Although Du Bois and Césaire were undeniably fellow travelers that maintained associations with and even memberships in their respective national Communist Parties, their insistent black radical anticolonialism interrupted the Cold War binary between East and West.

Almost immediately upon arriving in Haiti, Mercer Cook set wheels in motion for Du Bois to make an official visit to Haiti by speaking with the cultural attaché, Horace Ashton, in the U.S. embassy. Around the same time, Du Bois also reached out to Rayford Logan at Howard. In response, Logan informed Du Bois of his recent conversation with Kenneth Holland, director of the education division of Nelson Rockefeller's Office of Inter-American Affairs, and his confidence in securing government support for the trip provided that Du Bois's proposed lectures did not overlap with those Alain Locke had given earlier that year (Logan 1943). After many false starts and delays and despite seeming official enthusiasm for his trip, the final arrangements for Du Bois trip were only completed in the summer of 1944; Du Bois spent a little under two weeks in Haiti from September 6 to September 19, 1944. The timing of the trip allowed Du Bois to lecture a summer school for secondary teachers, but unfortunately prevented him from attending the Congrès International de Philosophie organized by Camille Lhérisson. On the eve of his departure, he penned a message of regret and regards to the conference and its attendees, whom he saluted for "taking a remarkable interest in the progress of science" ("qui s'intéressent, de façon si remarquable, au progress de la science") (1944, 40). As I will discuss later, this conference is also where Césaire first presented his well-known essay "Poésie et connaissance" ("Poetry and Knowledge").

In his Haitian lectures, Du Bois worked through ideas that he would later expand and further develop in his *Color and Democracy: Colonies and Peace* (1945). The three lectures Du Bois gave in Haiti were titled "The Colonial Groups in the Postwar World"; "Democracy and Peace"; and "The Meaning of Education." In these lectures, Du Bois argues for the critical importance of culture in reshaping the world according to a different, more democratic and peaceful pattern, a view that informed his participation in the cultural Cold War. The reception of these lectures and the larger context that made it possible for Du Bois to deliver them in Haiti make painfully clear how much the early Cold War years represented a radical shift to the right in U.S. political culture. This shift made it possible to isolate and discredit Du Bois for being a communist fellow traveler, an example of which was the canceling of his passport mentioned in chapter 1. These lectures also anticipate the forceful critique that Du Bois later lodged against U.S. dominance of the postwar world order, which, he argued, deviated only slightly from the pattern established by European colonial powers. It bears repeating here that the substance of this critique contributed significantly to the official reaction to Du Bois in this period.

As he looked to the future and the end of World War II, Du Bois focused his concern on the status of those people subjected to one form or another of European colonialism. In "Colonial Groups in the Postwar World," Du Bois sets out to provide an inventory of the colonial groups in the world. Working with a more expansive notion of "colonial" to include those "groups of people, countries and nations, which while not colonies in the strict sense of the word, yet so approach the colonial status as to merit the designation semicolonial" (Du Bois 1985a, 229). In considering their "economic and political condition," this group includes in addition to the colonies in Asia and Africa, the South and Central American republics, the majority of the Balkan and Near East states, China, the independent black nations of Liberia, Haiti, and Ethiopia, and finally, African Americans. In 1944, Du Bois could make a claim about African Americans' "semi-colonial" status as part of a U.S. government–sponsored trip and have it be considered "a triumph," which "people are still talking about" three weeks later, as Mercer Cook dutifully informed him afterwards (October 10, 1944). A clear indicator of the ideological impact of the Cold War can be seen in the fact that twelve years later at the First Congress of Black Writers and Artists, as discussed in chapter 1, Mercer Cook, by then a bona fide Cold Warrior, and his fellow American delegate to the conference, John A. Davis, took issue with Aimé Césaire's similar characterization of the African American situation. The colonial relation produced a situation, Du Bois argued, in which "the parts of the world where human toil and natural resources have made the greatest contribution to the accumulation of wealth, such parts of the earth, curiously enough, have benefited least from the new commerce and industry" (Du Bois 1985a, 233). By framing the question this way, Du Bois shifted away from the exclusive focus on individual prejudice, the primary concern of Gunnar Myrdal in his Carnegie Foundation–supported *American Dilemma* published that same year. This analysis placed Du Bois in a vagabond relation to Myrdal's racial liberalism, which was adopted as the guiding principle of the civil rights reforms pursued in the context of the U.S. Cold War.

The central concern of the postwar period in Du Bois's estimation was the need to address the fundamental problem of poverty, which closely shadowed the color line. He argued that conditions of widespread poverty retarded the expansion of democracy, and the absence of democracy dimmed the prospects of an abiding peace in the postwar world. The mutually constitutive relationship between democracy and peace was the subject of his second lecture, "Democracy and Peace." In this talk, Du Bois expressed the utopian idea that "modern miracles of technique make a world without poverty possible if industry is carried on not simply for private profit but primarily for public welfare" (242).[24] The abolition of poverty, however, was not an end unto itself. Freedom from poverty would produce the conditions necessary for educating the masses of people, which would in turn encourage the democratic process, which "depends primarily on more thorough and complete education, not only for children but for adults" (237). According to Du Bois, education was the only means by which the masses of people could contribute to raising the level of culture in the world and to establishing government by and for the majority, the absence of which made peace impossible.

The importance of education in Du Bois's vision of the postwar order made it a fitting subject for his address to a summer school for secondary school teachers. His lecture was one of several scheduled over the course of the summer, the second year of the school's operation under the direction of the minister for urban education, Félix Morisseau-Leroy. In the "Meaning of Education," Du Bois rehearsed his arguments on the value of a broad liberal education in the "humanities and art and literature" (251), arguments he famously articulated in "Of Mr. Booker T. Washington and Others," the third chapter of his seminal *The Souls of Black Folks*. He began this lecture with a pointed defense of both the costs and results of his own twenty years of formal education and travel. While it "must have cost in the aggregate something like forty thousand" and failed to prepare him "to do any specific piece of work," it did provide him with "a rather firm grasp, and idea of what this world was, and how it had developed in the last thousand years" (250). This understanding and its product, a "trained and disciplined mind which knows the world" (252), Du Bois argued, could not be substituted for technical training that ignores both the person "for whom the technique exists" and the fundamental questions of why certain work "is done, and for whom, and to what end" (251). In raising these fundamental questions to Haitian secondary school teachers, Du Bois connected their local pedagogical efforts to the global postwar project of expanding democracy among colonial peoples, the condition of possibility for a lasting peace in the postwar world. At the height of the anticommunist witch hunts of the early Cold War years in the United States, posing questions about the beneficiaries and products of the labor of the world's darker peoples would lead to Du Bois being regarded as a threat to both national security and the new postwar world order.

As World War II was drawing to a close, Du Bois was not the only African diaspora intellectual in Haiti raising fundamental questions about the constitution of the postwar world order. Du Bois's nearly two-week-long visit to Haiti overlapped with the much longer visit of Aimé Césaire, the Martinican poet and politician regarded as one of the principal founders of the Négritude movement. In mid-May of 1944, Césaire and his wife, the poet and activist Suzanne Césaire, traveled to Haiti, spending several months there before returning to Martinique. Henri Seyrig, the cultural attaché at the Free French consulate in New York, arranged the Césaires' trip to coincide with the Congrès International de Philosophie at the request of Camille Lhérisson, who had been charged by Lescot's government with organizing the conference. According to Kora Véron, however, Cesaire's attendance at the conference was only the pretext for his larger "mission of cultural diplomacy aimed at restoring French influence in the world" and supporting Haitians in their self-appointed role "as representatives of French civilization in their region" (Véron 2013, 433). Over the course of his seven-month stay, Césaire taught daily classes at the University of Haiti, gave weekly lectures on modern poetry, and wrote part of the play that would eventually become the play *Et les chiens se taisaient.*

Even as Césaire presented his thinking to various audiences and his stay in the country "where Négritude first stood up" proved productive in creative terms, it also proved troubling. He confided to Seyrig about his strained relations with Haiti's "'la petite bourgeoisie de couleur' ('the lower-middle class mulattoes')," which "he judge[d] as mediocre and subject to prejudice" (Véron 2013, 439). Besides these relations, the conditions Césaire encountered in Haiti informed his political thought with regard to independence. As Gary Wilder notes, "the cautionary example" of Haiti "demystified the idea of state sovereignty as a self-evident good" (2015, 29) and led him to support departmentalization for Martinique and the other "old French colonies" (Guadeloupe, French Guyana, and Reunion). It would be a mistake to divorce Césaire's reflections on Haiti as a negative example of a possible future for an independent Martinique from the island nation's recent past of U.S. occupation and the wider transformations of the Caribbean Sea into an American lake discussed above. His Haitian experience perhaps made clear for Césaire the reality of independence under the shadow of U.S. imperialism. In this context, departmentalization within France might have appeared to him as a practical solution to erecting a barrier between Martinique and the ravages of U.S. imperial domination, whose tragic results were on painful display in Haiti.

During his stay in Haiti, Césaire, like Du Bois, also lectured the secondary school teachers attending the summer school in Port-au-Prince. According to the Haitian director of urban education, Morisseau-Leroy, in an article published in the September 1944 issue of *Cahiers d' Haïti*, the title of Césaire's lecture was "Alain, professeur" (1944, 3). Alain was the pseudonym for Émile Auguste Chartier, a philosopher and journalist, who taught philosophy at the Lycée Henri IV, a prestigious and rigorous secondary school in Paris that prepared students for the extremely competitive entrance exams for the French "Grandes Écoles." Responding to a question about the evident influence of Nietzsche, Péguy, and Alain on the first issues of *Tropiques* in an interview with Jacqueline Leiner, Césaire suggested that "Alain was a great thinker to a number of people at that time, including [René] Ménil, who had been his student" ("Alain, vous savez pourquoi? C'était le grand maître à penser, à cette époque, d'un certain nombre, de persons, de Ménil y compris; il avait été son élève.") (Leiner 1993, 111).[25] Indeed, the second issue of *Tropiques* featured an article by Suzanne Césaire titled "Alain and Esthetics" that engages with his theory of art developed in *Le système des beaux-arts* (1920) and explores the fine arts from drawing to poetry. In this article, she celebrates Alain having "consigned [poetic creation] to its proper place: first place! First place in a ruinously extravagant world of bankruptcy, and fraud" (Césaire 2012, 11). In her reading of Alain, Suzanne Césaire invests poetry with a power that anticipates Aimé Césaire's argument in his frequently referenced essay "Poetry and Knowledge," considered below. In addition to art criticism, Alain also published a work outlining his philosophy of education, *Propos sur l'éducation* (1932). According to Philippe Foray, the fundamental goal of education for Alain was cultivating the "freedom of the mind" necessary "to give citizens the power to judge the State" (1993, 23). For this reason, he, much like Du Bois, was disdainful of attempts to align education to the dictates of the labor market, and he maintained that "the time children spend in the classroom should not be overshadowed by the time they spend in the workshop, where they only acquire specifically technical skills" (24). While I have not been able to locate a copy of Césaire's lecture to secondary school teachers, it seems likely that he would have echoed Du Bois in championing the humanities.[26]

Césaire presented "Poetry and Knowledge" on the fifth day of the seven-day Congrès International de Philosophie, held from September 24 to 30, 1944, in Port-au-Prince. In his lecture, Césaire elevated poetic knowledge as both deeper and richer than scientific knowledge, which limited itself to a merely utilitarian view of the world. In elaborating this position, he argued that "science affords . . . a summary and superficial view" of the world and that the single-minded pursuit of this "poor and half-starved" knowledge had "impoverished humanity" (1990, xlii).[27] As an antidote to this deprived and depriving knowledge, Césaire prescribed the "fulfilling knowledge" of poetry as a curative (xliii). The beneficial effects of poetic knowledge, according to Césaire, resides in its orientation toward possibility, a notion he returns to throughout the essay: the "poet approaches the poem" and finds "all the possibility" there (xlvii); the poet "gambles all our possibilities" "on the word" (xlix); and, finally, "when the sun of image reaches its zenith, everything becomes possible again" (lii). It is difficult not to see in Césaire's insistence on the connection between poetry and possibility a reference to the Haitian past. In the Haitian revolution, as Césaire surely would have appreciated, overworked, ill-fed, and brutalized former slaves realized the possible out of a "scientific" impossibility when they defeated in succession the armies of the most powerful European nations to defend their hard-won freedom.

In "Poetry and Knowledge," the poet emerges as the critical figure in this struggle, which, as it involves the production of myths, is essentially over hearts and minds. "Only myth," Césaire declares, "satisfies mankind completely; heart, reason, taste for detail and wholeness, taste for the false and true, since myth is all that at once" (liii). Césaire's words regarding "no peacemaker, no plumber of the deep," being "more rebellious or pugnacious" than the poet make sense in the context of this struggle (l). In setting the postwar moment in these terms, Césaire understood precisely the nature of the coming battles. From Haiti, he could clearly observe the penetration of the United States throughout Latin America and the Caribbean, albeit not by military means with the end of the occupation of Haiti, but with the perhaps even more pernicious weapons of cultural institutes and exchanges. In many ways the African diaspora intellectuals such as Cook, Du Bois, and Césaire who visited Haiti in this moment went through a dry run of the cultural Cold War battles into which they would all be conscripted in the postwar years.

The poetic form that Césaire chose for "Poetry and Knowledge," a departure from the conventional academic form of the other papers presented, did not prevent the conference participants from appreciating the robustness and complexity of his thought. In his summary of the conference proceedings, Cornelius Kruse of the American Philosophical Association judged Césaire's address "one of the most brilliant of the Congress, being characterized both by impetuous eloquence and keen analysis of the contribution poetry can make in our day to man's happiness and dignity" (Kruse 1945, 38). While Kruse's comment captures the import of poetry, his thinking is perhaps too "subject to habit of thought" (Césaire 1990, xlix), to use Césaire's words, to discern the specific import of this message to its Caribbean audience. For the colonized, poetic knowledge had a particular significance, since "scientific" knowledge had been wielded as a weapon to systemically deprive them of both happiness and dignity.

The politics of "Poetry and Knowledge" are expressed in Césaire's meditation on the specific history of the Caribbean and his articulation of a romantic and nostalgic Caribbean modernism. The essay elaborates this theoretical position through the metaphors and analogies around which it is structured. For example, Césaire argues for the "superiority of the tree, which is rootedness and deepening, over mankind who is agitation and malfeasance" (xlviii). In its specific context, this argument is a call to root oneself in the Caribbean past and discover the poetry to be found there, as opposed to the perpetual search for sustenance in the Euro-American myths in which the Caribbean exists only as a lack, scientific and otherwise. J. Michael Dash suggests that "the domination of the northern Caribbean by the United States" directly influences Césaire's elevation of the natural world and his articulation of a "poetics of origination," which figures "an elemental Caribbean space outside of time, history, and discourse" in the essay (Dash 1998, 62–63). While one can find traces of a "prelapsarian innocence" that Dash describes as central to Césaire's poetics in the essay, its theoretical force resides elsewhere, in the call to recognize the fullness of history and time. Césaire proposes that this fullness has been sacrificed on the altar of a scientific knowledge that only verifies what is and ignores the possibilities present in any given moment. The vital contribution of African diaspora cultural producers was to insist on these possibilities in the face of the cultural Cold War ideological enclosures.

For Césaire, the superiority of poetry resides in the fact that it both arises from and elevates these possibilities. Science, by contrast, operates within the limits imposed by "the law of identity, the law of non-contradiction, and the logical principle of the excluded middle" (Césaire 1990, li). These limits are why poetry for Césaire, Gary Wilder argues, offers the means to "leap outside of (colonial) modernity altogether—not in order to escape it but in order to disrupt it. His celebration of poetry [being] a grand if politically weak gesture of refusal designed to open up utopian possibilities" (Wilder 2005, 266–67). In 1944, looking forward to the end of the war and the postwar reconstruction of the world order, Césaire offered poetry and the utopian possibility of an antiracist and anticolonial future as the forever receding horizon toward which the practical politics of his moment might be oriented.

To this day, Césaire's "Poetry and Knowledge" continues to be a resource for analyzing the afterlife of colonial modernity in its present neoliberal form and devising methods to disrupt its disastrous consequences for the majority of humanity. Sylvia Wynter, for example, has recently proposed her own engagement with and extension of Césaire's "Science of the Word" as the basis for a new intellectual praxis of being human. Such a praxis is urgently needed, Wynter argues, to provide a "way out" of our current predicament of "fossil-fuel driven capital accumulation" and its "ever-increasing ratios of global warming and climate change . . . [and] human immiseration based on increasing degrees of *racially, socially,* and *religiously* stratified economic inequality" (2015, 66, emphasis in original). Such a praxis and science of being human presents the only hope for African diaspora people to blossom, in Césaire's words, "to the dimensions of the world" (1990, xlix).

Most treatments of this period in Haiti tend to concentrate on the protests of radical students like Jacques Stephen Alexis and René Depestre, among others, which sparked the revolution of 1946. Because of the acknowledged influence of surrealism on this generation and the distance from official government circles of its representatives in Haiti, these accounts highlight both the role of Pierre Mabille and the series of five lectures André Breton gave during his visits to the island over the course of several months prior to and during the revolt, from December 1945 to April 1946.[28] In underplaying the significance of the American presence through official government agencies and exchanges, this approach misses a valuable opportunity to clarify why the forces of counterrevolution ultimately prevailed. Those forces had established firm control over the means of producing knowledge. This period in Haitian history and the Caribbean more broadly proved to be a testing ground for some of the strategies and personnel mobilized later in the U.S. pursuit of global dominance during the Cold War period. Breaking with the early twentieth-century practice of military intervention, under the Good Neighbor policy the United States weaponized culture as a more effective means of securing influence in the Caribbean and Latin America. In the context of the Cold War, the United States adapted this policy to its relations with the newly independent nations of Africa and Asia. The policy assured "peaceful" relations so long as these nations did not call into question the fundamentally unequal economic relations that U.S. capitalism produced and on which its profits depended. The policy had its domestic counterpart in the racial liberalism that guided mainstream civil rights reform efforts. Within this framework African American elites offered support for, and at the very least refused to publicly criticize, the project of U.S. global dominance in exchange for domestic civil rights reform. Not coincidentally, these same elites stood to gain more from these reforms than the working-class majority of African Americans. These reform initiatives set the terrain upon which vagabond and fellow traveling African diaspora literary culture producers struggled against the ideological enclosures of the cultural Cold War. Langston Hughes and Alice Childress were two such cultural producers, and the next chapter considers their alignment with the black working class as an aesthetic attempt to defy the ideological limits of the U.S. Cold War context.

CHAPTER 3

Fellow Travelers, Treacherous Ground

Strategic Critique in the Black Press Writing of Langston Hughes and Alice Childress

If, as we have seen in the previous chapter, the cultural Cold War had a chilling effect on African diaspora cultural production outside the United States, its domestic corollary, a full out anticommunist witch hunt, decimated much of the intellectual and organizational infrastructure of the left in the United States. Notwithstanding this assault, the African-American left persisted in its critique of the racist underpinnings of U.S. anticommunism, particularly the strain emanating from Washington and directed by southern congressmen and their northern allies (i.e., Joseph McCarthy and Francis E. Walter). In order to weather this moment, many on the African American left adopted a strategy of dissimulation, being less than direct and often evasive about the exact nature of their relationship to the organized, Euro-American left. This strategy, as James Smethurst notes, allowed these artists and intellectuals to "not only ... preserve their careers, but also their political effectiveness" (2002, 1227). One of the institutions that permitted these artists to navigate the space between opportunism and martyrdom was the African American press.

The cultural Cold War's chilling effect on black artistic and intellectual circles can be traced in the intersecting and diverging career trajectories of Langston Hughes and Alice Childress. In the postwar years, Hughes was extremely cautious about his public identification with his communist past. (This caution, however, did not prevent his being called before Joseph McCarthy's Senate Permanent Subcommittee on Investigations). This disassociation did not entail abandoning the incisive critiques of racism and injustice that characterized his earlier work. Writing for the black press, Hughes offered his primarily African American audience his insights into the racist underpinnings of the Red Scare and the connections between domestic issues and foreign events. The vehicle for these insights was the regular column and Simple stories he published for the *Chicago Defender*.

While Hughes wrote for the established *Defender*, Alice Childress launched her career as a writer in the pages of Paul Robeson's newspaper *Freedom*. Childress's contribution furthered the paper's concern with the experience of black women workers. This particular orientation reflected the politics of the radicals that gravitated around *Freedom*, whose "particular brand of radical politics," according to Dayo Gore, "celebrated the political activism and cultural work of black women radicals" (2011, 136). Childress clearly appreciated the radical substance of Hughes's Simple stories, as she drew on them in crafting a theatrical production for a black radical cultural organization as well as her "A Conversation from Life" columns for *Freedom*. In this chapter, I read Hughes and Childress writings from this period as piercing through racial liberalism's strategy of containment by creating black working-class characters that brought a sophisticated critique of the Cold War both to and *from* the bars and tenements of black urban America.

CONNECTING HERE TO YONDER: LANGSTON HUGHES'S *DEFENDER* COLUMN AND SIMPLE STORIES

The first installment of Langston Hughes's *Chicago Defender* column, "Here to Yonder," appeared on November 21, 1942. Begun in the midst of World War II, the weekly columns were published mostly without interruption for the next twenty years, bringing Hughes's worldly insight and analysis to the newspaper's primarily African American audience. The columns also provided a space for artistic exploration, as Hughes developed his beloved Simple stories for the column. These stories and their principal character, Jesse B. Semple, were, according to Christopher De Santis, the "most successful manifest[ation]" of "Hughes's desire to bring the concerns of the black working class to the forefront of African-American consciousness" (1995, 15). A rich archive of the remnants of the radicalism from Hughes's past travels and political commitments exists in these columns, while they also reveal how the pressures of the Cold War prodded him along on the journey away from the communist associations of his youth. My reading of these columns emphasizes their articulation of a radical framework that foregrounds the mutual constitution of the domestic and the global. This framework makes clear the stakes involved as the cultural Cold War delegitimized certain types of knowledge in the process of making racial liberalism the dominant discourse on matters of race.

Hughes announced his column with a piece titled "Why and Wherefore" that outlined its motivating factors and guiding principles. Looking back on the last twenty years of his life as "half writer and half vagabond" in which he "traveled from here to yonder, . . . from pillar to post," Hughes arrived at the conclusion that "what happens at the post affects the pillar, and vice versa" (De Santis 1995, 221). His reflections on the topical issues of the day will therefore proceed from this insight as he establishes connections to those events and the everyday life-world of his African American readership. As Donna Harper notes, Hughes "distinguished his column from the rest of the *Defender* discussions by stating and demonstrating in his first column his commitment to represent the viewpoints of average black people" (Harper 1995, 41). The piece ends with a statement by Hughes of his intention to use the column to give presence to a black life-world heretofore absent in the newspapers. He writes: "I know lots of folks, whose names have never been in the newspapers. . . . I shall write about them, also. Your folks and mine—as colored as me—scattered all over the world from here to yonder" (De Santis 1995, 223). In Hughes's hand, African Americans are not simply the subjects of his writing but the subjects of modernity whose experiences shaped and were shaped by the dynamic interplay between the local and the global as the United States ascended to its dominant role in the capitalist world order.

The story around which Hughes constructs his first column explores the tensions and competing demands placed on African Americans as the United States began to occupy its new role. In this story, Hughes relates his experience at the hospital where the draft board has sent him for a physical. There, the poet Hughes talks with the other potential draftees. Not surprisingly, given both Hughes's radical inclinations and the predominantly working-class composition of the African American population, the conversation revolves around the determining influence of race on American labor, both military and civilian. According to Hughes, "the cat . . . standing in line in front of [him]" was talking freely about the racism in army assignments: "He said, 'I know they gonna send all us cats to a labor battalion. . . . Look at the pictures you see of colored soldiers in the papers, always working, building roads, unloading ships, that's all. . . . I want to be a fighter!'" (222).

Indeed, while civil rights organizations pressured President Roosevelt into mandating that African Americans make up 10 percent of soldiers, reflecting the country's demographics, the majority of those soldiers served in labor units. The historian Kimberley Phillips describes a pattern, which "intensified over the course of the war," wherein African American soldiers were trained for combat then reassigned, so that "by the eve of the Normandy invasion, the army had assigned three-quarters of black soldiers to the Service Force branches" (55). This pattern suggests an overlap between military and civilian life, as both depended on a symbolic and economic order that relegated African American labor to an inferior position in order to reproduce the notion of white freedom.

Hughes represents the "cat" in question as making a similar assessment of the racial stratification of civilian labor. He declares, "That Italian I work for don't care whether the draft board calls you or not, you better be to work on time. He ain't been in this country but six or seven years and owns a whole fleet of trucks, and best I can do is drive one of 'em for him. Foreigners can get ahead in this country. I can't" (De Santis 1995, 222). Hughes represents this encounter with potential draftees in a manner that emphasizes the development in the African American working class of a critical analysis linking racism, capitalism, and fascism. This analysis locates the Italian's whiteness as the invisible hand behind his rapid advance from recent immigrant to America to owner of the means of production. In contrast, the "cat's" blackness confines him to selling his labor as a driver to the Italian and prevents him from being able to "get ahead" or outside these particularly racialized relations of production. By drawing attention to how his Italian boss prioritizes the discipline of his workers above patriotic duty, the "cat" subtly questions his boss's loyalties (Italy was an Axis power and thus a declared enemy of the United States) and demonstrates how the interests of capital took precedence over those of the nation. And lastly, the information concerning his boss only having arrived to the United States six or seven year ago associates him with the Italian fascists that invaded Ethiopia in October of 1935.[1] This reference was perhaps pitched directly to the readers of the *Defender*. As the historian James H. Meriwether notes, "Black Americans turned their attention to Ethiopia on a sustained level unmatched by that accorded any previous event in Africa.... By the end of the year, the *Defender* had decided the most important event of 1935 was the Italian invasion of Ethiopia" (2002, 44). Thus, in this inaugural column, Hughes represents black workers as possessing a political consciousness attuned to the interpenetration of the local in the global and vice versa, or in Hughes's parlance that "here is yonder, and yonder is here" (De Santis 1995, 221).

The Chinese revolution was a post–World War II event that Hughes reframed for his readers, giving them an alternative interpretation from the dominant Cold War narrative about the spread of communism. In his reflections, the revolution became a global event of local concern as an instance of the dramatic reconfiguration of the world color line. In his column "With the Crumbling of the Old Chain [*sic*], Jim Crow Crumbles, Too," published in the *Defender* of October 8, 1949, Hughes linked the Chinese revolution to the struggle against racial segregation in the United States. He writes, "What is happening in China is important to Negroes, in fact, to people of color all around the world, because each time an old bastion of white supremacy crumbles its falling weakens the whole Jim Crow system everywhere" (De Santis 1995, 60).[2] Staking a position based on his own experience in China ("I saw it with my own eyes . . . when I was there before the war"), Hughes writes approvingly of the "revolutionary armies now sweeping over China" for being "not only against color-lines and Jim Crow . . . [but] also against child labor, child-prostitution, dope rackets with headquarters in Europe and dividend collectors who grow rich in faraway lands from the dawn to dusk hours of Chinese workers" (61). By yoking Jim Crow to various forms of exploitation, Hughes reminds his readers that segregation was not only, or even primarily, about defining the use of public space but was the constellation of practices and laws meant to subordinate and maintain control over African American labor. This reminder anticipates in certain respects Kenneth Warren's claim that "the problem of race . . . is at bottom a problem of politics and economics—of constitution making and of wielding power legislatively and economically in order to mobilize broad constituencies to preserve an unequal social order" (2003, 21). Hughes envisions social justice in this passage as not only ending legal restrictions on public space, but also as abolishing the exploitative relations characterizing racial capitalism. In these instances, Hughes emerges not so much as a poet retreating from the radical excesses of his youth, but as one articulating a radicalism that enfolds the struggle for socialism in the world-spanning color line.

At least as judged by his columns for the year, Hughes's concern for the problems of the African American masses had not completely diminished his sympathy for the communist left, the prime targets of the anticommunist repression being conducted at a fever pitch in 1949. His February 5, 1949, column, titled "A Portent and a Warning to the Negro People from

Hughes," declares the trial against twelve communist leaders in New York City to be "the most important thing happening in America today," because communism and communists were not the only ones being tried, but so were "all who question the status quo—who question things as they are—all poor people, Negroes, Jews, un-white Americans, un-rich Americans." (De Santis 1995, 184). In order to contextualize these proceedings for his readers, Hughes draws a parallel to Nazi Germany, making a historical reference to the recently ended war. In one of the most striking moments of the essay, he compares those "American Negro leaders [that] denounce Communists" to those "Jews in Germany who joined with Hitler at the beginning" (185). Hughes's conclusion in this column implies that the two struggles, while not identical, cannot be separated from one another. Thus any attempt to make such a separation amounts to little more than a position in favor of the status quo. This conclusion cuts two ways, offering not only a critique of African American leaders' embrace of anticommunism, but less evidently also recalls the history when the Communist Party USA (CPUSA) had encouraged African Americans to temper their struggles against racism in support of the war effort during World War II. In his *Defender* columns, Hughes operates within a field cleared by these two cuts, providing for his readers a radical analysis that both resists subordination to the class struggle and challenges national belonging predicated on wishing away the realities of class domination in a capitalist society.

JIM CROW HAUNTS

As I will develop further in the discussion of Paul Robeson's Cold War ordeal in the next chapter, the House Un-American Activities Committee (HUAC) and its Senate counterparts the Internal Security Subcommittee and the Permanent Subcommittee on Investigations, under Joseph McCarthy's chairmanship, operated during this period to help establish the contours of national belonging by casting as subversive nearly all attempts to address racial and class subjugation in the United States. In the late summer of 1949, a couple of weeks following the hearings held primarily to repudiate Robeson, Hughes's column for the *Defender* took direct aim at the HUAC. If World War II had unleashed forces that could create a postwar world shorn of the practices necessary for reproducing racial capitalism, the HUAC was mobilized to rein in those forces and restore society to something approaching the prewar status quo. In this way, the HUAC fulfilled its roles as a "State apparatus [that] secures by repression (from the most brutal physical force, via mere administrative commands and interdictions, to open and tacit censorship) the political conditions" for "the reproduction of relations of production which are in the last resort relations of exploitation" (Althusser 1971, 149–50). From this perspective, Hughes's column situates the HUAC's proclaimed mission to defend the national body against communist threats as producing the ideological conditions necessary for continued exploitation under a postwar regime of racial capitalism.

In his column, Hughes imagines the spectral embodiment of the African American freedom struggle defiantly confronting the committee. He describes the "unannounced, also unsummoned" appearance of "Old Ghost" before the committee and its chairman, "Mr. Georgia," an obvious allusion to the actual chairman of the committee, John Wood, a representative from Georgia. His insistence on this connection links the committee's declared anticommunism to southern racial segregation, the same connection leftists African American union activists would make three years later in 1952 when Wood took the HUAC to Detroit under the cover of investigating communist infiltration of defense industries. Hughes portrays the chairman as astonished to see the ghost because "since Jackie Robinson's speech, Negroes had no place on the Committee's agenda" (De Santis 1995, 185). Of course, Robinson had been the star witness summoned before the committee to discredit the idea of communism's appeal to African Americans and to denounce Robeson's alleged comments at the Paris Peace Conference that previous spring. The column critiques the idea of African American belonging in the national community being conditioned upon support of an anticommunist agenda led, at least in the legislative branch, by staunch defenders of racial segregation.

The critique of anticommunist racial liberalism emerges in an exchange between Old Ghost and Mr. Georgia. In this exchange, Old Ghost explains his motivation for appearing before the committee:

> "Boy, why are you here?" asked the Chairman Georgia. . . .
>   "I am here to insult you," said Old Ghost. "I can see that my black presence is not amenable to your comfort. . . ."
>   "You must be a radical," said Chairman Georgia.
>   "I am," said Old Ghost, "which is why I want to be called, 'Mister.' According to the dictionary, radical means complete, thorough, extreme, also one who favors a basic change. That is me! (De Santis 1995, 186)

In this exchange, Hughes characterizes the committee as a performance or-chestrated by the powerful southern leaders of Congress that aimed to exor-cise from the national conversation the "basic change" to the social structure demanded by African American radicals. As the representative of this radical tradition, Old Ghost challenges the committee to "investigate the Ku Klux Klan which is so active in . . . Georgia" as being un-American (186). By iden-tifying the KKK's racist violence as the primary concern of African Ameri-cans, Hughes makes racism and not communism the paramount threat to realizing the national ideal of democracy. At the onset of the Cold War, Af-rican Americans were not dissimilar to people of color across the globe in that they considered racism and colonialism as being more important than the conflict between the United States and the Soviet Union.[3] Although African Americans were prevented from making a meaningful contribution to the postwar reconstruction of American society, Hughes figures African American radicalism as a haunting presence that appears as an "unexpected stranger" to throw "the whole meeting into a state of confusion" (185, 187). In an echo of Marx, Hughes presents African American radicalism as the specter haunting the United States as it proclaimed itself the bastion and defender of freedom in a world beset by the forces of tyranny.

SIMPLE HAS HIS SAY

Hughes's nonfiction column was not the only place he explored African American radicalism in the pages of the *Defender*; his Simple stories also expressed radical sentiments. First appearing in February of 1943, three months after he began writing his nonfiction column, Simple was con-ceived, according to Hughes's biographer Arnold Rampersad, "as a device to encourage African Americans to support the Allied cause during World War II" (Rampersad 1994, xvi). Rampersad describes the genesis of Simple as an invitation extended to Hughes to join a man, whom he knew mainly by sight, and his girlfriend at their table in a Harlem bar. Inquiring into what the man did for a living, Hughes learns he works in a defense factory making cranks. When he later admits to not knowing what kind of cranks since white folks withhold that information from him, his girlfriend derides him for sounding "right simple" (xvii). This anecdote about Simple's genesis reveals both Hughes's sympathy for the African American everyman and his admiration for the poetic, if cutting, quality of the vernacular language of the African American everywoman. The anecdote's suggestion that these two impulses informed Hughes's choice of the title character for his stories is consistent with the representation of Hughes as a "race man . . . involved with other blacks on a daily basis as a citizen and an artist" (Rampersad 2002, 297). This mining of his quotidian contact with African Americans for artistic inspiration distinguished Hughes from other prominent writers during this early Cold War period.

The Simple genesis story has further implications in that it suggests Hughes's specific commitment to representing the life-world of the increasingly prominent African American working class. Simple's work in a defense factory ties him to President Roosevelt's Executive Order 8802, the direct result of pressure exerted by A. Phillip Randolph's march on Washington movement (MOWM). This movement had threatened to marshal a hundred thousand African Americans to march on Washington if the president failed to prohibit employment discrimination in defense factories. But perhaps more significantly, through this link Hughes associates Simple with "the followship" that A. Phillip Randolph described as having gotten ahead of black leadership when he launched MOWM in 1941 (Singh 2004, 102). As a consequence of this order more than a million African American workers entered the industrial workforce during World War II. Many of these workers joined trade unions and, according to Martha Biondi, by 1948 had "displaced the 'talented tenth' as agents of Black community advancement" (2003, 26). Additionally, Hughes frames the question of Simple's relationship to the product of his labor in a way that foregrounds racism as a factor in his alienation. The analysis of American industrial society contained in Hughes's depiction of Simple echoes the one put forward by the "cat" he describes encountering while taking a physical for the draft board in his first *Defender* column. In both instances, Hughes insists that not only is the United States stratified between the owners of the means of production and those forced to sell their labor-power, but also between white owners favorably positioned within (by) America's capitalist society and African Americans prevented from moving beyond the position of exploited labor.

This fundamental division along racial lines made it impractical for African American workers to rely solely on interracial workers' organizations such as trade unions or the Communist Party to support their struggles. While carrying out struggles around the primacy of race in worker's organizations, African American workers also waged struggles within racial organizations such as the NAACP to make those organizations responsible for and accountable to the needs of the masses. The necessity of working within African American organizations is the subject of the Simple story "Ways and Means," which Hughes first published in *Simple Speaks His Mind* (1950). Hughes culled the material for this story from several *Defender* columns from August 1943 that dealt with the riots that month in Harlem. The story begins with Simple proudly showing the narrator his membership card for the NAACP, which Simple calls "the National Organization for the Association of Colored Folks" (Harper, 1994, 67). More than just a way of indicating his unfamiliarity with the organization, Simple's act of renaming suggests his desire to realign the organization toward the aspirations of the "folk" as opposed to more respectable colored "people." The necessity for this realignment becomes evident in the discussion between Simple and the narrator about the summer's riots. Simple admits to having descended into the streets during the riots with "two bricks" "looking for justice" (71). At the time of the riots, the narrator was out of town, but had he been present he "would have emerged to see the excitement, yes, but not to break windows looking for Justice" (70). For this reason, the narrator is glad that Simple has "joined the NAACP, so that the next time a crisis comes up, [he] will have a more legitimate outlet for [his] energies. There [being] more effective ways and means of achieving justice than through violence" (71). The story, however, does not end with the narrator's "wise" counsel, but with Simple's unequivocal restatement of his having sought justice with the help of two bricks. This ending would seem to reinforce the idea of a persistent gap between rank-and-file members, "folk" like Simple, and the respectable leadership of the NAACP with regard to "legitimate" forms of protest.

Between the glass-strewn streets of a rioting Harlem and the more measured deliberative actions of the NAACP, the shop floor provides Simple with a more suitable political space. Revolving around a labor dispute, the action in the story "When a Man Sees Red" takes readers to the factory where Simple works. Although the location has changed, Simple's destination remains the same; he continues to search for justice, in the form of the right "to eat for his work, to have some clothes, and a roof over his head . . . [to] keep body and soul together" (83). While expressed in simple terms, his demands actually entail a profound altering of the social relations of capitalism. Simple's boss clearly perceives the radical implication of his words and warns him that "you are talking like a Communist, and I will not have no reds in my plant" (84). Emboldened by the strength of organized labor, Simple feels empowered to make such demands because he recognizes that his boss "didn't want to have no trouble out of that union" (84). When the narrator suggests that Simple's assertiveness might result in his being called before the Un-American Activities Committee, Simple relishes the idea of the opportunity to confront the southern chairman of the committee.

Running with the idea of this imagined confrontation, he proceeds to narrate the details of that encounter. During the course of his back and forth with the chairman, Simple declares his willingness to embrace the label "un-American" if it means "[he] can run a train." He focuses on the operation of trains because as a potent symbol of modernity, it crystallizes the racialized labor structure that determines the African American experience of modernity: "All I see Negroes doing on the railroads is sweeping out coaches and making beds. [...] I do not like being a Pullman porter all the time. Sometimes I want to run a train" (85). Like Simple's boss, the chairman equates African Americans being more than mere objects of modernity with communism, which he reveals in his designating Simple as a "Red Russian" "Negro." Simple, however, associates this demand to those American ideals, outlined in the Declaration of Independence, which entitled him to "liberty whilst pursuing happiness" (86). Through this association, Hughes counters the strategy of ascribing African American freedom claims to foreign manipulation; he legitimizes these claims as the realization of the American democratic project. Thus, in the early Simple stories, like in his nonfiction column, Hughes explored the ways society's commitment to racial subjugation mixed with anticommunism to discredit the African American freedom movement. In the early Cold War period, this volatile mixture produced the conditions in which racial liberalism became the dominant discourse on race in the postwar United States, thereby marginalizing as mere propaganda cultural production from an unapologetically left perspective.

SUBVERSIVE TRANSLATION: HUGHES AND COOK'S TRANSLATION OF *MASTERS OF THE DEW*

As we have seen, Hughes treaded cautiously across the landscape of Cold War America given his past domestic and international alliances with artists and activists on the left. At the same time, it is also clear that Hughes maintained many of the ideological positions that had initially attracted him to the left and the Communist Party. The substance of these positions was Hughes's enduring commitment to rendering the dignity and poetry of black working-class life, a commitment evident, as we have just seen, in the Simple stories. Another testament of his commitment to the left were the personal relationships he maintained throughout the period bridging the prewar period to the subsequent Cold War era. One such relationship was Hughes's friendship with the writer and founder of the Haitian Communist Party, Jacques Roumain. As discussed in chapter 2, Roumain had inspired and been a mentor to a younger generation of post-U.S. occupation radical activists and writers, like René Depestre and Jacques Stephen Alexis. Using a letter of introduction from Walter White, Hughes briefly met Roumain in the spring of 1932, at the end of his three-month visit to Haiti. When Roumain was arrested by Sténio Vincent's regime in August of 1934 because of his communist activities, Hughes supported the Committee for the Release of Jacques Roumain and published letters in various outlets calling for his release, becoming "one of the first to appeal to American blacks to rise to Roumain's defence" (Dash 1997, 54).[4] In February of 1945, ten years after working to free Roumain, Hughes received a letter from Mercer Cook, relaying a request from Nicole Roumain, Roumain's widow, that he translate into English Roumain's posthumously published novel, *Gouverneurs de la rosée* (Rampersad 2002, 106). According to Rampersad, Hughes accepted the translation project even though he had not read the novel and it "would bring little or no money" (106).

If at the onset of the Cold War Hughes distanced himself from his past on the radical left, his decision to translate a novel by a prominent figure in the opposition to the U.S. occupation and founder of the Haitian Communist Party indicates the difficulty of that journey. In June of 1947, Hughes and Cook's translation of *Masters of the Dew* was published to "pleasant reviews ... in most journals, and glowing ones ... in the leftist organs" (Rampersad 135). Their translation made available to English readers a novel whose main character, Manuel, typified the African diaspora revolutionary vagabond, a figure that reoccurs in many of the present work's discussions. On his return to his native Haitian village after having worked for years on Cuban sugar cane plantations, Manuel "attacks the resignation endemic among his people by preaching ... political awareness and solidarity," while remaining "emotionally and spiritually integrated into his community" (Dash 1978, 14–15). American readers of *Masters of the Dew* might have drawn a parallel to Manuel's character and the African American veterans who, after fighting in a war abroad to end fascism and racism, enmeshed themselves in domestic struggles against racism and discrimination. Hughes himself might have found the figure of Manuel attractive, given his own decision to curtail his own wanderings and devote much of his artistic output to giving voice to the struggles and aspirations of the African-American working class in organs such as the *Defender*.

Translating a work like *Masters of the Dew* is exactly the type of African diaspora literary culture that U.S. cultural Cold War forces worked to marginalize and discredit as they worked to convince the world and particularly the peoples of Africa and Asia of American capitalism's beneficence. When Hughes and Cook's translation appeared in 1947, it would have undoubtedly found a receptive audience among the African American left intellectuals and activists working in Harlem. The prominence of these activists and intellectuals assured that the rhetoric of the New York civil right movement, according to Martha Biondi, "frequently linked the domestic antiracist struggle, the labor movement, and anticolonialism" (2003, 64). By force of his past as a celebrated star of the Harlem Renaissance, his work on the radical left, and his extensive international and diaspora connections, Hughes would have enjoyed an honorary status among this group even if he increasingly identified with more moderate and liberal political positions and causes. In a certain sense, his translation of Roumain's novel closed a chapter on a radical past, which despite his best efforts continued to haunt him during the Cold War period.

Hughes's artistic response to news of Roumain's death reveals what was at stake in celebrating his memory. The spring following Roumain's death and less than a month after receiving Cook's letter with the translation request, Hughes completed "A Poem for Jacques Roumain: Late Poet of Haiti," which paid homage to the deceased poet. In the poem, Hughes ponders "when did"—but perhaps more pertinently how did—Roumain "learn to say / Without fear or shame, / *Je suis Communiste?*"[5] The only other French in the poem, "morne" (hills), refers to the Haitian countryside, where the "blackest peasant" makes his home. His decision to use French in these instances should not be read simply as Hughes demonstrating the erudition and facility with languages that allowed him to translate not only Roumain, but also the poets Federico García Lorca and Nicolás Guillén, who wrote in Spanish. By leaving the declarative statement "I am Communist" untranslated, Hughes suggests Roumain's example, a son of the bourgeoisie proudly and defiantly identifying as communist,[6] is without referent or equivalent in the American English-speaking community, being intimately tied to the Haitian soil and that country's unique historical and political realities. This refusal or inability to translate, however, gestures toward the necessity of thinking beyond linguistically defined boundaries when considering African diaspora literary culture. Hughes's act of nontranslation invites us to discover literary culture and politics outside the United States for a more thoroughgoing critique of racism and imperialism. In trying to understand the conditions that provide meaning to Roumain's assertion, readers are confronted with a history that reveals U.S. capitalism as not simply stained by racism and imperialism but constituted by it.

If artistically Hughes could illuminate the meaning of Roumain's life and work, his public reaction to his death provides an early indication of the distancing from the left that he would adopt as he bowed to the political pressures of the early Cold War years. Despite his obvious appreciation for Roumain, as evidenced in this poem and his agreeing to the translation project, Hughes did not attend a memorial held for Roumain in New York. The memorial was organized by the Association Democratique Haïtienne, an organization founded by the Haitian exile and one-time Roumain collaborator Max Hudicourt, and featured speakers such as the U.S. Communist Party leader Earl Browder. In Hughes's absence, his friend, the actor and leftist activist Canada Lee, read Hughes's poem dedicated to Roumain's memory (Rampersad 2002, 106). These two seemingly contradictory impulses, penning a celebratory poem while shunning a public memorial, encapsulates the type of decision-making calculus that Hughes and other racial liberal writers and activists employed with increasing frequency during the early years of the Cold War. Certainly, the odiousness of Communist Party positions and decisions, often the consequence of policy emanating from the Soviet Union, and deep-seated anticommunism explain much African American disassociation from the left. This undeniable reality, however, should not diminish the role of repressive state apparatuses such as the HUAC, the FBI, and the CIA in compelling the retreat from leftist cultural politics. In this context, Hughes's refusal to attend the apparently integrated and communist-affiliated memorial for Roumain was only one example of many.

VOICING DOMESTIC CONCERNS:
ALICE CHILDRESS'S BLACK LEFT FEMINIST CRITIQUE

Despite his own retreat from the left in the latter part of his career and the adaptation of his aesthetic and political choices to the Cold War environment, Langston Hughes's work continued to inspire black leftist artists. One such artist was Alice Childress, who launched her career amid anticommunist repression working alongside the artists and activists of the Harlem left, nearly all of whom faced "persecution, investigation, repression, or censorship" (Biondi 2003, 137). Childress honed her craft as a politically committed leftist artist without even the minimal protections Hughes benefited from as one of the most celebrated artists of the Harlem Renaissance. As Mary Helen Washington has noted, nearly all the institutions that enabled Childress to develop as an artist and activist—*Masses & Mainstream*, Club Baron, the Jefferson School of Social Science, *Freedom*, Sojourners for Truth and Justice, the American Negro Theater, and the Committee for the Negro in the Arts—were considered "subversive" by the FBI or the attorney general (Washington 2014, 126). With this designation, these organizations became the targets of constant government surveillance and were forced to devote considerable time and resources to long, drawn-out legal battles to keep from being forced to register with the government as either "Communist-action" or "Communist-front" organizations, as required by the Internal Security Act of 1950, also known as the McCarran Act.[7] Under these conditions, Childress produced work that put the desires and struggles of the African American working class, particularly its women, at the center of the leftist and internationalist activism and art of the Harlem left. The following section examines Childress's contributions to this movement in the form of her theatrical adaptation of Hughes's *Simple Speaks His Mind* and her columns for *Freedom* newspaper. In these works, Childress represents an African American working class conscious of itself and its interests, refusing to be subsumed under the white working class or to accept the class interests of the African American bourgeoisie as those of the entire race.

FOR A BLACK RADICAL THEATER

Childress first entered the world of the African American left through the theater, and it was in the theater that she made her first foray into black radical cultural production. While the biographical information is scarce, the evidence suggests that as early as her teenage years Childress was involved with the Negro Theatre Youth League of the Federal Theatre Project (FTP), where she would have surely encountered radical ideas and politics. In fact, the FTP was one of the first targets of the Dies Committee, led by Texas

representative Martin Dies, who in 1939 "grilled [its director] Hallie Flana-
gan and her supervisor Ellen Sullivan Woodward about Communism in the
Federal Theatre Project, which soon was terminated as a result" (Storrs 2013,
88). Two years later, Childress joined the American Negro Theater (ANT),
founded by theater artists Frederick O'Neal and Abram Hill, where she
would work in nearly all aspects of the theater from director to stagehand
(Washington 2014, 134). Her diverse and comprehensive training was more
than likely a result of "O'Neal's pedagogic vision," which valued "teaching,
learning and integrating all aspects of theatrical artistry alongside prepara-
tions for stage production" and was realized in the founding of the ANT
School of Drama in 1942 (Shandell 2007, 104). Given her subsequent career in the theater, Childress likely attended the school, which, according to
Jonathan Shandell, was directed by the African American actress and teacher Osceola Archer (Adams) and offered a two-year curriculum in acting,
speech, movement, directing, radio, stagecraft, design, playwriting, theater
history, and drama appreciation (108). Although the school and the larger
company did not survive into the next decade, those like Childress carried
their training with them into new and different theatrical spaces.

When the ANT ceased operations in 1950, the theater division of the
Committee for the Negro in the Arts (CNA) filled the void. The CNA grew
out of the Cultural Division of the Communist Party–affiliated National
Negro Congress (NNC), which formed an important nucleus of the later
Civil Rights Congress (CRC). These organizations provided a venue for
Childress to pursue both her radical political work and involvement in the
theater, since she served on the Finance Committee of the CRC and as the
chair of the Production Committee for the CNA (McDonald 55). Childress
played an important part in the staging of the CNA's first theatrical production, *Just a Little Simple*, in September of 1950. A variety show of song,
comedy, drama, and dance, the production showcased her multiple artistic
talents. According to the handbill for the production, in her adaptations of
Hughes's recently published *Simple Speaks His Mind*, Childress had "skil-
fully [sic] woven a connecting link through the whole show which includes
two superb one-act plays, songs, dances, sketches, and patter ranging from
hilarious farce to the most tense and exciting drama."[8] One of the one-act
plays featured was Childress's *Florence*, which had been conceived as both a
response and challenge to a "the prevailing notion within the Harlem Left
that only black male issues were central to the racial struggle" (McDonald
2002, 51). While the production promised audience members "a whale of an

evening," it also offered them an unrepentant left perspective on contemporary race and labor issues.

The venue the CNA secured for its productions was the Club Baron, a nightclub at 132nd Street and Lenox Avenue, "spang in the middle of Harlem" (Childress 1950, *Just* 3).[9] According to McDonald, the club's owner John Barone offered Childress and Clarice Taylor use of the space for free during the week (56). In a column announcing the production of "Just a Little Simple," Arthur Pollock describes Barone as an Italian American who immigrated from Calabria as a teenager and worked his way up from shoe shine boy to Harlem club owner.[10] Securing space in one of the more fashionable Harlem venues suggests that Childress sought a popular audience for the CNA's activities in Harlem. Paul Robeson also supported Childress, according to his biographer Martin Duberman, by bringing people along with him to see the production, attending fund-raisers, and providing financial support in the form of a $500 personal check (Duberman 1989, 703). This support of Childress highlights the ripple effects felt throughout the Harlem left that came from blacklisting and revoking Robeson's passport, thereby decimating his finances. Deprived of this potential source of funding, Harlem left organizations struggled to sustain themselves, and most buckled under anticommunist pressures. As a result, left voices had difficulty competing for African American hearts and minds with those racial liberal organizations that benefited from major foundation support, to say nothing of the covert government funding channeled through CIA-front organizations like AMSAC.

An alternative to the framing of race in the dominant paradigm of racial liberalism can be found in "Just a Little Simple." In this production, Childress adapted the musings of Jesse B. Semple to present him as a kind of African American everyman with a highly developed racial and class consciousness. In her adaptation, Simple, as his friends call him, is brought from the pages of Hughes's book at the request of the CNA to supervise their new production. One of his first acts on stage is to object to the lighting technician's use of green lighting: "Mr. Taylor! I did deliberately ask the Harlem Stage Hands Union local . . . not to let you gentlemen put no green lights on me" (Childress 1950, 1). This opening shifts attention away from the principal actor and draws attention to the technical aspects of stagecraft, something Childress's training at ANT would have emphasized. This emphasis on stagecraft reappears when Simple draws spectators' attention to the Club Baron's electronic curtain (5). The initial scene also presents organized labor as a powerful intermediary through which Simple realizes his desire to be bathed in "a rosy pleasin' light" (1) as he presides over the CNA's production. Of course, Simple's preferred color offers a clear indication of his politics, while "rose" also serves as a reminder that workers' struggles are not simply about economic issues, but questions of dignity as well.

The dignity of workers, above and beyond matters of "bread," is the theme of the Simple scene that opens the second part of *Just a Little Simple*. The basis for this scene is the story published in *Simple Speaks His Mind* as "When a Man Sees Red," an original version of which appeared in Hughes's *Defender* column on April 26, 1947, under the title "Simple Sees Red." In her adaptation, Childress replaces Hughes with a bartender as Simple's interlocutor in a conversation about a recent dispute with his boss. Simple's recollection of the dispute draws attention to unions' role in preserving the dignity of workers and the equation of dissent with subversion. It ends with him imagining an act of defiance before the disciplinary apparatus of the HUAC.

The dispute begins when his boss accuses Simple of neglecting his work. Simple insists that he was just "thinkin' about [his girlfriend] Joyce" and not, as his boss accuses him, "layin' down on the job" (13). The confrontation, however, sparks Simple to reflect angrily on his meager wages and the boss's eagerness to fire him for seeming insubordination. The union, however, provides a check on the boss's power and Simple eagerly reminds him of that fact. The bartender cautions Simple that his defiance, in the logic of the times, might be understood as communist. Simple loudly challenges the equation of "want[ing] decent wages" and "to keep your job and not want[ing] to take no stuff off a boss" with communism (14). When the bartender warns Simple that his insistence on standing up for his rights will result in his being called to appear before the "Unamerican Committee," Simple imagines such a summons as a welcome opportunity to confront the racist power enshrined in the committee. Like Hughes's original, Childress also emphasizes the racism motivating the committee's work by describing it as led by "that old Southern Chairman" (15). Although a New Jersey congressman chaired the committee for five years between the chairmanships of Texas representative Dies and Georgia representative Wood, for the African American left, power and authority clearly resided with the committee's "spiritual leader" (Woods 2003, 26), Mississippi representative John Rankin. If Simple provided the connecting link in *Just a Little Simple*, the critique of racist southern congressional power exists as a recurrent theme uniting the production's three parts. Part one advances this critique through the two Dixiecrats that appear in Les Pine's "Grocery Store," while in the third and final section Simple expresses his frustration that "everytime them civil rights bills come up them old white Southerners filibuster them to hell and gone" (Childress 1950, 19). In *Just a Little Simple*, Childress adapted one of Langston Hughes's most beloved characters to offer a militant African American working-class voice that refused to be silenced in the face of racist attempts to equate dissent with communist subversion. The play likely served as a springboard to her development of the character Mildred, who would prove to be no less beloved, if not as well known, as Simple.

DOMESTIC DISSENT

Childress developed the character of Mildred Johnson, an African American domestic worker, for the "A Conversation from Life" columns she wrote for Paul Robeson's black leftist newspaper, *Freedom*. The newspaper's first issue appeared in November 1950, just months after the Club Baron production of "Just a Little Simple." Although promoted as Robeson's paper, *Freedom* seems to have been an initiative of a cadre of African American communists working in Harlem with whom Robeson worked closely.[11] Indeed, according to Lamphere, "the *Freedom* staff included both members of the Communist Party and others who could be called 'fellow travelers'" (2003, 131). In her interview with Robeson's biographer Martin Duberman, Childress characterized the creation of *Freedom* as an act of independent black radicalism, distinct from the party and committed to African American liberation. According to her, the black radicals that founded the newspaper "never took a position 'We're anti-C.P.' They simply said, 'We're going to do it our way. We're not going to have other people saying, you know, what they're going to ... you know, the party line.' ... But they were not going to have a separation from the black struggle. That's what *Freedom* was about" (16).[12] The black radicals that drafted the prospectus for *Freedom*—Louis Burnham, Esther Cooper and James Jackson, and Edward E. Strong—envisioned it as a critique of the mainstream African American press, whose "Neglect of Negro Workingclass [sic] Struggles and Activities" meant that "it would be almost impossible to find the problems and activities of a Negro domestic worker or sharecropper [sic] wife reflected on the elaborate women's pages of these publications" (2). Childress's column, with its fictionalization of the experiences of a domestic worker, clearly addressed this neglect, presenting a domestic worker who is actively engaged in all aspects of African American community life. Mildred emerges in the monologues that make up the columns as someone who not only forthrightly challenges the daily slights and abuses of her job as a day worker, but also volunteers for her church, participates in benevolent and educational clubs, cares for an extended network of family, friends, and neighbors, all while taking time to simply enjoy life.

Her work on *Freedom* was an indication of Childress's growing stature in Harlem's black radical cultural circles. As his financial support for *Just a Little Simple* suggests, Robeson clearly thought highly of Childress and surely played some part in securing her contribution to the fledgling newspaper. Indeed, Robeson compared Childress to O'Casey and Chekhov in her creative work in "the tradition of another noble, struggling, long too-patient people, of a folk laboring."[13] Recognition of her artistic merit, however, was not accompanied by financial remuneration. As she admitted to Duberman, Childress "was doing columns for *Freedom* for free and doing housework during the day" (1983, 4). Her columns, then, must have been an expression of her commitment to the newspaper's politics of African American socialist liberation. This political orientation meant the newspaper did not dedicate much space to celebrating the individual achievements of the African American bourgeoisie, which was beginning to reap the rewards of the country's adoption of anticommunist racial liberalism. Instead, the African American radicals gathered around *Freedom* devoted its energies to cultivating race and class consciousness and an internationalist perspective among the African American working class. Childress's Mildred character contributed to this effort by offering an image of the domestic worker as a militant both on the job and in her associational life.

In a hostile political environment, the African American radicals working on *Freedom* managed to publish the newspaper on a more or less monthly basis for nearly five years, from late 1950 until the summer of 1955. In the later years of its existence, as it struggled to attract subscriptions and other sources of revenues, the newspaper's publishing schedule became more erratic. When *Freedom* ceased publication, Childress was able to sell her columns to the *Baltimore Afro-American* for republication, and with the help of her friend, the communist historian Herbert Aptheker, arranged for their publication in book form with a small radical publisher in 1956. As a book, the columns appeared under the title *Like One of the Family: Conversations from a Domestic's Life*. Although Childress's relationship with this publisher was exploitative (she received neither advance nor royalty (Harris 1986, xvii)), the book version has encouraged a level of scholarly consideration of the columns that greatly surpasses work on *Freedom*, the original vehicle for her writing. Mary Helen Washington has insightfully argued for the importance of reading "the Mildred monologues as they first appeared . . . in a Left-wing newspaper in the midst of Cold War tensions, dramatically transformed by their position on the page and by their dialogic relationship to their audience and to the other stories in the paper" (Washington 2003, 189). Recognizing the sagacity of Washington's suggestion, I refer to the original column when it offers an important supplement to my discussion of the version of the column republished in the Beacon paperback version of *Like One of the Family* (1986).[14]

Traces of the columns' origin in *Freedom*, Paul Robeson's newspaper, can be found in at least two of the Mildred's stories published in *Like One of the Family*, one which explicitly mentions Robeson and another that makes an oblique reference to criticism in the mainstream press of his activist stances. The explicit mention of Robeson is found in the chapter "Story Tellin' Time," which appears just past the book's halfway point.[15] In the story, her employer, Mrs. B., immediately picks up and begins reading the African American newspaper Mildred has placed on the hall table upon arriving to work. When she comes across an advertisement for a Robeson concert, she asks if Mildred would attend such an event and eventually cautions her that "Paul Robeson is the kind of man who get his people in trouble" (1986, 119). The original version of the column was published in the August 1954 edition of *Freedom* and was titled "Old Master Said to Jim: 'You Got Your Faults and I Got Mine'" and begins on a somewhat different note. In the original version, instead of an advertisement provoking Mrs. B's warning, Mildred informs her employers that "she was goin' to the **Salute to Paul Robeson** (bold in original) and ask[s] them to buy some tickets." Her employers respond with sputtering and stammering "a whole lot of foolishness about what is good for her," which does not anger Mildred but tellingly provokes her to tell them a story.

The *Like One of the Family* version of the column begins with Mildred trying to avoid the question of Robeson all together. Mildred arrives to work with a copy of a black newspaper, which her employer Mrs. B. flips through while Mildred starts her work day. After coming across a notice for a Robeson concert in the newspaper, Mrs. B. enters the bedroom where Mildred is working to gain assurance that she wouldn't attend such an event. Mildred avoids responding and instead comments on the weather before moving to the kitchen to do the dishes. When Mrs. B. follows Mildred into the kitchen and insists on pursuing the subject of Robeson despite her repeated attempts to change the subject, Mildred decides to tell Mrs. B. a parable about an old slave master and his slave Jim. The story begins in slavery with the master constantly whipping Jim and selling Jim's children to pay for his son's college education. The relationship, however, endures throughout U.S. history, from the violent dismantling of Reconstruction, the instituting of share cropping and Jim Crow law on up until the massive white resistance to the Supreme Court's school desegregation decision. This history is punctuated by two reconciliatory moments, during both World Wars, when the master asks Jim to accept democracy's fault and "go off and fight for Democracy." These moments end, however, with the "same old burnin' and killin'" when Jim returns and makes demands based on his military service (121). In the original *Freedom* column, Mildred credits Paul Robeson with having "stood up and said that Jim had caught wise to old Master and was ready to call his bluff" (Childress 1954, 8). The reference to Robeson's role does not appear in the *Like One of the Family*, and Mildred concludes her tale with an explicit and direct statement to Mrs. B about its moral: "the object of this tale is simply this: *I know who makes trouble for me!*" (122, emphasis in original). Mildred insists through the parable that "trouble" for African Americans has come at the hands of white Americans who have refused to recognize their humanity and have deprived them of the right to family, the vote, and an education.

Mildred's tale highlights the role of narrative in determining how Cold War realities were understood. Well-meaning, if ultimately misguided, whites like Mrs. B. were conditioned to accept the narrative that if not for radicals like Robeson the nation would readily embrace African American equality. Leftist radicals like Childress, however, insisted that the demonization of Robeson could only be understood within the long history of white resistance to African American freedom struggles. If the primary object of Mildred's story was to assert that she saw beyond white lies to the truth of African American history, a secondary object was to unsettle Mrs. B.'s comfortable white liberalism and show its affinities with the paternalism of white slaveholders and their descendants and defenders.

The more obscure reference to Robeson's ordeal in *Like One of the Family* deals with the criticism he faced in mainstream venues when he spoke out on political matters. The monologue titled "Where Is the Speakin' Place?"

presents Mildred's reflections on a magazine article she has just read calling for "famous folks keepin' their mouth shut about *anything* that goes on that calls for folks speakin' out." The article resolves a question about which she had "always wondered," namely "why these big, famous, grand, important people never have a word to say about the most important things that's splashed all over the newspaper" (194). Of course, the editors of the *New York Times* had admonished Robeson in a similar vein following his purported statements at the Paris Peace Conference in 1949. The editorial suggests that "Robeson will do himself and the cause of the American Negro a disservice if he carries out his resolution not to sing again but to devote his life to making speeches" and asserts that in regard to fighting racial prejudice and discrimination, "nothing Mr. Robeson can say will be half as important as the very fact of the existence of Roland Hayes and Ralph Bunche, of Joe Louis and Jackie Robinson, of Marian Anderson and Dorothy Maynor; yes, and of Paul Robeson" ("The Case of Paul Robeson," April 25, 1949). By the end of the column, Mildred recoils from the idea of celebrity if it means submitting to the Cold War imperative of "giving up [one's] speakin' place" and insists that no amount of "swimming pools or champagne cocktails or motorcars" could reconcile her to it (196). In reaching this conclusion, Childress is obviously endorsing celebrity in the mold of Robeson and making sense of his stance for readers of her work.

It is not so much her thoughts on celebrity that make Mildred such a compelling character, but it is her strong identification and valorization of her work as a domestic worker. Critics such as Washington and McDonald have linked Mildred's characterization as a militant domestic worker to the writings of the black communist leader Claudia Jones, specifically her groundbreaking article, "An End to the Neglect of the Problems of the Negro Woman!" which she published in the June 1949 issue of the CPUSA journal *Political Affairs*.[16] In her article, Jones decried the "almost complete exclusion" of African American women "from virtually all fields of work except the most menial and underpaid, namely, domestic service." Using Department of Labor statistics, she demonstrated that roughly 70 percent of the 1.6 million African American women in the workforce in 1945 were employed in either domestic or personal service (Jones 1949, 53). In light of these statistics it seems clear that if the lily-white suburbs were the image of postwar prosperity in the United States, their immaculately clean interiors and abundant dinner tables owed their existence to the massive exploitation of the labor of African American women. Thus when Childress developed Mildred, she created a character with which a vast majority of African American women working outside the home for a wage could identify.

In her monologues, Mildred takes pride in her work and displays a keen awareness of its importance in providing the foundation on which African American community life was built. At least a couple of the columns collected in *Like One of the Family* demonstrate Mildred's highly developed class consciousness. The "All about My Job" column finds Mildred volunteering at her church bazaar. Engaging in conversation with a bourgeois African American woman who stops by her booth, Mildred affirms herself and her occupation. She also exhorts a fellow domestic worker, who had been ashamed to tell the same woman how she made her living, to exhibit similar pride. Much of Mildred's pride in her work comes from her sense of the critical role domestic workers have played in African American history. In the course of her monologue, disguised as conversation with her friend Marge, Mildred asserts that domestic workers have "taken care of our brothers and fathers and husbands when the factory gates and office desks and pretty near everything else was closed to them; . . . built that church that the bazaar was held in!" More significantly, "after freedom came, it was domestics that kept [African Americans] from perishing by the wayside," their "dollars and pennies [having] built many a school!" (36-37). The point she makes is clearly that, although not the sort of actions typically associated with class struggle like a strike or unionization drive, in the context of U.S. racial capitalism these actions must be understood as such. In Jones's analysis, the inability to recognize the revolutionary significance of these actions is the consequence of the failure to apprehend "the *special character*" of African American women's work under conditions of "Jim Crow lynch system in the U.S." (57).

This special character did not, however, prevent Childress from using Mildred to advocate for traditional means of class struggle like unionization. In the short monologue "We Need a Union Too," Mildred presents the conditions that warrant a union for domestic workers, acknowledges the challenges to organizing, and imagines the power of an organized workforce. Mildred looks to the union as a means of securing "set hours and set pay" and protecting domestic workers from being obligated to perform physically demanding tasks she considers men's work like waxing the floors with "paste wax, window washin', scrubbin' walls, takin' down venetian blinds and all such" (140-1). If she can see how domestic workers would benefit from a union, Mildred also recognizes that it "would be awful hard to get houseworkers together on a count of them all workin' off separate-like in different homes" (140). Despite this structural impediment to organizing, Mildred closes her monologue with the image of organized domestic workers waging a strike action in front of the apartment building where an employer has tried to secure less expensive, nonunion labor to do her housework.

Following McDonald's lead, one can trace back to Jones's article the question of organizing domestic workers raised in this column. In that article, Jones had pointed to the "failure . . . to *organize* the domestic worker" as "one of the crassest manifestations of trade-union neglect of the problems of the Negro woman worker" (McDonald 2012, 58). Indeed, organizing domestic workers was an important issue for the Harlem left. Thelma Dale, a communist member of the Harlem left, who became *Freedom's* business manager near the end of its publication run in March 1955, made it a major component of her political writing and activity. According to McDonald, "for several years, Thelma Dale had been campaigning for the unionization of domestic workers, speaking publicly on the issue and writing about it in the pages of *Political Affairs*" (68). What made this unionization work radical and indeed subversive in the eyes of the U.S. government, was that it oriented the struggle for civil rights around the problems and concerns of the African American working class and refused to concede the inextricability of race and class. This orientation, of course, ran counter to the dominant discourse of racial liberalism, which made it all but impossible to take account of the economic foundations of racial domination. Considered within this context, the radical critique embedded in Childress's columns becomes evident. This critique has often been overlooked in the scholarly tendency to focus on the columns' positive address to their intended working-class audience.

Besides their focus on the working class, those in the Harlem left circles Childress inhabited publicly, and sometimes scathingly, criticized U.S. foreign policy. This criticism distinguished them from more mainstream civil rights organizations in the early Cold War period. These organizations were induced to align their civil rights platforms with U.S. anticommunist foreign policy goals for the same reasons they were required to craft an approach to civil rights shorn of broader economic justice concerns: it allowed them to both deflect charges of communist subversion and further the class interests of an expanding bourgeoisie. Childress and her comrades on the left, however, insisted that domestic racism and foreign imperialism were both rooted in American capitalism. Although the columns collected in *Like One of the Family* do not explicitly critique American foreign policy, they present Mildred as someone who takes an active interest in learning about the African diaspora, an interest that would more than likely entail lessons in the means and ends of U.S. imperialism.

One of the ways *Like One of the Family* defies the representation of domestic workers as downtrodden, and therefore subservient, laborers is to provide Mildred with a varied and rich associational life outside of work. For example, in the column "Good Reason for a Good Time," Mildred returns to her apartment after a weekend with her friends Mabel and Jim. She happily shares the details of a Saturday night of good food and cold drinks, laughing, singing, and dancing. Mildred is most excited, however, about their plans to form a social club that will not only sponsor parties and outings, but also host speakers who will inform the group "about what's goin' on in the world," with the first speaker scheduled "to tell [them] all about African and West Indian people" (74). The first speaker's subject indicates the importance given to the African diaspora on the Harlem left and the reality that post–World War II global ascendancy had increased U.S. political and economic involvement in these regions. As a result, one imagines that Mildred will come away from this first lecture with more knowledge about U.S. economic and military interest in the mineral resources of the Congo and South Africa and the process of intervention and occupation that transformed the Caribbean Sea into an American lake. Such a talk would reflect the interests and concerns of organizations like the Council on African Affairs (CAA), with whom *Freedom* shared not only the same office building but personnel as well, with the likes of Eslanda Goode Robeson and W.E.B. Du Bois contributing to both efforts. Through these organizations, intellectuals on the Harlem left maintained their international focus at a time when attention to foreign affairs waned among mainstream civil rights organizations. In part, this retreat reflected the "domestication" of racism, which the discourse of racial liberalism rendered primarily a matter of personal prejudice and legal discrimination divorced from the realities of American political economy.

One of the first educational meetings Mildred attends in *Like One of the Family* is devoted to African cultural and political developments. The description in the "What Does Africa Want? . . . Freedom!" column reads like a fictional representation of a meeting of the CAA. The original column had appeared in the June 1953 issue of *Freedom*, which was devoted almost entirely to Africa and at 12-pages was slightly larger than the typical 8-page run. Appearing on the issue's last page, Childress's column condensed the thought running through articles such as those penned by Eslanda Goode Robeson on African civilization and the causes of current unrest on the continent. It also provided context for an adjoining picture of "grim-faced and strong-willed, men of the Kikuyu tribe in Kenya," whom British colonial authorities had placed in concentration camps in an effort to crush the Mau-Mau insurgency. In the column, Mildred returns from the meeting disabused of prior notions about Africa, which she now perceives as little more than "a pack of fancy lies" propagated in "bad moving pictures" (99). In contrast to this misinformation, the meeting provides Mildred with knowledge about African art, history, and contemporary political struggles. During the discussion of these struggles, Mildred becomes exasperated with the back and forth about what Africans want and their capacity for self-government. Her frustration leads her to jump and "make a scene" when she admonishes those at the meeting to "stop all this pussyfootin' pretense" and recognize the simple truth that "*Africans want to be free!*" (100-1, emphasis in the original). While Mildred's stance on African freedom was obviously consistent with the position of the CAA and others on the Harlem left, it was radical in relation to the thinking of the times.[17] In this regard, it is worth considering that Ghana was the first black African nation to achieve independence in 1957 and that the most celebrated and authoritative African American voice on colonial affairs at the time, Ralph Bunche, was a proponent of trusteeship programs for dependent nations. Mildred emerges in these columns, therefore, as the embodiment of the militant, politically advanced working class those on the Harlem left hoped to foster.

In the ideal of the Harlem left, the working class does not merely learn more about the world but deploys their knowledge in actively transforming it. We witness Mildred in such a role in the course of her involvement with a benevolent social club at her church. The club comes together to raise funds to support civil rights activists, "people who have lost their homes because of tryin' to get their children into school and families of men that have been killed or run out of town" (201). In "The Benevolent Club" column, Mildred reveals that the planning meeting for the new club had raised intraracial tensions between African American and West Indians. Mildred tells Marge about the meeting's host, Ruth, who is of West Indian origin, having "made a crack, [that] 'if all those bombings had taken place in the *West Indies*, the people wouldn't have taken it.'" Ruth's crack elicits a response from Betty, presumably African American, who ventures, "It's a strange thing, everything is so fine in the West Indies, but they keeping coming over here." Playing the role of peacemaker, Mildred offers, "I guess Ruth came from the West Indies for the same reason that I came here from South Carolina" (201–2). More than just diffusing the tension in the room, Mildred offers the club's members a worldview that links the two regions and pushes them to see the connection between racism in the South and imperialism in the Caribbean and their similar effects on working-class black women. Mildred's attempt to link the two struggles was consistent with the overall ethos of *Freedom* newspaper. In his column opening the issue in which Childress's original column appeared, Robeson demonstrated this ethos when he brought attention to "the McCarran Act, denying freedom of entry, for example, to our West Indian brothers and sisters" (Robeson 1952). Making such links illuminated the real consequence for the black working class when the U.S. South became the northern shore of a Caribbean Sea transformed into an American lake.

In writing their respective columns centered around working-class protagonists, both Hughes and Childress gave readers of the African American press something they did not encounter often. Their choice, however, was not simply a matter of aesthetics, but spoke powerfully about this class's potential contribution to the world-altering changes afoot in the world. This contribution was the critical element in realizing the vision of a postwar global order not structured along the world color line. While this period brought about a shift in leadership of the global order from European to U.S. power, it left the color line, with slight modifications, intact. Reflecting an understanding that wealth and power in the global order rested on the backs of a politically weak black working class, the U.S. ruling class made sure this class was isolated from potential racial and class allies, and it effectively silenced those intellectuals and activists who dared stand with this class. In order to achieve these objectives, the ruling class adopted an approach that was not solely disciplinary, but also co-optive and productive. It co-opted an emergent black bourgeoisie, whose own class interests were furthered through the discourse of racial liberalism and whose very existence was used as an arm in the propaganda war with the Soviet Union. It also produced the racial entitlements in the form of government-supported home loans and highway constructions, facilitating the growth of suburbs for the white working class and eroding the foundations of interracial class solidarity. Euro-American radical leftists, within both communist parties and other organizations, have been notoriously unable to produce a cogent analysis, never mind an adequate response, to these latter developments. In failing to grasp the centrality of antiblack racism to the constitution of the modern global order and insisting that black struggles be subsumed under the class struggle, these movements have pushed many African diaspora intellectuals and activists to maintain a guarded distance from predominantly white radical organizations. One such figure caught up in the push and pull between white political movements and black freedom struggles was Paul Robeson. His ordeal is the subject of the next chapter.

CHAPTER 4

Black Radical Vagabond
Paul Robeson's Cold War Ordeal

The Cold War tragedy of Paul Robeson, "the black star"[1] of the United States, was enacted on the stage set by African Americans' heightened expectations in the period immediately following World War II. Robeson's tragedy reveals the mechanisms by which a series of interest-convergences moderated these expectations and effectively marginalized the African American left position on racial equality. While he was perhaps the most well-known African American of the period, Robeson's unapologetic identification with the communist-affiliated left both provoked the disapprobation of the U.S. government and assured his marginalization from the dominant currents of the postwar struggle for racial equality. To counter the successful Cold War campaign that delegitimized the left position as foreign and ultimately un-American, Robeson penned an autobiographical text that locates his activist work within the long tradition of black antiracist struggle dating back to the fight to abolish slavery in the United States. This chapter provides a detailed account of a critical part of the cultural Cold War that has often been treated in a shorthand fashion with a simple reference to the silencing of African Americans radicals like Robeson and W.E.B. Du Bois.

This account begins in the World War II years. As in previous wars, African Americans supported the war effort with the hope that their loyalty and military service would strengthen their claim for citizenship rights at war's end. They also embraced the war's explicit goal of defeating Hitler and fascism, since victory for the Allies would discredit the ideas of racial superiority promoted by the Axis powers. On the home front, the labor leader A. Phillip Randolph organized the march on Washington movement (MOWM), which leveraged the threat of thousands of African Americans descending on Washington, D.C., to extract political concessions from President Roosevelt;

these included an executive order against racial discrimination in the defense industries and the creation of the Fair Employment Practices Committee (FEPC) to investigate discrimination complaints. Expanded industrial opportunities during the war encouraged African Americans to leave agricultural work in the rural South for factory work in urban centers throughout the country. For many African Americans, this wartime experience foretold Jim Crow's imminent death. Although it did not entail revolutionary changes in government, there was an "opening," which Slavoj Žižek describes as the time between the fall of one Master-Signifier and the installation of another (1993, 1). In the United States, this brief moment opened with the delegitimization of Jim Crow on the home front and closed when the Cold War installed racial liberalism as the reigning political ideology.

On the African American cultural scene, perhaps no figure loomed as large in the course of these developments as Paul Robeson. As one of its most prominent and vocal figures, Robeson was a high-value target in the ideological campaign to make the African American left position untenable. The cultural Cold War struggle for the hearts and minds of African and Asian peoples makes apparent the stakes involved in isolating Robeson and the African American left. As someone whose fame among the world's colored peoples was perhaps unparalleled, Robeson represented a prized asset, the jewel in the crown as it were, in the struggle to bring the newly independent nations in Africa and Asia into the respective superpowers' camp. By maintaining his attachment to the Soviet Union, airing his suspicions about U.S. interests in Africa and Asia, and giving his support to left-labor causes, Robeson rendered himself persona non grata in the eyes of the U.S. government and the liberal establishment. The resulting attack on Robeson emanated not only from government entities such as the FBI and House Committee on Un-American Activities, but also from the leaders of establishment intellectual and civil rights organizations such as AMSAC and the NAACP. This chapter examines this confluence of anticommunist and racial liberal forces, which succeeded, as Thomas Borstelmann argues, in submerging "a credible, coherent black Left . . . below the surface of American political life" (2001, 67) and made unlikely bedfellows of conservative racists like U.S. senator James Eastland and liberal antiracists like Roy Wilkins.

To illuminate this odd coupling, I retool the notion of interest convergence developed by the legal scholar Derrick Bell. In his original formulation, Bell demonstrated how elite white and African American interests converged to produce the judicial and legislative civil rights gains of the 1950s and 1960s. Interest-convergence provides a potent analytical frame to explain how the African American left position on racial equality was effectively marginalized during the Cold War. Through a series of convergences and divergences—African American and white liberal elite convergence; poor white and elite white divergence; and crucially, poor African American and white divergence—the African American left began to inhabit its primary role as the producer of utopian visions of an American society liberated from the crippling realities of racial capitalism. That transformations within this system triggered domestic reforms is but one insight to be gleaned from Bell's insistence that the Cold War foreign policy goals of the United States made advances on civil rights possible.

Despite the appreciable judicial and legislative advances toward racial equality and the expansion of New Deal–type programs justified by anticommunism, it seems incontrovertible that the reach of these actions did not extend to the nation's most vulnerable citizens. Indeed, the outcome for poor and working-class African Americans was, in the words of historian Carol Anderson, "one of the most tragic . . . legacies of the Cold War" (2003, 7). In the Cold War drama's headlong rush toward its seemingly inevitable tragic conclusion, critical voices did rise to challenge the liberal consensus and expose the mechanism by which it was produced.[2] Despite the metaphorical drowning described by Borstelmann, African American left voices emerged to trouble the waters. As one of many such voices, Paul Robeson's Here I Stand, which figures Robeson as a producer of texts and not simply an interpreter of them through singing and acting, is the focus of this chapter. In this text, Robeson emphasizes his roots in the African American community to counter the suggestion that his leftist politics were an exotic import, more suitable to foreign soil. By drawing on the rhetorical devices of the slave narrative, Robeson also establishes a parallel between his political activism and those of abolitionists. A recurrent feature of his speeches and other utterances from this period, this parallel roots his African American left critique within the long history of struggle against the brutalities and deprivations engendered by the development of racial capitalism in the United States particularly and in the New World generally.

A (TRAGIC) HERO'S WELCOME:
THE EMBRACE OF ROBESON UPON HIS RETURN HOME

In 1939, after having spent twelve years abroad in Europe, Robeson returned to the United States. He had been drawn back home by the feeling that he "must be among the Negro people during the great world crisis that was looming, and be part of their struggles for the new world a-coming that they sought" (Robeson 1988, 54–55). Just three weeks after his return, Robeson recorded "Ballad for Americans" for a half-hour radio program on CBS called *The Pursuit of Happiness*, an upbeat salute to democracy. The song was an instant sensation and made radio history according to the program's producer, and when it was recorded for the record label Victor, it soared to the top of the charts (Duberman 1989, 236). "Deeply patriotic and hopeful," according to historian Barbara Savage, the song "memorialized [a] new version of [U.S.] history" that was "a blend of idealism and ethnic contribution (1999, 61). Following this success, Robeson played a small but critical role in the success of *Freedom's People*, a federally sponsored national radio show emphasizing black contributions to the nation and drawing attention to the wide gap between American ideals and its democratic practices in regard to African Americans, which aired from 1941 to 1942.

Freedom's People owed its existence to Ambrose Caliver, a black professional employee at the Office of Education. He first pitched his show to NBC and then to the Office of Education at a time, the summer of 1940, when "federal officials were growing ever more nervous about black morale and the extent of black support for the war buildup" (Savage 1999, 69). Understanding the first show's importance to the program's overall success, Caliver and his group of advisers devoted this episode, which was broadcast on September 21, 1941, to African American musical contributions to the nation. After persistent negotiations, Caliver secured Robeson's participation, which brought "gravity and social consciousness . . . to the show" and guaranteed "the large audience the show would need in order to help convince NBC to reserve a slot for the programs that were to follow" (75). While his radio work was important, it was no doubt Robeson's role as Othello in a wartime revival of Shakespeare's play that was the biggest factor in boosting African American morale about their progress under America's flawed democracy.

After premiering to rave reviews in the summer of 1942 in the ostensibly more open-minded university towns of Cambridge and Princeton, Robeson debuted in the lead role of *Othello* on Broadway on October 19, 1943. It was the first time that a person of African descent played the lead role in Shakespeare's play for a North American audience. The production ran for 296 performances, a record for a Shakespearean production on Broadway, and then toured the United States and Canada for thirty-six weeks. Beyond his principled refusal to perform before segregated audiences, which he included as a clause in his contract, Robeson understood his role as Othello as explicitly engaged with the "external conditions of the contemporary moment," and making a "statement concerning the present circumstances of both the war and segregation" (Swindall 2011, 70). This understanding grew from the resonances between *Othello* and Shakespeare's historical moment that Robeson saw as parallels with his own moment and the world situation that emerged out of the destruction of World War II.

Robeson developed these parallels and articulated his vision of the possibilities for postwar America in an essay titled "Some Reflections on *Othello* and the Nature of Our Time," published in the autumn 1945 edition of *The American Scholar*. Looking "beyond the personal tragedy," Robeson discovers in "the terrible agony of Othello, the irretrievability of his world, the complete destruction of all trusted and sacred values," evidence of "the shattering of a universe" (1945, 391). Taking his clues from Theodore Spencer's *Shakespeare and the Nature of Man*, Robeson argued that "Othello's world was breaking asunder," poised as it was between "Medievalism [that] was ending, and the new world of Renaissance [that was] beginning." Such moments, according to Spencer, were "propitious for the writing of great tragic drama" since in them "a conventional pattern of belief and behavior" existed alongside "an acute consciousness of how that conventional pattern can be violated" (1942, 50). For Robeson, post–World War II America was not dissimilar to late sixteenth-century England in this regard, which explains why American audiences found this latest revival of Shakespeare's *Othello* "strikingly contemporary." These audiences were standing "at the end of one period in human history and before the entrance of a new" (Robeson 1945, 391). No doubt, a symbol of this epochal shift was that North American audiences could accept and respond enthusiastically to a play in which an African American cast in the lead role marries then murders a white woman.

The appreciable shift in racial attitudes was, for Robeson at least, part of a general pattern the roots of which lay in the soil of political economy. In this respect the war had not been simply destructive, but immensely constructive. Robeson wrote, "We have been engaged in a global war, a war in which the capacity of *our* productive processes and techniques ... clearly presaged the realization of new productive relationships." In the new relationships envisioned here, profit would no longer be the driving force; instead these relationships would be constituted in and by the needs of "the whole people, in their potential and realized abilities." According to Robeson, such conditions would allow for "the emergence into full bloom of the last estate, the vision of no high and no low, no superior and no inferior—but equals, assigned to different tasks in the building of a new and richer human society" (392). During the war years the U.S. government and liberal allies had tolerated Robeson's socialist vision as long as he put his considerable talents to the service of racial unity and maintenance of African American support for the war effort. At war's end, however, his suggestion that the productive forces organized to defeat fascism held the potential to radically remake society provoked a distinctly different reaction. Such talk was considered subversive in the United States because it raised the specter of communism, which was starting to be regarded as the greatest threat to the American way of life. This essay no doubt set the stage for the sustained effort to isolate Robeson and the African American left as traitorously un-American during the Cold War.

The FBI's investigation into Robeson's apparently subversive activities began little more than a year after his return from Europe in late 1939. Most commentators tend to agree that this secret surveillance gave way to public denouncement following his speech to the Soviet-sponsored World Congress of the Partisans of Peace (Congrès Mondial des Partisans de la Paix) held in Paris in April 1949. Indeed, the Associated Press's misquoted version of the speech provoked an "immediate" and "fierce" reaction from all quarters, as the white press labeled him a traitor, black leaders questioned his leadership credentials, and U.S. government agencies pondered rendering him a noncitizen (Duberman 1989, 342). While there is no gainsaying the far-reaching impact of the fallout from the words attributed to him, Robeson had already crossed the line separating permissible criticism and traitorous dissent two years earlier.

In April 1947, Robeson decided to suspend his concert and stage career and use his considerable talents in the cause of eradicating Jim Crow from American society and institutions. In his new work, Robeson gravitated toward those struggles that reflected his dual commitment to fight racial discrimination and advance the cause of labor. Along these lines and through his collaboration with Ewart Guinier, international secretary-treasurer of the United Public Workers, Robeson traveled to the Panama Canal Zone in May of that same year.[3] According to one source, Robeson refrained from making "speeches," treating his audience to a "repertoire . . . of many songs from distant lands" that "contained the longing and aspirations of human beings who . . . never fail to experience the human trait of thinking above and beyond the conditions to which they are circumscribed" (Nolan 1947).

Immediately upon returning from Panama, however, Robeson denounced the U.S. importation of Jim Crow to the region and collaborated with African American leftists W.E.B. Du Bois and Charlotta Bass in a committee to end segregation and the discriminatory silver-gold pay system in the zone. If the nations of Africa and Asia were searching for an example of what being brought into the U.S. orbit might entail, Panama "seemed to represent," in Borstelmann's words, "a pure case of U.S. overseas imperial policy, directly analogous to European colonial policies abroad" (2001, 80). Robeson's support for the struggle to end racial discrimination in Panama showed an internationalist perspective that understood the color line as a global phenomenon. This perspective, however, did not preclude his support of struggles with a markedly local character.

Soon after returning from Panama, Robeson ventured to Winston-Salem, North Carolina, to lend support to Local 22 of the Food, Tobacco, and Agricultural and Allied Workers of America Union. This union of predominantly African American women had just concluded a difficult six-week strike against the R. J. Reynolds Tobacco Company, which left "their funds and morale exhausted," when it "sent a desperate appeal [to] Robeson" (Wright 1975, 58). Robeson arrived on a sweltering Sunday in late June of 1947, attracting thousands to a fund-raising concert for a union whose beleaguered members, despite the end of the strike several weeks earlier, still relied on the union's soup kitchen and commissary for sustenance (Korstad 2003, 335). In his banter between songs, Robeson did not attribute his presence to the CPUSA, whose members occupied leadership positions in the union and to which Robeson was (and continues to be) linked. Instead, he linked his presence to the irrepressible memory of "his father who [had been] born a slave in the tobacco country" in another part of North Carolina (quoted in Korstad 2003, 336). In anchoring his politics in his familial connection to America's slave past and not in the dictates for international communism issued from Moscow, Robeson deployed one of his signal rhetorical strategies of the early Cold War period.

Despite its overwhelming African American, noncommunist rank-and-file membership estimated at eight thousand, the presence of communists in its leadership sealed Local 22's fate.[4] Not a month after Robeson's relief concert, three union leaders were subpoenaed to appear before the House Un-American Activities Committee (HUAC) to face questioning. The *Hearings Regarding Communism in Labor Unions in the United States* were the result of a request made by North Carolina representative and HUAC member

Herbert Bonner and a motion by Georgia representative John Wood that a subcommittee be established to investigate Local 22. On July 23, 1947, FTA international representative Edwin McCrea and Local 22 cochairmen W. C. Sheppard and Robert C. Black testified before a committee that included the arch-segregationist Mississippi representative John Rankin. The hearings opened with the testimony of Ann Mathews, a communist-turned-informant, who at the insistence of Rankin provided the committee with the name and race of suspected communists in the union. She also raised the specter of Paul Robeson when she mentioned that the union sent "a [ten-dollar] contribution . . . to the Council on African Affairs, requested by Paul Robeson, who also requested that a resolution be passed . . . on the South African situation [Jan Smuts' government plans to annex South-West Africa]" (U.S. Congress 1947, 77).[5] Her mention of Robeson would not be the last time his name was invoked as a synecdoche for the supposed Soviet and CPUSA conspiracy to hijack the legitimate struggles of African Americans for racial equality in the United States.

GOING TO MEET THE MAN:
ROBESON STANDS UP TO THE HUAC

In late April of 1949, in the midst of his European concert tour, Paul Robeson took time off to attend the World Congress of the Partisans of Peace (Congrès Mondial des Partisans de la Paix) being held in Paris.[6] At the urging of the nearly two thousand delegates from fifty countries attending the congress, Robeson addressed the assembly with an impromptu speech. This speech reiterated his support of the anticolonial struggle, the right of workers to an equal share of the wealth they produced, and the peace movement's rejection of warmongering governments. Soon afterwards an Associated Press dispatch circulated throughout the United States quoting Robeson as having declared that "it was unthinkable that American Negroes would go to war . . . against the Soviet Union" (quoted in Duberman 1989, 342). Just a month prior to the Parisian conference, Robeson had attended an event, the Cultural and Scientific Conference for World Peace, held at the Waldorf-Astoria Hotel in New York City, which historian Hugh Wilford describes as "the Communist Information Bureau['s] . . . most startling provocation of the whole Cold War" (2008, 70). By lending his support to a Soviet conference on U.S. soil and then appearing at high-profile event in Europe, Robeson assisted America's declared enemy and recent WWII ally in one area where the United States did not possess a decided advantage: "the ideological struggle between capitalism and communism for the 'hearts and minds' of nonaligned peoples around the world" (Wilford 2008, 5). The official reaction to these acts of alleged disloyalty was sustained and unrelenting; it brought an end to a lucrative performance career and precipitated a decline in Robeson's legendary physical and mental abilities.

Although it would be several years before Robeson was hauled before a committee to answer to charges of subversion, the U.S. government started preparing the ground almost immediately when Georgia congressman John Wood, chairman of the HUAC, organized hearings. The committee heard testimony from a cross-section of African American "leaders": a professional informer, a black veteran, the president of Fisk University, the president of the Urban League, and, most sensationally, Jackie Robinson, the first African American to break the color barrier in twentieth-century professional baseball. The witnesses reassured Congress, and the public more generally, of African Americans' loyalty to the United States and denounced Robeson's purported statement as unrepresentative of African American sentiments. According to historian Andrea Friedman, "Robeson functioned [in these hearings] not just as the bad Negro in contrast to their good Negro, but as an icon of disloyalty, a traitor to his race as well as his nation" (2007, 455). The hearings also united a community of believers, the Dixiecrats, for whom the hearings were "sacred scrolls" in the effort "to paint the maturing civil rights movement red" (Woods 2003, 38). For the black-hating, anticommunist crusaders in Congress, there was perhaps no higher-profile target than the supposed black-turned-red, Paul Robeson.

When he appeared before the HUAC in the summer of 1956, Robeson took a defiant stance that had been previewed by some of his closest associates on the African American left. These radicals did not refrain from expressing their contempt for the committee and its Senate counterpart during their testimonies. In July of 1953, the African American leftist Eslanda Goode Robeson, Robeson's wife, refused to be intimidated when she testified before Joseph McCarthy's Senate Permanent Subcommittee on Investigations. She sharply responded to his committee's insulting suggestion that she relied on communist assistance to write her book *Africa Journey*, and she invoked her Fifth Amendment and Fifteenth Amendment rights when posed questions about her membership in the Communist Party. The latter right, although not strictly relevant in a legal sense, served to highlight the committee's racism and the fact that African Americans in the South were prevented from electing senators (Ransby 2013, 223–224). The previous year Georgia congressman John Wood encountered similar resistance when he brought the HUAC to Detroit to investigate Local 600, which historian Martin Halpern describes as "a bulwark of Left-wing influence in the United States" and "an important base of support for radicalism within the African American community" (1997, 20–21). In Detroit, Wood confronted the radical African American unionist Coleman Young. Young leveled charges that the committee had singled out Negro leaders and reminded Chairman Wood that his own position in Congress had been won as a consequence of violent repression and legal restrictions that prevented African Americans from voting in Georgia (29). In both cases, Eslanda Robeson and Coleman Young highlighted the seemingly indistinguishable relationship between white supremacy and anticommunism.

On the surface it appears that by June 1956, when Robeson appeared to testify before the HUAC as part of an *Investigation of the Unauthorized Use of United States Passports*, the committee had moved beyond the strategies and procedures of its past southern chairmen, Rankin and Wood. But those appearances would be deceiving. When Robeson went before the committee, Rep. Francis E. Walter of Pennsylvania was the presiding chairman. In the context of the questioning, Robeson identified the chairman as the author of the Immigration and Nationality Act of 1952 (also referred to as the McCarran-Walter Act), which he described as "going to keep all kinds of decent people out of the country . . . colored people like myself, from the West Indies and all kinds, and just Teutonic Anglo-Saxon stock that you would let come in" (U.S. Congress 1956, 4498). As Robeson emphasized, this act was used to deport from the United States Caribbean-born radicals, among them the communist Claudia Jones, the Trotskyist C.L.R. James, and the radical trade unionist Ferdinand Smith of the NMU and later Harlem Trade Union Council.[7] Indeed, the cultural critic Carole Boyce Davies has judged the McCarran-Walter Act as "deadlier than the Smith Act" for having laid "the foundation for immigration checks, deportation, harassment of African Americans, [and] even 'authorized concentration camps for emergency situations'" (2001, 957). While it is not clear how much Robeson knew at the time about Walter's associations, his reference to "Teutonic Anglo-Saxon stock" clearly associates Walter and his signal legislation with the discourse of white supremacy.

Historical evidence confirms Robeson's suggestion that Congressman

Walter's congressional career reflected his commitment to white supremacy. Indeed, the largest contributor to Walter's election campaign had been
Wickliffe Draper, founder of the Pioneer Fund. Draper created the fund in
1937 to support the study of problems of heredity and eugenics, and according to William H. Tucker, he "opened wide his pursestrings between the late
1950s and his death in 1972" and poured "huge amounts of money into various anti-integration products conducted by some of the most ardent racists"
(2002, 67).[8] Walter also served on a committee set up by Draper to surrep-
titiously fund scientific projects concerned with questions of "immigration
and race" (71–72). Thus Robeson was quite correct to insist throughout his
testimony that his appearance before the HUAC had little, if anything, to
do with the use of his passport and that it should be understood in the
wider context of a white supremacist assault on the African American freedom struggle emanating from the legislative branch of the U.S. government.

Robeson's appearance before the HUAC gave the committee the opportunity to cast the black left as something akin to Soviet communism
in blackface. Consider, for example, Mr. Arens, the HUAC staff director
and Robeson's principal inquisitor during the hearings, who taunted him to
reveal the names of "the Communists who participated in the preparation
of the statement" (U.S. Congress 1956, 4499) he was not allowed to read.[9]
Later Mr. Arens read a statement supposedly made by Robeson in which
he declares himself "a member of the American resistance movement that
fights against American imperialism, just as the resistance movement fought
against Hitler." Robeson interrupts Mr. Arens and proclaims "just like Frederick Douglas [sic] and Harriet Tubman were underground railroaders, and
fighting for our freedom; you bet your life" (4502). Robeson's interruption
obstructs the path Arens was apparently taking to establish the dominant
role of communists in the antifascist resistance in Europe and reroutes it
back to American soil and the black antislavery movement, thereby grounding his own politics in the African American freedom struggle.

When his critics tried to paint him as a dupe of the Soviets, Robeson
returned the favor by framing his critics as little more than racists who had
simply cloaked their principal objective of perpetuating black subjugation in
the garb of anticommunism. Robeson cleverly made this point when he was
questioned about his alleged statement seven years earlier in Paris. Raising
the specter of virulent and powerful racists, he "clarifies" for the committee
that he had actually stated that "it was unthinkable to [him] that any people
would take up arms in the name of an [James O.] Eastland to go against

anybody" (4501).[10] The Mississippi senator, who served on one of Draper's eugenics committees (Tucker 2002, 71), was a perfect foil. Eastland had used his position on the Senate Internal Security Subcommittee to portray the civil rights movement as part of a vast conspiracy directed by the forces of international communism.[11] In the winter just before Robeson's HUAC hearing, in a speech before the Statewide Convention of the Association of (White) Citizens' Councils of Mississippi, Eastland argued that the Supreme Court's decision in *Brown v. Board of Education* was evidence that the court "present[ed] a clear threat and present danger ... to the foundations of our Republican form of Government" (Eastland 1955, 4). In his reference to Eastland, Robeson frames his own politics and rhetoric as first and foremost those of a committed antiracist.

In *Here I Stand*, Robeson obliquely refers to his ordeal before the HUAC and responds to the attempt to paint the African American left as "un-American" by designating as the "real Un-Americans" (Robeson 1958, 4) those anticommunist, primarily southern congressmen and their allies who led and orchestrated the congressional resistance to civil rights for African Americans.[12] These men gave official credence to the idea, and supported it with the enormous resources of the federal government, that there was no greater evidence of the communist plot to destroy the American way of life than the African American challenge to the Jim Crow social order. Historian Gerald Horne remarked long ago on the "sharp racist edge" (1986, 2) of McCarthyism. And more recently, Jeff Woods has argued that Mississippi senator James Eastland's "anti-Communism was not simply a convenient front for his racism" (44). The relationship between anticommunism and racism, however, was not incidental: the Jim Crow regime was as premised on economic exploitation as it was on racial subordination. Thus men like Eastland and Rep. John Rankin, and Georgia senator Richard B. Russell and Rep. John Wood, leaders of key congressional committees, allied with J. Edgar Hoover's FBI to smear nearly every challenge to racial discrimination as being directed by Moscow.

The broad strokes with which Hoover and his coconspirators painted red the entire African American freedom struggle further limited the left's already marginal influence. It was, however, in a cluster of organizations with a decidedly leftist orientation that Robeson focused his primary engagement in the freedom struggle. In 1952, when Robeson relaunched his concert career, he did so as part of a two-month, fifteen-city fund-raising tour to raise money for the United Freedom Fund (UFF), an umbrella group that provided financial support to *Freedom* newspaper, the Council on African Affairs (CAA), the National Negro Labor Council (NNLC), and the Committee for the Negro in the Arts (CNA).[13] These organizations formed an important nucleus of black left cultural and political activism and presented an alternative to the anticommunist racial liberalism that achieved dominance during the Cold War.

The first issue of *Freedom*, "Paul Robeson's Newspaper," was published in late 1950, and the paper ran until 1955, when it closed under the weight of meager resources and government repression. Robeson contributed a regular column to the newspaper, "Here's My Story." According to Martin Duberman, the columns were first worked out with the African American leftist writer Lloyd Brown, who wrote them and passed them by Robeson to be checked over (Duberman 1989, 393).[14] Louis Burnham, an activist and journalist who had occupied leadership positions in the Southern Negro Youth Congress (SNYC), was the primary editor of *Freedom*. Burnham, with Ed Strong, a fellow comrade from his SNYC days (and possibly Esther Cooper and James E. Jackson), prepared the prospectus for the newspaper in 1949.[15] The CPUSA's hand in the founding of *Freedom* is clearly evident in the fellow-traveler language of the prospectus. It locates the rationale for *Freedom* in the necessity of countering "the propaganda of right-wing reformism, petty bourgeois nationalism, and social-democratic opportunism, particularly addressed to Negro readers through Negro newspapers and periodical" (Burnham 1949, 1). *Freedom* provided its readers with a perspective that consistently "focused on international news and emphasized solidarity with people of color" and also published a cadre of African American women writers and labor activists, such as Lorraine Hansberry, Alice Childress, and Vicki Garvin, who "helped shape the paper's black-leftist-feminist viewpoint" (Washington 2014, 145).[16] These writers and activists' work on *Freedom* flowed seamlessly into their involvement with other UFF organizations (for example Garvin's role in the founding of the NNLC) and brought them into regular contact with activists and scholars working with the CAA, which from the fall of 1952 shared the newspaper's office space at 53 West 125th Street in Harlem.

Max Yergan with Robeson's help founded the first incarnation of the CAA, the International Committee on African Affairs, in 1937. Under his stewardship the organization attracted prominent African American intellectuals across the political spectrum, including Mary McLeod Bethune, Ralph Bunche, and E. Franklin Frazier, to support its work on behalf of

African causes. After the group underwent reorganization in 1942, Robeson served as its chair and veered the organization toward a more militant anti-capitalist and anti-imperialist orientation. In 1948, a dispute over the organization's relationship to the left caused a split that resulted in Yergan being expelled from the CAA.[17] From this point, Robeson, along with Alphaeus Hunton, who joined the organization in 1943, and W.E.B. Du Bois, who moved his office to the CAA's after he was expelled from the NAACP, largely charted the organization's course. If the CAA reflected Robeson's commitment to international issues, the NNLC was the organization through which he supported domestic black working-class struggles.

In June 1950, Robeson gave the keynote address to the National Labor Conference for Negro Rights, which brought nearly a thousand representatives of organized labor to Chicago. His speech, "Forge Negro-Labor Unity for Peace and Jobs," was later published and distributed in pamphlet form by the Harlem Trade Union Council and the South Side Negro Council. One of the calls issuing from this conference was to build Negro labor councils throughout the United States and to unite them in a national organization. When the NNLC held its founding convention a year later in Cincinnati, Ohio, Robeson attended as an "artist like many in the world today who give constantly of their talents and energies to the struggles for freedom of the working masses of the world." As the highlight of the first night's cultural program, Robeson sang for the delegates, but not before reminding them of the "necessity of unity between all sections of labor in this land and throughout the world."[18] At this founding convention, the NNLC dedicated itself to breaking barriers to employment in industries that excluded African American workers, pushing model FEPC clauses in union contracts, and addressing the particular rights and grievances of African American women, who occupied the lowest position in the economic hierarchy.[19]

While cultural elements played an essential role in the journalistic work, diasporic political work, and domestic labor organizing of the above organizations, the Committee for the Negro in the Arts (CNA) concentrated its efforts on improving the quantity and quality of African American participation in the various arts. According to Brian Dolinar, the CNA was the new name for the Cultural Division of the National Negro Congress when that organization was folded into the Civil Rights Congress in 1947 (Dolinar 2012, 64). The CNA notably provided a space to develop theatrical talent, nourishing the budding careers of actors such as Ruby Dee, Ossie Davis, Sidney Poitier, and Harry Belafonte, among others. Playing an important role in the organization was the cultural activist and producer Ruth Jett, who represented the CNA at the founding of the UFF in February of 1952. In 1950, Jett produced Alice Childress's play *Just a Little Simple*, an adaptation of Langston Hughes's novel *Simple Speaks His Mind*, for the CNA's first theatrical production, which ran for three weeks at Club Baron on 132nd and Lenox (Washington 2014, 92). The CNA also supported the career of the leftist visual artist Charles White, who had spent time as a Cold War exile in Mexico, aiding him with his first solo exhibition at a major New York gallery (Schreiber 2008, 55).[20] The CNA's work, like that of all the other organization's supported by the UFF, was short-lived, as it buckled under the weight of government repression that resulted from being on the attorney general's list of subversive organizations.

The government's success in effectively curtailing the African American left's influence within the freedom struggle should not be construed as a simple morality play of good versus evil, black versus white, or communists versus racists. The effectiveness of the campaign was due in large measure to the combination of insecurity, opportunism, ambition, and convenient alliances that are the making of all tragic dramas. This confluence of forces came together to produce the Cold War civil rights that made "unthinkable" "discussions of broad-based social change, or a linking of race and class" (Dudziak 2000, 13). Robeson's experience playing Othello during the war, before he put his acting and singing career on hold to engage in politics, was perhaps a dress rehearsal for the Cold War political drama in which he would play a leading role.

"SCANDALIZE MY NAME": THE CIVIL RIGHTS ESTABLISHMENT DISTANCES ITSELF FROM ROBESON

Civil rights establishment leaders played a critical, supporting role in the tragic drama in which Robeson was portrayed as at best a naïve dupe of Soviet machinations. Penning a series of articles that shored up their anticommunist bona fides, leaders like Walter White, the executive secretary of the NAACP, took up the anti-Robeson crusade. In an article published in the February 1951 edition of *Ebony* magazine, White endeavors to make sense of "The Strange Case of Paul Robeson" and ultimately concludes that "the sum total ... seems to be a bewildered man who is more to be pitied than damned" (White 1951, 78).[21] White doubts that Robeson's "Left-wingism is based on honest, reasoned conviction," locating its origin instead in an "unconscious lashing out at those whites that have hurt him and other Negroes through racial proscriptions" (82). White's psychoanalyzing of Robeson makes use of an ideology that the performance and cultural critic Tony Perucci argues "encouraged the translation of political and social problems into individual, personal ones, and emphasized coping and adjusting, rather than social and political transformation" (2012, 23). By focusing on the unconscious motivations for Robeson's politics, White avoids confronting the more interesting and ultimately more generative question of the "reasonableness" and value of the critique of racial oppression emanating from the black left. Such failures of dialogue participated in the Cold War climate of fear and acrimony, which hindered the development of a robust conversation about the direction of the African American freedom struggle. As a consequence, many of those who assumed the mantle of African American liberal leadership did so by limiting the field of possible alternatives.

In the absence of a thoughtful engagement with alternative perspectives, critics like White resorted to personal attacks. For example, he writes that Robeson's "outlook on life has always been slightly out of balance. . . . He seemed more concerned with finding some oasis in the world where he personally and his family would be free of race prejudice rather than consider fighting the malady itself" (1951, 80). In White's description, Robeson emerges as someone unconcerned with the masses and only interested in self-aggrandizement. White refuses, however, to consider that their disagreement might reside in their diagnosis of the "malady." He presents it as a matter of empirical obviousness that the fundamental problem, the malady from which most Negroes suffered, was race prejudice. Of course, by failing to take account of social class, White's analysis conflates the interests and concerns of well-to-do African Americans like him and Robeson with those of working-class and poor families for whom such issues as employment, decent housing, health care, and education determined their life prospects. In *Here I Stand*, Robeson describes this conflation as a situation in which "a few crumbs for a few is too often hailed as 'progress for the race'" (1958, 102). The absence of dialogue meant that what constituted "progress" was taken as obvious and had the perhaps unintended consequence of narrowing the range and reach of progress.

In his indictment, White presents himself as baffled by Robeson's apparent naiveté about Soviet designs. Thus he writes, "But one of the puzzling aspects of Robeson's thinking during recent years is his inability to see through the opportunism of Soviet domestic and foreign policy" (1951, 83). White's eagerness to indict Robeson is all the more striking if one considers that his own influence on and access to the Truman administration was due in large measure to the Soviet Union highlighting U.S. racism in its foreign policy propaganda.[22] Perhaps White's seeming incredulity here betrays his discomfort with the degree to which his own agenda was being crafted and constrained by the dictates of U.S. domestic and foreign policy. Given these constraints, White probably took it as a point of pride and cause for celebration that "the overwhelming majority of Negroes have been wise enough to see Russia's faults as well as those of the United States and to choose to fight for freedom in a faulty democracy instead of surrendering their fates to a totalitarian philosophy" (84). White's celebration might have been tempered by the undeniable fact that "freedom in a faulty democracy" did little to address the socioeconomic structures that determined the quality of life for the working-class majority of African Americans. From the perspective of the black left, the freedom for which White and mainstream civil rights organizations fought was, to quote Marx, "a big step forward, . . . not the last form of . . . emancipation, but the last form . . . *within* the prevailing scheme of things" (1975, 221). Paul Robeson and the black left at the very least offered a critique of the limits of the prevailing scheme and raised the question of liberalism's capacity to address the political and economic problems that have confronted African Americans since Reconstruction.

In many ways, Walter White was simply continuing an attack against Robeson's leadership credentials that Roy Wilkins, editor of the *Crisis*, the NAACP's official magazine, had initiated in an unsigned editorial in the May 1949 issue of the magazine. Wilkins's editorial provides a rich example of the stakes involved in rendering the black left position "unthinkable" during the Cold War. Wilkins begins by denying the truth of the statement attributed to Robeson about African Americans' willingness to go to war against the Soviet Union, adding, "Negroes have always fought for their country against any enemy" (1949, 37). Oddly, Wilkins does not address the relationship between his debatable claim and the subject of his lead editorial: the ending of the official policy of segregation in the armed forces by secretary of defense Louis A. Johnson. Coincidentally, this change of policy was announced in a memorandum released to the public on the very same day, April 20th, that the news wires carried word of Robeson's purported statement. In his rush to assert unwavering Negro loyalty, Wilkins dismisses the very idea of the conditionality of African American support in military efforts.[23] Emphasizing this conditionality, however, had provided a foundation for the "Double V" campaign that characterized African American participation in World War II as an effort to end fascism abroad and racism at home.[24] In this context, it seems not unreasonable to suggest that African Americans would be reluctant to fight in a still segregated army in a new conflict. The Truman administration, at least, appears to have not taken for granted African American support, as it moved quickly to shore up this support with its Executive Order 9981 of 1948, which created a committee to study equality of opportunity in the armed forces and led to the defense secretary's decision a year later.

Truman's executive order and the decision to end the policy of Jim Crow in the armed services demonstrate the important place of representation in the Cold War struggle. The U.S. military was, as Borstelmann notes, "the largest multiracial group of Americans overseas" and its "racial policies . . . served as a lightning rod for domestic and foreign critics of inequality" (2001, 80). In this regard, the armed forces of the United States were meant to be doubly representative: being a "portrait" of American diversity to foreign audiences and likewise "speaking" on behalf of their fellow Americans to those same audiences. Therefore, a segregated military undermined the administration's ability to project itself as offering a democratic alternative to totalitarian rule for people of color, which was critical in the struggle for the hearts and minds of the people of Africa and Asia emerging out from under the yoke of colonial rule.

It is no surprise then that Wilkins focuses on the question of representation in his critique of Robeson. He states unequivocally that Robeson "does not represent any American Negroes," with "represent" being in the strict sense of "speaking for." As an athlete and concert singer he had inspired African Americans and "given them a 'great one' to cite in their briefs for better treatment," thus performing his role as a representative African American, in the sense of "portraying" the race's possibilities when not hampered by racial discrimination. Robeson ceased to serve this function, however, when he began to mix his artistic performances with "the Communist party line." So instead of representing African Americans, Robeson, "if he represent[ed] any group at all, [spoke] for the fellow travelers of Communism," who "it is well-known . . . [are] overwhelmingly white." Here Wilkins suggests that Robeson's involvement with communism not only disqualified him from representing African Americans (speaking for them), but also annulled his status as representative of African American achievement. To support his accusations, Wilkins describes "ordinary American Negroes and their organizations, plugging away at the job of lifting a few ceilings on the everyday life of colored people" as being unable to "get even a reply [from Robeson] to a letter," whereas "mixed and all-white Left-wing groups could snare the great man." In conclusion, Wilkins criticizes Robeson for being distant from "ordinary Negroes" and for preferring "a circle of international intellectuals."[25]

Despite its clearly personal nature, Wilkins's attack in the editorial peddles in a Cold War era truth that caricatured the black left as lackeys for white communists.[26] He renders this portrait most vividly in his description of Robeson as turning a deaf ear to African American pleas for help from the U.S. South while "writing about Africa, singing Russian working songs, and dispensing the comfort-to-be when and if the Soviet cabal replaced the Talmadge-Rankin cabal." In one sentence Wilkins dismisses the diasporic and internationalist consciousness of the black left and establishes an equivalency between leaders of international communism and the archsegregationists Governor Eugene Talmadge of Georgia and Mississippi congressman John E. Rankin. Wilkins's refusal to accord any legitimacy to the black left might be understood as a move of self-aggrandizement. Through this move he both increases his own authority to determine which ceiling weighed most heavily on African Americans and establishes himself as arbiter of what constitutes "service to the race" and who qualifies to "speak for American Negroes." Obviously, the black left challenged Wilkins's position in its insistence that African American workers had specific concerns that neither bourgeois race groups nor white organized labor were able to articulate better than the workers themselves. Wilkins's editorial furthers the project of making the black left position "unthinkable."

LITERARY ANCESTORS:
THE SLAVE NARRATIVES RESISTANCE MODEL

In early 1958, the Othello Associates, an independent publishing company created to circumvent the blacklisting of Robeson, published his *Here I Stand*, a hybrid autobiography/political manifesto. Serving as a rejoinder to his Cold War critics, it appeared after a nearly decade-long period during which he had been blacklisted, stripped of his passport, and repudiated as a fellow traveler, if not a card-carrying communist. *Here I Stand* challenges the dominant representations of Robeson as at best a naïve dupe of the Soviet Union and at worst a deluded performer with designs to become a "Black Stalin," as a paid government informant once declared. These images of him circulated in the dominant narrative that justified the Peekskill riots of late summer 1949, when a rabid anticommunist mob thwarted a planned Robeson concert by dragging concertgoers from their cars and beating them, while state and local police looked on in amusement. In June 1956, the HUAC gave the final government imprimatur to Robeson's image as either dupe or potential Stalin during its questioning of him in the context of an investigation into the unauthorized use of United States passports. The committee rarely questioned Robeson about his passport. Instead, its members took the occasion to interrogate him about past praise for Stalin and to goad him into revealing his links to known communists and the Communist Party. Over the course of the near decade that he was vilified by the government and the press for his affiliation with the Soviet Union and American communists, Robeson mostly responded to his accusers in a reactive, ad hoc manner through articles, interviews, public statements, and speeches given at political events. Ultimately, however, in response to the need to present a fuller depiction of his life and thinking, Robeson collaborated with the African American leftist writer Lloyd L. Brown to write *Here I Stand*. Robeson and Brown had first begun to work together on Robeson's regular column for his newspaper *Freedom*; Brown also penned a pamphlet, *Lift Every Voice for Paul Robeson* (1951), to protest the denial of Robeson's passport.[27]

The vehicle of this defense, *Here I Stand*, is a hybrid text that frames Robeson's political views within the context of his autobiography, from his humble beginnings as the son of a former slave to his experiences abroad as a world-renowned actor and singer. Over the course of five chapters, he articulates his political views, which had been "the subject of wide discussion and controversy in public life generally and in Negro life as well" (1958, 28) during the height of the anticommunist hysteria. These political chapters are preceded in the 1958 version of the text by an "Author's Foreword" and prologue. These two sections, positioned in the paratext, contain the bulk of the straightforward, linear autobiographical writing in the text.[28] The structural placement of the autobiographical sections outside the main body of text is consistent with Robeson's declaration in the foreword that the book was not conceived as an autobiography. He admits to feeling compelled to include the mainly autobiographical prologue out of the conviction that "his early days and the lasting influences from [his] childhood" (5) determined the shape and form of the politics he adopted later in life. Thus the prologue serves to frame Robeson's political positions as not those acquired in foreign lands by a globetrotting entertainer, but those of the son of an ex-slave rooted in American soil.

In *Here I Stand*, Robeson draws on the rhetorical strategies of the slave narrative to defend a black left position marginalized and discredited by liberals and conservatives alike during the early years of the Cold War.[29] In crafting his life story for use in a political cause, Robeson explicitly inscribes himself and his text in the tradition of the slave narrators who produced texts of their lives to further the abolitionist cause. With its origins in the slave narratives, "the tradition of African-American writing is," as Kenneth Mostern notes, "thus one in which political commentary necessitates, invites, and assumes autobiography as its rhetorical form" (1999, 11). While I might quibble with the "necessity" of his choice, it seems indisputable that Robeson's decision to engage this form furthered his political goal of linking his own struggle to the abolitionist cause. *Here I Stand* adapts the form to contemporary realities, which is evident in its subtle reworking of the generic conventions of the author's foreword in the slave narrative. The prefatory matter of antebellum slave narratives was usually consigned to white authorities that could both attest to the character of the black narrator and the veracity of the narrator's tale. Thus literary critics have described slave narratives as carrying a black message in a white envelope.[30] By including his own prefatory remarks, Robeson symbolically upends this familiar operation. He authenticates his own discourse and structures his text so as to contradict the portrayal of him as simply a black messenger of the mostly white CPUSA, whose ultimate goal was to further the foreign policy interests of the Soviet Union.

Key to Robeson's strategy of self-authentication in the prologue, titled "A Home in that Rock," is a compelling portrait of his relationship with his father, the Reverend William D. Robeson. While he mentions in passing his mother's family's connection to the American Revolutionary War,[31] Robeson places greater emphasis on his paternal heritage, which directly links him to slave resistance. Robeson's father, "the glory of [his] boyhood years" (6), was a runaway slave who gained his freedom in the North by means of the Underground Railroad. The text presents him as both a paragon of black upward mobility and principled resistance to the racist social order. After studying at Lincoln University, he served as a Presbyterian reverend and then as a pastor in A.M.E. Zion churches in the black communities of southern New Jersey. At times, he also worked as an "ash-man" and coach-man to provide for his family, but he never demonstrated a "hint of servility," since, according to Robeson, "just as in youth he had refused to remain a slave, so in all the years of his manhood he disdained to be an Uncle Tom" (11). Robeson's portrait of his father establishes the continuity between his father's defiance of slavery and his subsequent refusal to make his way forward in Jim Crow America by donning the mask of servility.

This defiant stance imparts to Paul Robeson, his youngest son, an important paternal lesson and secures Robeson's enduring admiration for his father. Daniel Holder has recently argued that Robeson stresses his devotion to his father in order to suture "himself to the patriarchal and conservative blackness embodied by his father" and "other, historical African American fathers on whom Robeson's father is himself modeled," most notably Frederick Douglass (2012, 73). This astute observation about the text's figuring of the father-son relationship speaks directly to how homophobic anticommunist discourse painted suspected communists as emasculated men. It ignores, however, that Robeson also crafts the text of his life in this manner in order to draw attention to the confluence between the leadership of the anticommunist charge and the white resistance to desegregation, particularly in the U.S. Congress. Just as his father resisted the slavocracy by escaping to the free states of the North, Robeson figures his own struggle as opposing the descendants of this class in the likes of Congressman John Wood or Senator James Eastland. Thus he situates his own struggle in relation to past movements that resisted first slavery and then Jim Crow.

Robeson makes an argument for the continuity between struggles when he mentions his father outside the autobiographical sections of the text, in the chapter devoted to his passport case. Recalling the long history of African Americans "assert[ing] their right of freedom of movement," Robeson valorizes those "tens of thousands of Negros slaves, like [his] own father, [who] traveled the Underground Railroad to freedom in the North" (66). This history serves as the ground upon which he rests his claim that "from the days of chattel slavery until today, the concept of *travel* has been inseparably linked in the minds of our people with the concept of *freedom*" (67). More than individual freedom, however, is at stake here. Robeson reminds his readers of those fugitive slaves and freeborn African Americans who traveled abroad to further the abolitionist cause and build support in foreign countries for African American rights. Thus he establishes the cause of African American freedom as historically and necessarily international and creates for himself a privileged and direct relationship to this history: not as learned history, but as history constituting his very being as a consequence of his close relationship to his father.

Throughout the discussion of his passport case in Here I Stand, Robeson uses black abolitionism as an ethical signpost for making political sense of his struggle to reobtain his passport, which the U.S. State Department revoked in 1950. He insists that international travel is inextricably tied to securing African American rights. According to Robeson, "speaking the truth abroad has been of great value to the struggle for Negro rights in America. . . . The good work [of black abolitionists] abroad lives on in our own time, for that pressure which comes today from Europe in our behalf is in part a precious heritage from those early Negro sojourners for freedom who crossed the sea to champion the rights of black men in America" (67). In this claim, Robeson reframes the issue of his passport not as the personal matter of an international celebrity deprived of the means of making a living, but as an effort to channel the African American freedom struggle into a stream compatible with the Cold War foreign policy objectives of the United States.

The U.S. State Department judged that Robeson's ability to travel was contrary to the best interests of the United States and revoked his passport. Indeed, according to one source, Mrs. Ruth B. Shipley, the chief of the State Department's Passport Office, informed Robeson that "when he spoke against colonialism, he was 'meddling in matters within the exclusive jurisdiction of the secretary of state'" (Rogers 1985, 499).[32] Robeson insisted, however, that one could not "oppose White Supremacy in South Carolina and not oppose the same vicious system in South Africa" (Robeson 1958, 64). In his view, the domestic fight against racial discrimination was of a piece with the anticolonial struggle, since both were waged against the globe-encompassing color line. Thus, Robeson was not denied a passport because he broke the law, but rather because he contradicted the official narrative on domestic racial progress and insisted on immediate independence for Africa.[33] In Here I Stand, Robeson thus characterizes his passport case as a matter of the fundamental right to an independent opinion and not being forced to parrot the views "of some Wall Street corporation lawyer . . . appointed Secretary of State [Acheson] or . . . of some political office-seeker who is rewarded with the job of issuing passports [Shipley]" (66). Of course, Robeson's position was neither the only nor final word on such matters.

In the early 1950s, the State Department sponsored tours of African Americans such as J. Saunders Redding, Carl T. Rowan, and Edith Sampson to Asia and Europe.[34] The Truman administration conceived these tours to counteract the "acutely embarrassing" (Borstelmann 2001, 76) petitions filed with the United Nations that impressively detailed the racial discrimination African Americans faced.[35] While abroad, these African Americans responded to questions about the status of African Americans in U.S. society, corrected "misinformation" disseminated by Soviet propagandists, and assured audiences that great strides were being made toward racial equality in the United States. These tours were conducted within the interest convergence framework. Within this framework, the executive and judicial branches filtered their support for African American civil rights through the lens of foreign policy objectives.

Here I Stand acknowledges and offers up for scorn this countertradition in African American public life. It is probably not a surprise to most readers that Robeson associates this tradition with Booker T. Washington, "one of the first of these Negro apostles of the 'American way of life' . . . who tried to serve both the needs of his people and the interests of their oppressors" (Robeson 1958, 70). This moment in the text implicitly draws a parallel between Washington's second European tour of 1910 and those of Sampson, Redding, and Rowan, who "have thought it advisable to travel abroad with tidings that all is well with their folks back home."[36] Presenting a view that challenged this optimistic assessment invited charges of working on behalf of the Soviet Union, whose vast propaganda machine, from the U.S. government's perspective, was responsible for raising doubts in other parts of the world about progress being made toward African American equality.

The United States government's response to Robeson's attempt to cross the border into Canada for a concert underscores the extent to which it perceived his leftist position as a threat. In late January of 1952, Paul Robeson set off from Seattle, Washington, en route to Vancouver, British Columbia, where he was set to appear at the Western District convention of the United Mine, Mill and Smelter Workers Union. Even though he was traveling without his passport, which the U.S. State Department had revoked in 1950, this should not have posed a problem; at that time American citizens did not require a passport to travel to and from Canada. Yet upon arriving at the border crossing in Blaine, Washington, Robeson was summoned into the Immigration and Naturalization Service offices and told that he would not be allowed to leave the United States because of a statute dating from World War I that empowered the government to prevent the entry or departure of its citizens during a national emergency (Duberman 1989, 399). Robeson informed the Canadian welcoming committee of the INS's ruling, returned to Seattle, and addressed the miners long-distance by means of a telephone connection patched into the convention hall's public address system. Before the convention concluded, the union proposed and subsequently set about organizing the first in a series of outdoor concerts at the Peace Arch Park, straddling the border between the United States and Canada.[37] That first concert brought Robeson back to the northwest in May and drew an estimated crowd of thirty thousand, with twenty-five thousand of those arriving from the Canadian side.

The travel restrictions placed on Robeson and other African American leftists who failed to endorse the anticommunist civil rights platform took place within the interest-convergence framework. These restrictions were part of the U.S. Cold War state's "monopolization of the legitimate means of movement," a mechanism that John Torpey argues "is crucial to an adequate comprehension of how modern states actually work" (2000, 5). Thus, the incredible energies spent to discredit Robeson and the larger African American left as "un-American" were essential to the process of legitimizing certain ideas and discrediting others. In this context, travel and passports helped establish the ideological boundaries that determined the legitimate methods by which African Americans could achieve civil rights in the early Cold War period. My reading of Robeson's discussion of his passport case in *Here I Stand* from the angle of this historical fettering underscores the fact that the dominant strategies for addressing the inequalities generated under American racial capitalism emerged as "the ravages and excesses of the McCarthy era drove a punishing offensive through the heart of an older cadre of Left-wing intellectuals" (Spillers 2003, 434). *Here I Stand* then must be read as a statement made after Robeson absorbed the full force of this offensive. His text offers an alternative account that calls into question the triumphalist narrative of the government's recognition of African American citizenship rights as the inevitable outgrowth of the democratic promise enshrined in U.S. institutions. As an alternative to this triumphalism, *Here I Stand* reminds us of the ideological limits established to press the African American freedom struggle into the service of U.S. foreign policy.

One of the dominant rhetorical gestures in *Here I Stand* is to locate Paul Robeson's physical body and by extension his politics in the African American community, specifically Harlem. Thus he begins his foreword with the seemingly simple declarations: "I am a Negro. The house I live in is in Harlem" (1958, 1). At first glance it might seem bizarre that probably one of the most recognizable African Americans in the world at the time would need to make such a declaration, but the statement concerning his race must be viewed in the context of the persistent anticommunist effort to paint Robeson as red before and over black. Indeed, Holder has suggested that *Here I Stand* be read as "autobiographical self-fashioning that sutures Robeson's self to the black community" (2012, 77) from which he was ostensibly still ostracized in 1958, the time of the text's publication. In this regard, Holder is mostly correct in his assessment that Robeson's vision of Harlem is one of "a utopian, romanticized space of racial solidarity" that "downplays intra-racial political differences" (77). Yet his own claim about Robeson's ostracism depends on a similar construction of a homogeneous, politically undifferentiated African American community.

What Holder understands as Robeson's ostracism from a community previously formed around a set of normative practices and ideas is in fact a moment of community constitution around the principles of racial liberalism. Mainstream civil rights leaders exhibited little patience for African American leftists like Robeson who insisted on the intersection of race with class and on the connections between domestic racism and Western imperialism. My reading thus positions *Here I Stand* as a document attesting to the presence of an African American left, the exclusion of which was the necessary condition for conducting the African American freedom struggle within the frame of a racially liberal anticommunism.[38] Racial liberalism became the dominant paradigm as leaders of mainstream civil rights organizations allied themselves with the Truman and subsequent presidential administrations to redress racial discrimination without directly addressing the socioeconomic concerns of working-class and poor African Americans. The Cold War climate rendered such concerns as at odds with the commitment to anticommunism.

A powerful weapon in neutralizing the impact of the left on the African American freedom struggle was to characterize Robeson and others of his ilk as dupes of the CPUSA and by extension the Soviet Union. He disputes this charge through his advocacy of independent action to achieve the equality that African Americans are entitled under the laws of the United States, a position he puts forward in the concluding chapter of *Here I Stand*, "The Power of Negro Action." Using the example of the Montgomery bus boycott, Robeson argues that "churches and other groups of similar independent character—fraternal orders, women's clubs, and so forth—will increasingly take the lead [in the struggle] because they are closer to the Negro rank-and-file, more responsive to their needs, and less subject to control by forces outside the Negro community" (1958, 96).[39] Robeson's singling out independence as the critical feature of these groups achieves two goals: it prioritizes the African American struggle over ideological differences and asserts that the problems of race in the United States are not simply reducible to questions of class. His position here was not in contradiction with his "deep conviction that for all mankind a socialist society represents an advance to a higher stage of life—that is a form of society which is economically, socially, culturally, and ethically superior to a system based upon production for private profit" (38). In fact, he combines the two positions in his analysis that African American trade unionists represent "potentially the most powerful and effective force in [the] community." He consequently urges these trade unionists to "provide the spirit, the determination, the organizational skill, the firm steel of unyielding militancy to the age-old strivings of our people for equality and freedom" and "to rally the strength of the whole trade union movement, white and black, to the battle for liberation of our people" (96–97). Indeed, according to the historian Martha Biondi, "in this era when unionized blue- and white-collar employment was becoming a stepping stone to a middle-class lifestyle, autoworkers and meatpackers, nurses and postal workers, displaced the 'talented tenth' as agents of Black community advancement" (2003, 26).[40] The critical importance that Robeson assigns to the African American trade union movement anchors the left solidly within the African American freedom struggle and directly counters the attempt to link its presence to foreign infiltration.

When individuals who had been affiliated with the left contributed to the movement in a leadership capacity, they proved to be a liability given the concerted effort of powerful segregationist anticommunists to discredit the entire movement as a communist conspiracy. Therefore, by the time the mass mobilizations typically associated with the southern civil rights movement got under way, the African American left had been, at least ideologically, marginalized. Such was the case with Jack O'Dell, who joined the staff of Martin Luther King's Southern Christian Leadership Conference (SCLC) as both a fundraiser in the North and organizer in charge of voter registration operations in the South in 1961. Prior to going to work for SCLC, O'Dell had been a member of the CPUSA and also of the National Maritime Union (NMU), from which he had been expelled in a purge of suspected communists. As a member of the NMU, he helped defend Paul Robeson in the return to Peekskill concert, which was held on Labor Day of

1949, a week after an anticommunist mob had disrupted a previously scheduled concert.

In early 1962, when FBI director J. Edgar Hoover became aware through a wiretapped phone call that King was considering appointing O'Dell the executive director of SCLC, he discreetly passed this information to James Eastland and John McClellan, the southern leaders of the Senate Internal Security Subcommittee. SISS was familiar with O'Dell, having "had a relationship with [him] that dated back to its 1956 hearings in New Orleans" on subversive activities in the region (Woods 2003, 161). In September, attorney general Robert Kennedy got word to King encouraging him to disassociate himself from O'Dell, but "it is a testament to how much King valued O'Dell that he held out for almost a full year before accepting the resignation . . . tendered" after the "FBI decided to leak information about O'Dell to the Southern press" (Singh 2010, 29). The southern press had dutifully run front-page stories charging communist infiltration of a top administrative post in the SCLC (Woods 2003, 163). The Hoover-orchestrated King-O'Dell split illustrates the great lengths taken to purge the left from the main currents of the African American freedom struggle. *Here I Stand* offers a firsthand account of the process by which the African American left was made "unthinkable," while providing the essential plot elements that drove this political drama toward its tragic end. This tragedy is crystallized in an image that Robeson refers to near the end of *Here I Stand*.

RACIAL CONTAINMENT AND THE TRAGEDY OF INTEREST-CONVERGENCE

In July of 1949, just a couple of months after Robeson's alleged statement in Paris and mere days after the conclusion of John Woods's HUAC hearings to denounce Robeson, Mr. Roscoe Johnson, an African American postal worker, and his wife, Ethel, purchased and moved into a two-flat building in the Park Manor neighborhood on Chicago's South Side. For two nights, a mob of between five hundred and two thousand whites, assembled to protest the Johnsons' moving into the neighborhood. A *Chicago Daily Tribune* article covering the disturbance describes the protesters as "catcalling and stopping motorists" while displaying signs that denounced "the Negro newcomers" to passing drivers. Intent on terrorizing the Johnsons, members of the mob threw stones, breaking the apartment's windows, "threw missiles, including a railroad flare, into . . . the building," and finally ignited a gasoline bomb on the lawn ("6 Teen-Agers" 1949, 3). In the Cold War context, such events were no longer simply images of local color prejudice, but powerful ammunition in a propaganda battle being fought on a globe-expanding scale.

Toward the end of *Here I Stand*, Paul Robeson focuses his narrative attention on an image that recalls the Johnsons' ordeal in the Park Manor riots. Describing what he refers to as an often reproduced image in newspapers and magazines of the day, Robeson paints the picture of "a Negro family—the husband, wife, their children—huddled together in their newly purchased or rented home, while outside hundreds of Negro-haters have gathered to throw stones, to howl filthy abuse, to threaten murder and arson" (1958, 93). Yet for all the power of this image to capture the determined resistance of whites acting as shock troops in the maintenance of residential segregation, Robeson's interest lies less in what the photograph captures than in the conspicuous absence it documents. He continues, "something is missing from this picture that ought to be there, and its absence gives rise to a nagging question that cannot be stilled: *Where are the other Negroes?*" (93). In his introduction to the 1988 edition of *Here I Stand*, historian Sterling Stuckey returns to this image of the besieged and isolated black family to draw a parallel between it and Robeson's own experience of isolation as a target of anticommunist repression in the 1950s. In Stuckey's opinion, "where were the Negroes when Robeson was under siege?" is "a central question in the history of the Afro-American in the last half of the century" (1958, xx). A possible answer to this "central question" might lie in the interest-convergence dilemma that the legal scholar Derrick Bell posited as shaping the Supreme Court decision in *Brown v. Board of Education*. At least one scholar credits Bell's insight with providing the foundation for the groundbreaking historical work that considers the civil rights movement within the context of the Cold War.[41]

When Stuckey locates Robeson in a position that is structurally parallel to the besieged and isolated black family evoked in *Here I Stand*, he seems to imagine an African American community undivided by ideological cleavages. By posing his question, Stuckey brings readers' attention to the lack of racial solidarity that made Robeson's isolation possible, and he reinforces the association of those leading the anticommunist cause with the most virulent strain of antiblack racism. The question also invites a consideration of just how racial liberalism became the dominant paradigm for addressing racial discrimination in the 1950s. According to legal scholar Lani Guinier, this strategy, which insists on "the damaging effects of segregation on black personality" (2004, 95), was developed to secure both legal victories in the courts and the sympathy of middle-class whites. The focus on the damaged black personality ran counter to the black left position, which emphasized the role of segregation in reproducing the American class structure and the dependence of that structure on maintaining the division between African American and white workers. Kenneth Janken argues that "the isolation of African-American radicals like Du Bois and Robeson, who denounced American racism as fundamental to American capitalism and demanded far-reaching changes in the country's polity and economy," was part of a strategy to contain "potential fallout from such a politically expedient move" as "the Supreme Court's *Brown* school desegregation decision of 1954" (1998, 1090). The potential for fallout was particularly high given that just ten days after the court's decision, "Mississippi senator James Eastland stood before the Senate and accused the Court of pandering to Communism and its allies when it handed down the 'Black Monday' *Brown* decision" (Woods 2003, 54). Given the congressional intransigence and massive white resistance mobilized to deter any challenge to the racist social order, establishment civil rights organizations felt compelled to adopt strategies and goals that would not foreclose liberal support. In the context of developing this program, organizations took positions that were portrayed as representing African American interests but which in the end primarily served the ideological and material interests of a privileged few.

This problem of casting the narrow ideological and material interests of the few as those of the many was a central problem of the United States Cold War strategy both at home and abroad. If at home this strategy involved convincing the nation that its interests were the same as those of the elite, abroad the strategy meant that the newly independent African and Asian countries had to accept American interests as their own. As a consequence, the production and management of images became critical to achieving foreign policy objectives and realizing domestic reform. As I mentioned earlier, George Kennan, had already linked the effectiveness of the policy of "containment" to the U.S. successfully addressing "the problems of its internal life" (1947, 581). From this moment, the United States began its effort of projecting to the world the image of improving race relations within the country.

The role of domestic reform in realizing the United States' foreign policy objectives highlights the confluence of circumstances that made advances toward racial equality possible during the Cold War period. One of the first scholars to theorize the connection between racial equality advances for African Americans and the self-interest of elite whites was Derrick Bell. In his seminal 1980 article "*Brown v. Board of Education* and the Interest-Convergence Dilemma," Bell argued that "the interest of blacks in achieving racial equality will be accommodated only when it converges with the interests of whites." Therefore, he continues, achieving "racial justice—or its appearance" was only possible at those moments when it was "counted among the interests deemed important by the courts and by society's policymakers" (1980, 523). For Bell, the Supreme Court's landmark decision in *Brown v. Board of Education* was a case in point of such interest-convergence. Lawyers for both the NAACP and the federal government had argued that a decision stripping segregation of its constitutional authority would "provide immediate credibility to America's struggle with Communist countries to win the hearts and minds of emerging third world peoples" (524). Bell's theory suggests how the image of progress in American race relations became important to the United States' effort to contain communist expansion. Given this importance, establishment civil rights organizations developed initiatives consistent with the government's anticommunist policies. In addition, the framing of African Americans' civil rights as part of the larger anticommunist struggle made them slightly more palatable to those powerful elements of American society for whom racism remained a cherished way of life.

Yet as the massive resistance to the desegregation of public schools and the mobs assembled to violently dislodge African Americans from their homes suggests, the government's efforts to link racial equality and anticommunism were not entirely successful. These images of white resistance to African American equality document a moment of interest divergence. As Bell suggests, when elite white interests converged with those of African Americans to produce the Supreme Court's decision condemning segregation in *Brown*, poor whites reacted not only out of "feared loss of control" over their local institutions, they also felt that white elites had betrayed their commitment to maintaining "lower class whites in a societal status superior to blacks" (525–26). Likewise, the violent mobs evoked in Robeson's image document a moment of interest divergence. These mobs might be understood as protesting against the forfeiting of what David Roediger refers to as the "wages of whiteness." Building on a formulation put forth by Du Bois in *Black Reconstruction*, Roediger describes this wage as the "status and privileges conferred" to white workers as "not slaves" and as "not Blacks" "to make up for alienating and exploitative class relationships" (1999, 13).

The question remains, however, "Where were the other Negroes?" in these images of white mobs surrounding isolated blacks. Undoubtedly, African Americans agreed with the principle that as citizens of the United States they had the right to attend any public school, live wherever they could afford, and protest the racial injustice that kept American ideals from becoming reality. Their absence, nevertheless, suggests that they still needed to be convinced that it served their interests to defend somebody else's property. Indeed, they were eventually convinced, and they produced the images of integrated schools and neighborhoods that documented the progress possible under America's democratic system. These images, however, did little in the way of producing the basic "set of public goods" such as "comprehensive health care, sufficient housing provisions," "quality elementary and secondary education, [and] public transportation" (Iton 2000, 2) that might improve the life prospects for poor and working-class African Americans. And what of Robeson? His isolation figures his role in a tragic dilemma, a role for which his experience playing the lead in Shakespeare's *Othello* might have prepared him. This dilemma presented him with the task of convincing poor and working-class whites that the provision of basic public goods was something other than welfare exclusively for African Americans. Given the historical appeal of racism to the white working class, the civil rights establishment made the convenient, if ultimately unwise decision to align their interests with those of elite whites, don the cloak of anticommunism, and abandon Robeson to suffer alone the tragic consequences of his radical vision. Although the accumulation of years of repression prevented Robeson from actively participating in later struggles, the black radical vision of which he was an emblem endured and re-emerged in a younger generation of activists who defied the civil rights establishment in their refusal to align their protest with the anticommunist goals of U.S. foreign policy. This rupture played out on the world stage in the events surrounding the Congo Crisis, with which the present study concludes.

CHAPTER 5

Crisis and Rupture

African American Literary Culture and the Response to Patrice Lumumba's Assassination

Of Vagabonds and Fellow Travelers departs from standard accounts of the Cold War by placing both culture and race at the center of its investigation. It seeks to understand the consequences for African diaspora culture and labor of the Soviet Union's comparative strength on the cultural front and the United States' relative weakness with regard to issues of racial discrimination.

Since the late nineteenth century, the formation of the American empire necessitated incorporating and disciplining the labor of African diaspora people. For example, with the occupation of Cuba in 1898 the United States assumed control of sugar production in the eastern and blacker part of the country. To develop this industry, the United States depended on attracting laborers from neighboring Haiti, Jamaica, and other Caribbean nations. In the early twentieth century, the United States extended its empire with the building and maintaining of the Panama Canal, which facilitated trade between the U.S. east and west coasts and with Asia. The construction of the canal was accomplished on the backs of Caribbean workers, a large portion of them from Barbados, who provided an indispensable source of inexpensive labor. With the opening of the Panama Canal the process of transforming of the Caribbean Sea into an American lake accelerated, with the U.S. military occupation of Haiti in 1915 being a critical part of that process.

When the occupation of Haiti ended nineteen years later, the United States sought to maintain its dominance through means other than direct military intervention. The new policy orientation emphasized Good Neighbor relations in the hemisphere and promoted cultural exchanges as a soft-power weapon aimed at hearts and minds. President Roosevelt promoted this policy as a more effective (and enduring) method of creating a stable environment for U.S. business without the political and economic costs of military occupation.

Following the transformation of the Caribbean into an American lake and the securing of the hemisphere during World War II, U.S. imperial ambitions turned toward the globe. As the Cold War advanced and the United States took over leadership of the world order, it presented itself as departing from the model set by its predecessors, the European colonial powers. At the same time, it projected an image of itself as being a force for good on the world stage and thus the polar opposite of its only competitor to superpower status, the Soviet Union. In their debut novels, the Caribbean writers George Lamming and Jacques Stephen Alexis, however, reminded a global audience of the consequences of U.S. rule for the world's darker peoples in their searing portrayals of the half-century of U.S. domination in the region. Their incisive critiques placed these authors in a vagabond relation to the ideological enclosure emanating from Washington, but their message was particularly salient to audiences in the newly independent nations of Asia and Africa.

In its pursuit of global power status, the United States drew on methods it first deployed in its dominion over the Western hemisphere through the Good Neighbor policy. Motivating this policy was the realization, drawn from lessons of the Haitian occupation, that the United States could not exercise its dominance exclusively through military means. Another motivating factor in the cultural Cold War, the struggle for hearts and minds between the United States and the Soviet Union, was that on the cultural front the two opponents were more evenly matched. The cultural front was unlike other aspects of the conflict, such as the military and economic spheres, where the United States enjoyed a distinct advantage over the Soviet Union.

Alongside the Marshall Plan, which provided financial assistance for the European reconstruction effort after World War II in part to hamper the communist influence in war-torn Europe, the government also created the Office of Policy Coordination (OPC) under the organizational structure of the CIA and policy guidance of the secretary of state. The OPC oversaw covert political warfare operations or propaganda efforts that directly challenged the Soviet Union's extensive and well-developed propaganda network. When Eisenhower became president in 1953, he adapted methods from the earlier Good Neighbor policy to fit his program of special operations channeled through the Operations Coordinating Board (OCB) and to disperse the funds from his Emergency Fund for International Affairs. This adaptation was accomplished primarily through an overlap of personnel, chief among them Nelson Rockefeller, who served as assistant secretary of state. Mercer Cook of AMSAC was another such figure associated with both the GNP and the cultural Cold War effort. These efforts concentrated on cultural exchanges and were the context for the creation of the Congress of Cultural Freedom, the government-sponsored jazz band tours, the world tour of *Porgy and Bess*, and other efforts.

The major skirmishes of this cultural battle were fought on the European continent. In its early years, a major objective of the cultural Cold War was winning the support of Western intellectuals to either the communist or anticommunist cause. Owing to its status as the cultural capital of the West, Paris was a major battleground of the cultural Cold War struggle. Of particular concern to the United States was the wide influence of communists enjoyed in French intellectual circles, largely a consequence of the role communists played in the resistance to fascism during World War II.

In addition to the concern over Western intellectuals, there was the equally important, if often overlooked, question of the destiny of the European colonies in Africa and Asia, which were crucial to the new world order over which the United States presumed to lead after World War II. It was manifestly clear from early on that the colonized were not going to accept a return to business as usual. As many of the intellectual leaders of the anticolonial struggles had been formed and resided in European capitals, sites like Paris became centers of the cultural struggle against colonialism. As the Cold War developed it became increasingly clear that "the stakes" of this conflict were, as Steven Belletto argues, "the hearts and minds of third world countries" (2012, 119), and by extension control over the resources in the formerly colonized areas of Africa and Asia and the nominally independent countries of Latin America.

In the contest for influence over these regions of the globe, the Soviet Union seized on the advantage provided by the segregation and legal discrimination that African Americans suffered in the United States. Race proved to be America's Achilles heel. While the civil rights movement could leverage this international context to achieve its goals, its goals were tempered by that same context. The doctrine of racial liberalism provided the ideological enclosure that produced narrowly defined and acceptable goals. Within this ideological enclosure, racism in American society was primarily a problem of discrimination against individuals resulting from racial prejudice. Such a framework effectively disconnected racism and the discrimination African Americans faced from the U.S. economy. This non-economic understanding of racism was bolstered by the examples of successful African Americans who had achieved prominence in the economic and political structures of the United States. Held up to the world, particularly to those in Africa and Asia, these individuals were meant to be a testament to the opportunities available in the U.S. liberal democratic and capitalist system.

Not all African Americans, however, abided by the tenets of racial liberalism. Indeed, as I have demonstrated here, some of the most recognizable and respected members of the race refused to toe the official line on racial progress and insisted on locating discrimination in the very foundations of the U.S. economy. For their pains, these cultural workers faced the contempt of their peers; they were regarded as mere vagabonds for their refusal to accept the discipline of the new situation and conveniently branded as communist fellow travelers. As such they were subject to government repression and surveillance and denied passports and the opportunity to make a living. Despite their strained circumstances, individuals like Paul Robeson and W.E.B. Du Bois supported a range of black leftist activities and organizations, including independent trade unions and arts organizations that launched the careers of such cultural luminaries as Alice Childress, Harry Belafonte, Sidney Poitier, and Lorraine Hansberry, among many others. By the mid-1950s, these organizations of the black left had been crippled by an assault orchestrated by racist and anticommunist forces wielding the power of the state.

While this assault submerged the black left that developed in the early Cold War years, the primary focus of this study, a new articulation of the black left resurfaced in the events surrounding the Congo Crisis. The Congo Crisis and the resulting assassination of Patrice Lumumba became one of two Pan-African "pressure points" (the other being the independence of Ghana and Kwame Nkrumah's leadership of the Pan-African movement) that the historian Christopher Tinson identifies as having "catapulted . . . into existence" the Liberation Committee for Africa (LCA) and its organ, *Liberator* magazine (2017, 14). The LCA and *Liberator* were part of a larger response to the crisis in African American literary culture, a response that continued the previous generation's critique of both U.S. imperialism abroad and racial liberalism at home. Unsurprisingly, their stance would occasion a rupture with the mainstream civil rights movement and expose both the organization and its magazine to the treatment reserved for those deemed vagabonds to the reigning order, and it would once again raise the charge of their being fellow travelers of world communism.

THE CONGO CRISIS AND THE CULTURAL COLD WAR

The Brussels Round Table in January of 1960 initiated the hasty independence process of the Belgian Congo. In these meetings with political representatives from the Congo, the Belgians, to the surprise of most observers, agreed to grant the Congo its independence and scheduled transfer-of-power ceremonies for that summer, a mere six months away. In July of that year, there was a mutiny of Congolese soldiers in the armed forces, which was followed in September by the Belgium-supported secession of the mineral-rich Katanga region from the Congo. The secession precipitated a political crisis that forced the Congolese prime minister Patrice Lumumba to seek aid from the United Nations in removing Belgian troops and reversing the secession. When the United Nations balked at being drawn into the conflict, Lumumba sought the aid of the Soviet Union. Within a month, he was placed under house arrest and then moved around the country as a prisoner. In January the Belgian, American, and Congolese forces of Moïse Tshombe, leader of the secessionist Katanga province, decided to assassinate Lumumba. News of his death, however, only reached the outside world in February and sparked protests across the globe.

Of Vagabonds and Fellow Travelers concludes with this chapter looking at events and texts surrounding the Congo Crisis because they illuminate the complex ways U.S. international and domestic policy bore down on African diaspora intellectuals and artists. In this moment, while some intellectuals and artists were made vagabonds and fellow travelers by Cold War state repression, their liberal and anticommunist counterparts were promoted as examples of what was possible for African Americans under American democracy. As these figures aligned their interests with those of the United States, they increasingly came into conflict with leaders in the formerly colonized countries of Africa and Asia. The undeniable discrimination African Americans faced in the United States made leaders in the decolonizing world deeply suspicious of the motives of officially sanctioned African Americans. These leaders simply were not convinced that the United States was unlike its white European colonial predecessors.

This chapter traces this conflict through a series of events, beginning with the All-African People's Congress that Kwame Nkrumah of Ghana organized in 1958. An important contingent of African Americans, representing different organizations, attended the congress, as did the Congo's future prime minister, Patrice Lumumba. From there it considers the meteoric rise and abrupt end to Lumumba's political career. Lumumba's rule over an independent Congo, which lasted less than three months, compresses the general course of events that brought the freedom dreams of colonized people into conflict with the priorities and material interests of the Cold War superpowers. In the United States, this collision precipitated an ideological rupture revealed in a range of texts and events, including Ralph Bunche's role as the special representative of the secretary-general of the United Nations at the transfer of power ceremony and director of that organization's peacekeeping mission in the Congo; a protest organized by a coalition of black activists, which included such prominent literary figures as Maya Angelou and Amiri Baraka, in the gallery of the United Nations the day following news of Lumumba's assassination; a James Baldwin essay published in the *New York Times Sunday Magazine* following Lumumba's assassination; a letter to the editor of the *New York Times* by Lorraine Hansberry denouncing Bunche.

All these texts and events highlight the stakes of the cultural Cold War struggle for hearts and minds. Considered together, they reveal the crucial part played in this struggle by African Americans, who both criticized U.S. imperialist might and were called upon to legitimize the exercise of that might. Out of these contradictory roles emerged an ideological consensus whose long shadow continues to influence ideas about the proper conduct of African American cultural politics. This consensus formed around the ideological enclosure of racial liberalism, which subsequent generations of African diaspora intellectuals and activists have had to contend with as they pursued racial justice both "here and yonder," to recall the title of Langston Hughes's *Chicago Defender* column.

RUMBLINGS IN THE JUNGLE: THE CONGO ACHIEVES INDEPENDENCE AND LUMUMBA FALLS TO ASSASSINS

The late 1950s inaugurated a sea change in the colonial relations that had marked the continent of Africa for more than a half-century. On the northern part of the continent, Algerians were fighting for their independence in a long, protracted guerrilla war against French settler colonialism. Egypt under Nasser was also a center of pan-Arabism that was making links across the continental divide to anticolonial struggles in sub-Saharan Africa. In 1957, under the leadership of the nationalist leader Kwame Nkrumah, Ghana became the first sub-Saharan nation to achieve its independence. The following year leaders from francophone Africa pushed Charles de Gaulle to write greater autonomy for African territories into the constitution of the Fifth Republic, which set the stage for the gradual end of their colonial relationship to France. Ahmed Sekou Touré of Guinea objected to this gradual process and organized a vote for immediate independence. Touré and Nkrumah combined their efforts and worked to support independence struggles throughout the continent. These efforts came together in the All-African People's Conference held in Ghana in 1958. Nationalist leaders from throughout the continent attended the conference, including the militant anticolonial theorist Frantz Fanon as the representative of the Provisional Government of Algeria. It is at this conference that Patrice Lumumba made the contacts and gained the support of other nationalists on the continent that would propel his meteoric rise to power.

With Lumumba as its prime minister, the Congo formally achieved its independence on June 30, 1960, midway through the year declared by the United Nations as "The Year of Africa." That historic year saw the map of European colonial domination redrawn as the United Nations accepted a dozen or so countries as new members, while seventeen countries in all gained independence. Of these nations, the transition to independence in the Congo proved most tumultuous. The breakneck speed and the array of forces that converged in that country caused conditions to quickly deteriorate and precipitated the Congo Crisis. In general, the Congo Crisis refers to the roughly eight-month period from Belgium's granting of independence in June of 1960 to the almost immediate dissolution of prime minister Patrice Lumumba's newly formed government, and his eventual, or perhaps inevitable, assassination in February of 1961.

Lumumba stepped onto the world historical stage not long after entering formal politics in the Congo. After spending a year in jail for embezzlement, he became active in the Mouvement National Congolais party. In 1958, under Lumumba's leadership, the party became the leading nationwide party in a political landscape dominated by parties with ethnic and regional ties. In December of that same year, he led the Congolese delegation to the first All-African Peoples Conference (AAPC), organized by the radical pan-Africanists George Padmore and Kwame Nkrumah in Accra, Ghana.

Padmore and Nkrumah had planned the AAPC and a separate conference bringing together the heads of independent African nations to lay down "the framework for African leadership within the nonaligned movement of new Asian and African states that sought to pose an alternative, a 'Third Force,' to the bipolar Cold War vision of global order" (Gaines 2006, 77). The conference brought together political and labor leaders from African nations who had yet to achieve their independence from European colonial powers. In all, more than two hundred official delegates from more than twenty-eight African nations attended the conference. These delegates were joined by Africans from the diaspora, including African Americans and Africans residing in Europe and representatives of cultural organizations, who were accorded "fraternal delegate" status, which allowed them to observe the proceedings but barred them from closed sessions where the conference resolutions were drafted (Gaines 2006, 95).

The conference was pivotal in Lumumba's political formation and recognition as one of the continent's rising nationalists leaders. At the conference, Lumumba earned the sympathy and support of Pan-Africanist heads of state such as Nkrumah of Ghana and Ahmed Sekou Touré of Guinea. According to his adviser, Thomas Kanza, Lumumba impressed participants with his "oratory, energy and faith in the pan-African ideal," and they began to regard him as the Congolese leader who grasped the significance of Nkrumah's repeated contention that because of its central position on the continent, the Congo's "struggle for freedom was not the struggle of just one country but of the whole continent" (1979, 50). Lumumba left the congress "inspired . . . with Pan-African visions" (Meriwether 2002, 212) and the nationalist support he would need to carry the Congo into the age of independence.

While the conference provided Lumumba with the opportunity to strengthen his contacts with African nationalists, it probably also brought him to the attention of the U.S. intelligence community. Among the sizable U.S. delegation, there were several delegates—Mercer Cook, Horace Mann Bond, and George McCray among them—covering the conference for organizations such as the Congress for Cultural Freedom, the American Society of African Culture, and the International Confederation of Free Trade Unions, all cultural front organizations receiving covert funding from the CIA.[1] The U.S. intelligence community was keen to send Americans to conferences such as the All-African Peoples Conference to counter criticism of American racism issuing from the Soviet Union and nations whose history of colonialism made them sensitive to racism. Through their members' participation and their publications, these cultural front organizations established an ideological enclosure in which "decolonization and global affairs" could be pursued from "a pro-American, noncommunist perspective that above all valued political stability in the image of Western political institutions and ideals" (Gaines 2006, 94). The radical Pan-Africanism of Padmore and Nkrumah that infused the conference and Nkrumah's embrace of Sekou Touré, who had recently rejected a referendum on a continued relationship with France in favor of full and immediate independence, was surely an unsettling model of decolonization for observers in Washington.

These observers were probably concerned that Lumumba carried such models with him to the Brussels Round Table convened in January of 1960, a little more than a year after the All-African Peoples Conference. The round table brought together Congolese political leaders and Belgian governmental officials to negotiate the terms of Congolese independence. Over the course of the month, representatives from the two countries discussed the issues surrounding the Congo's future independence. According to Kanza, however, the Belgians were granting the country independence in name only, since they took the issues "of really vital importance to any state's survival—the economic, financial, military and diplomatic ones" (Kanza 1979, 81)—off the table for discussion. Belgium's intent to remain in control of the Congo following independence perhaps explains the short timetable of formally handing over power in independence ceremonies by June 30, 1960, just a little over six months after the Round Table opened.

Belgium's decision to turn control of the colony over to the Congolese so rapidly surprised observers. Many Western governments were anxious about the colony's capacity for self-government given the paucity of Congolese university graduates and upper administrators in the colonial government. There was widespread fear that the lack of an indigenous bourgeoisie steeped in the capitalist values of Western societies left the Congo vulnerable to being overrun by "radical Pan-Africanism and Communist infiltration" (Plummer 2013, 88). To avoid such an outcome, other European colonial powers had generally negotiated to transfer power in some version of the tutelage/trusteeship model. In this model, the European powers allowed increased autonomy and the development of governmental structures of self-rule, preparing the way to eventual independence. Ghana, for example, had undergone such a process for about three years before becoming in 1957 the first sub-Saharan nation to gain its independence from a European colony. In 1960, the former French colonies in Africa gained their independence after a two-year period following the new constitution of 1958.

For Western observers, the June 30th independence ceremonies presaged the difficult, uncertain road that lay ahead. During the ceremonies, King Badouin of Belgium delivered a speech extolling the Belgians as dedicated servants who labored to bring light to the dark corners of Africa, and he challenged the Congolese to demonstrate their political maturity. He was followed by the president of the Congo, Joseph Kasa-Vubu, who expressed gratitude to the Belgians and reassured them that the Congolese would assume the solemn work of continuing the progress of civilization. Disrupting the apologetic tone of the proceedings, Prime Minister Lumumba, who had been excluded from the program, seized the microphone and inserted himself and the history of Congolese suffering into the ceremony. One observer recalled his speech as a "bitter" "lashing out" against Belgian brutality, while the Belgian press characterized it as "international suicide" (Plummer 2013, 89). In boldly declaring to the departing King Baudoin, "We are no longer your monkeys!" Lumumba assuredly did not endear himself to the sitting U.S. president Dwight Eisenhower, who enjoyed a close relationship with the king (quoted in Borstelmann 2001, 129). While anticolonialists celebrated Lumumba's "impromptu and impassioned speech," it only confirmed Western suspicions about his demagogic tendencies. In the context of the cultural Cold War, the same improvisatory, oratorical skills that bound Lumumba to the Congolese masses, and upon which his domestic political career depended, also served to alienate him from the Western powers who would determine whether Congolese independence was preserved or not.

The political situation in the Congo descended into chaos soon after the independence ceremonies. Just days after power was handed over to the Congo's new leaders, twenty thousand Congolese soldiers in the Force Publique, the army, mutinied against their all-white Belgian officers, who had "made it clear that independence would have no effect on their control of the army" (Borstelmann 2001, 131). The mutiny provoked an exodus of Belgian bureaucrats. Several days later, on July 11th, the mineral-rich Katanga province seceded when the pro-Western Moïse Tshombe declared its independence from Lumumba's Congo. Three days later the United Nations Security Council passed a resolution responding to a Congolese request for a U.N. intervention "to preserve order, secure the withdrawal of Belgian troops, and provide emergency technical and food aid" (Young 2010, 136). Lumumba, however, had invited the United Nations with the perhaps unrealistic expectations that U.N. troops would defend the Congo against Belgium and Western neocolonial aggression and restore national unity by putting an end to the Katanga secession.

Undoubtedly, it was the Congo and Lumumba's entrance into the Cold War matrix that made the end of the crisis a foregone conclusion. After his negotiations with Hammarskjöld, secretary-general of the United Nations, Lumumba grew disillusioned with the United Nations' inability or unwillingness to intervene in the Katanga secession. Lumumba took the United Nations' inaction as confirmation that the organization was complicit with Western interests. His sense of having been betrayed by the United Nations led Lumumba to reach out for support first to his Pan-Africanist comrades, namely Kwame Nkrumah. When that aid proved insufficient, Lumumba made his fatal decision to seek the assistance of the Soviet Union.

By even considering the option of Soviet support, Lumumba appears to have sealed his fate. The U.S. government was quick to brand Lumumba a communist and made his elimination a matter of national security. While President Eisenhower's White House and National Security Council developed plans to assassinate Lumumba, Belgian security forces and Moïse Tshombe, Katanga's secessionist leader, presented themselves as willing collaborators; Tshombe's agents cut Lumumba down in January of 1961. When news of his death finally reached the outside world, many throughout the world, but particularly those in the African diaspora, erupted in protest. For these protesters, Lumumba's assassination was the latest act in a long history of Western violence directed against radical Pan-African nationalists on the continent and elsewhere. For many activists in the diaspora, Lumumba embodied the radical African position that refused to be defined by the limits of the Cold War antagonism between the United States and the Soviet Union.

BUNCHE: WHOSE MAN IN THE CONGO?

One of the central players in the Congo Crisis was an African American diplomat, Ralph Bunche. With a degree in sociology from the University of Chicago, Bunche first came to prominence in African American intellectual circles in the early 1930s as one of the younger generation of thinkers who challenged W.E.B. Du Bois and his program of black solidarity and cooperative economics at the second Amenia conference. Two years later in 1935 at the Joint Committee on National Recovery, according to Nikhil Singh, Bunche would offer a "penetrating, Marxist influenced critique of the New Deal's liberal reform project" (2004, 81). From 1928 to 1941 Bunche was a professor in the Political Science Department at Howard University in Washington, D.C. With his Howard colleagues E. Franklin Frazier and Abram Harris Jr., Bunche formed part of a new direction in African American scholarship. This direction, according to Jonathan Holloway, represented a concerted attempt "to reorient America's obsession with the Negro problem away from an answer based upon racial solutions toward one grounded in class dynamics" (2002, 2). This orientation would cause Bunche and some of his Howard colleagues to clash with other black leaders during the Buy Black campaigns of the late 1930s over the salience of race over class.

During World War II, Bunche stopped teaching at Howard after he was recruited to work for the Organization of Secret Services (OSS), the precursor to the CIA. At the OSS, he helped with the military war effort in Africa. Following the war, Bunche, who had by then left behind his radical past and intellectual positions, became a model of the progress possible for African Americans in the United States' democratic, if flawed, system. He was appointed the U.S. ambassador to the United Nations under the Truman administration.

At the United Nations, Bunche contributed his expertise to matters concerning the future status of those parts of the world under European colonial rule. In this capacity, he helped draft the sections of the U.N. charter dealing with colonial issues, specifically the chapters on trusteeship. Neta C. Crawford has argued that for Bunche trusteeship represented a mechanism through which the United Nations could "fulfill [its] original mission of 'sacred trust,' paving the way for more gradual and peaceful decolonization" (2010, 102). The situation in the Congo departed in nearly every way from this model, and it produced exactly the kind of negative results that Bunche hoped to avoid in proposing trusteeship to facilitate the transition from colonial rule.

Bunche joined the world dignitaries gathered for the Congolese independence ceremonies on June 30, 1960, as the representative of the United Nations. What he witnessed surely caused him some trepidation about the country's future prospects. Lumumba's performance at the independence ceremony clearly left an impression on Bunche, who "characterized Lumumba's oratory as electric and spellbinding, intoxicating even to Lumumba himself."

Whereas the performance contributed to the legend of Lumumba, Bunche probably disapproved of his perceived impetuousness, which likely ignited his "visceral distaste for those he regarded as demagogues" (Young 2010, 131). In subsequent months, this initial negative reaction to Lumumba would degenerate into mutual antipathy and mistrust, a most unfortunate conclusion.

Soon after the Congolese independence ceremonies, the secretary-general of the United Nations, Dag Hammarskjöld, appointed Bunche to lead the U.N. mission in the Congo. Bunche no doubt shared the anxieties of Western observers about the road ahead as a consequence of the rapid pace of decolonization in the Congo, and so his worst fears were realized when the situation in the country spiraled out of control. As the United Nations' special representative in the Congo, Bunche assumed the responsibility of trying to restore order. He arrived in the Congo with "impeccable credentials" and "the complete confidence" of Hammarskjöld, "who gave him wide latitude to act on the spot" (Young 2010, 130) as he oversaw what was then the largest operation in the organization's history. The Congo operation, however, would ultimately prove to be a glaring blemish on Bunche's otherwise long and distinguished career in diplomatic service.

In large measure, Bunche failed to successfully conclude the U.N. mission in the Congo for both personal and professional reasons. Given his own temperament and ideas about leadership, Bunche's relationship with Lumumba degenerated rapidly "from initial cordiality into mutual contempt and animosity" (Young 2010, 128). Their strained relationship is not entirely surprising given their very different understandings of the United Nations' role. As a representative of the United Nations, Bunche understood its role as primarily peacekeeping and helping nations in Asia and Africa "to advance the process of decolonization and to support their developmental aspirations" (Young 2010, 137). Lumumba, however, had invited the United Nations into the Congo to preserve national unity and to aid him in suppressing the Katanga secession.

Despite these differences and his wariness about Bunche's undeniable links to the levers of power in Washington, Lumumba, a committed Pan-Africanist, attempted, at least initially, to move beyond his suspicions. For their part, the Congolese people, whose feelings of a racial bond transcended nationality, welcomed Bunche as an African American. According to Lumumba's adviser to the United Nations, Thomas Kanza, Bunche was "received . . . with the greatest sympathy and the most profound respect . . . and in his dealings with the new government of the Congo, the fraternity of race played a part that must not be underestimated" (1979, 142). The bonds of race, however, would prove brittle when put to the pressure tests of Cold War realpolitik.[2]

Bunche's refusal to intervene in the secessionist province of Katanga exacerbated this pressure. Lumumba, among others, interpreted his decision as the manifestation of his divided loyalties. For those holding to this line of reasoning, Bunche's ostensible presence in the Congo as a representative of the United Nations did not contravene his being ultimately accountable, as an American, for furthering the economic and national security interests of the United States, even at the expense of racial fraternity. It is not to discount either his qualifications or accomplishments to acknowledge that Bunche's position at the United Nations was tied to the organization's dependence on the United States. This dependence and Bunche's role in the Congo Crisis opened up the larger and deeply unsettling question pursued in this book of how African American elites have tethered their professional advancement and self-interests to the economic and national security interests of the United States. As recent work on the intersection of the Cold War and civil rights makes abundantly clear, the United States utilized the example of Bunche and others in its foreign policy as evidence of the progress made and the advancement possible for people of color under America's capitalist democracy. As the example of AMSAC discussed in chapter 2 reveals, well-placed African Americans proved crucial to U.S. propaganda efforts to win hearts and minds, particularly in Africa and Asia, and counteract foreign criticism, not all of which emanated from the Soviet Union.

While Bunche might have considered his loyalties as lying entirely with the United Nations during his sojourn in the Congo, it was impossible for him to escape the long shadow cast by the United States. Bunche was "utterly impatient" with the government's fixation on "communist penetration" and Lumumba's supposed communist tendencies, Crawford Young argues, and this often led to conflicts with the U.S. embassy in the Congo (131). Nevertheless, the United Nations' initial lack of a logistical infrastructure meant that Bunche had to make use of the embassy's communication and other facilities. For their part, Congolese officials surmised that Bunche was under the constant watch of American agents, and so they were guarded in their interactions with him. This distance between Bunche and the Congolese, especially Lumumba, only widened as the crisis, which began as a conflict between a European imperial power and its former African colony, became engulfed in the Cold War struggle between the United States and the Soviet

Union. For both sides in this conflict, the Congo represented a critical entry point to expanded influence over a wide swath of the African continent.

Lumumba's accusations that the United Nations was complicit with Western interests rankled Bunche and contributed to his decision to leave the Congo. Around the time of his departure, Bunche confided in private correspondence with his wife that Lumumba was a "madman" whose "insane fulminations" had destroyed the "greatest of international efforts" (Young 2010, 142). When Bunche left the Congo, the American Secretariat executive Andrew Cordier replaced him as interim head of the U.N. operation in the Congo. Cordier, who had been an international security advisor at the U.S. State department, did not waste time in pushing the crisis to its ghastly conclusion. He approved a request from Kusa Vubu that the United Nations guarantee his personal safety and shut down the radio stations and close the airports to Lumumba and his supporters. Thus isolated, it was only a matter of time before Lumumba met his ignoble fate at the hands of Tshombe's henchmen and their Belgium and American backers.

After the disappointing outcome in the Congo, Bunche returned to the United States and became an emblem of the progress racial liberalism in U.S. domestic and foreign affairs made possible. In this capacity, Bunche and others served as the proof of diminishing racism in the United States, since their achievements confirmed that racism no longer prevented individuals of exceptional character from achieving their full potential. The prominence of such figures suggested that opportunities were increasingly available under American democracy as racial impediments receded. These figures were thus deployed to focus the conversation on individual accomplishments and shift it away from the structural elements effectively barring African Americans from inclusion in U.S. society.

The consequences of racial liberalism were not limited, however, to domestic issues. While not fully appreciated, racial liberalism played an important role in the conduct of U.S. foreign affairs. Bunche's bit part in the U.S. government's assassination plot against Lumumba is an example of that role. While no evidence suggests Bunche's direct involvement in the decision to eliminate Lumumba, his minor role in the U.S. government's deliberations provided cover from the charge of racism. According to the historian Brenda Gayle Plummer, the White House and National Security Council feared their motives being reduced to naked racism, so "they sought and received corroboration for Lumumba's alleged maniacal character" in a Bunche letter to Andrew Cordier (2013, 90). The use made of Bunche in this instance typifies a broader pattern at work in the United States in which emblems of racial liberal progress were deployed to deflect charges of racism. By obscuring the racism that structured Western governments' relationship to the Congo and its leader, racial liberalism provided the framework for dismissing Lumumba's claim to control his country's resources as the maniacal ravings of a meddlesome politician.

A RIOTOUS MOOD:
IDEOLOGICAL RUPTURE IN AFRICAN AMERICA

By the time of the Congo Crisis and Lumumba's downfall, racial liberalism had been installed as the dominant paradigm through which the United States approached matters related to decolonization in Africa and Asia. For the most part, this dominance was achieved through a dual-pronged approach: government repression of left-leaning black organizations concerned with foreign policy and government support, sometimes covert, of liberal organizations. The most notable victim of the former was the Council on African Affairs (CAA). The CAA, you will recall from chapter 4, was an organization founded by Max Yergan and Paul Robeson. At the height of its prominence, the organization counted among its members such African American luminaries as Du Bois, E. Franklin Frazer, Mary McLeod Bethune, and Rayford Logan (Von Eschen 1997, 116). Through publications and meetings, the organization brought African Americans a critical perspective on apartheid in South Africa, the Mau Mau rebellion in Kenya, and other conflicts on the continent and throughout the diaspora. By 1948 a rift developed between Robeson and Yergan, with Yergan charging that the Communist Party USA had taken control of the organization and was using it to further the Soviet Union's foreign policy goals. Around the same time, the organization was placed on the attorney general's list of subversive organizations. By 1956, the organization disbanded under the weight of defending itself against legal complications arising from the attorney general's designation.

A host of racial liberal organizations stepped in to fill the void created by the now defunct CAA. Most prominent among them were the American Society of African Culture, the American Council on Africa, and the African American Institute. Organizations like AMSAC, the CIA's chief African American cultural front organization, discussed in chapter 1, were created with the express purpose of bringing a liberal perspective to international conferences concerned with Africa and decolonization and providing the U.S. intelligence community with information on developments on the continent and in the diaspora. With the extensive funding provided by CIA shell foundations, AMSAC dominated the field, practically drowning out any voices that stood outside racial liberalism's ideological enclosure.

Despite the dominance of government-supported organizations, vagabond voices continued to exist, and they inserted themselves into the conversation with the announcement of Lumumba's assassination. When word found its way out of the Congo, it incited demonstrators to pour into the streets of the world's capitals—Brussels, Paris, London, Moscow, Washington, Cairo, and Accra—to voice their outrage and condemn the Western powers complicit in his murder.

In the United States, this outrage was put on spectacular display in the halls of power. On February 15, 1961, a group of mostly African American activists "set off the most violent demonstration inside United Nations headquarters in the world organization's history" ("Riot," 1). The demonstration disrupted the deliberations in the U.N. Security Council chamber, which had been convened to discuss Lumumba's death and charges brought by the Soviet Union regarding U.N. secretary-general Dag Hammarskjöld's complicity in his demise. The *New York Times*, quoting Daniel H. Watts, identified as the "chairman of the nine-month-old Liberation Committee for Africa,"[3] that demonstrators entered the public gallery in silent protest with "the women [wearing] black veils and the men black arm bands." According to the *Times* report, when the newly appointed U.S. ambassador to the United Nations, Adlai E. Stevenson, started to express his support for Hammarskjöld,[4] a woman from On Guard for Freedom stood up and was rushed by guards, sparking the "riot."

Outside the United Nations, other protesters marched on Forty-second Street westward across Manhattan. Shouting a "modified Cuban slogan, Congo, yes! Yankee, no!," these protests against Lumumba's death "occasioned the articulation of a new black identity" that fused "1960s anticolonialism and black cultural politics" (Young 2006, 50). This fusion was a repudiation of the racial liberalism that had come to dominate black politics, cultural and otherwise, at that moment. One strain of that racial liberalism held that the realization of black identity lay in recognizing its "omni-Americanness"[5] and positioning it as a resource that could enable the United States to attain its democratic ideals.

Indeed, these demonstrations were a signal event in post–World War II African American literary and cultural history, involving such figures as Maya Angelou, Amiri Baraka, James Baldwin, and Lorraine Hansberry. While the *New York Times* reporter quotes Watts as putting members of his organization and On Guard at the center of the demonstration, Cheryl Higashida has recently argued that it was the black internationalist women working under the banner of the Cultural Association for Women of African Heritage (CAWAH) who "instigated [this] event that became pivotal in the revival of Black nationalist consciousness in the United States" (2012, 54). The driving forces in CAWAH were the literary artists Rosa Guy and Maya Angelou and the singer Abbey Lincoln. According to Higashida, it was only after the demonstration that Sarah Wright and fellow novelist and Harlem Writers Guild member Calvin Hicks formed On Guard for Freedom to solidify the coalition of activists that had come together for the demonstration.

The demonstration highlighted the organizational acumen and revolutionary consciousness of African American women leaders. Years later, Amiri Baraka remembered the "sisters . . . bashing the guards in the head with their shoes and throwing shoes down in the gallery" and wrote admiringly of "one sister, Mae Mallory," who "put up a terrific battle and the police were sorry they ever put their hands on her. . . . She was one of the people in On Guard and she is still very active in the Black Liberation Movement today" (Baraka 1984, 181).[6] Recently, Ashley Farmer has centered the demonstration in Mae Mallory's political trajectory from militant domestic, in the vein of Childress's Mildred discussed in chapter 3, to revolutionary political activist (Farmer 2017, 41-42).

The demonstration also proved pivotal in the political development of the poet LeRoi Jones (Amiri Baraka). It might not be too much of a stretch to claim that Baraka's journey north from Greenwich Village to Harlem began with this demonstration outside the United Nations' midtown Manhattan headquarters. Indeed, as Ira Dworkin has recently argued, Baraka's arrest at the demonstration marks it "as a radicalizing moment for one of the era's foremost artists and intellectuals" (2017, 227). In the *Autobiography of LeRoi Jones*, Baraka reminisces about the demonstration as the moment when he began to meet and befriend young black intellectuals connected with the Black Liberation Movement (181).

The organizing of the protest against Lumumba's assassination brought together a diverse coalition of African American nationalist organizations operating in and around Harlem at the time. In addition to the CAWAH, Harlem Writers Guild, and Liberation Committee for Africa activists, the protest included such organizations as James Lawson's United African Nationalist Movement, while members of the Universal African Legion, the International Muslim Society, the Brooklyn-based United Sons and Daughters of Africa, and the Order of Damballa Ouedo had been present in the galley when the "riot" broke out (Plummer 1996, 302). These organizations represented and carried forth a spirit of black radical independence that had not been entirely crushed by the anticommunism of the 1950s. In some cases these organizations were directly linked to organizations of the old black left. Apparently, there were tensions between the younger activists and old left, as indicated in the story about Benjamin Davis, the communist former Harlem city council member, being prevented from joining the demonstration. The precise nature of their relationship to the old left notwithstanding, the activists protesting Lumumba's assassination situated themselves within the black radical tradition that is the subject *Of Vagabonds and Fellow Travelers*.

In the month following the protest, James Baldwin and Lorraine Hansberry, two of the most celebrated names in African American letters at the time, declared in the pages of *The New York Times* their support for these activists and the black radical sentiment they expressed. Baldwin used the assassination of Lumumba and the protests in the gallery of the United Nations as the starting point for a discussion linking African independence to the self-assertion fueling the African American freedom struggle. Baldwin begins his article, "A Negro Assays the Negro Mood," which the *New York Times Sunday Magazine* published just three weeks following the U.N. demonstration, by assuring his readers that only "the chaos on [his] desk prevented [him] from being in the United Nations gallery that day." He then assails "the prevailing view" that "the Negro is so content with his lot [in the United States] that only the cynical agents of a foreign power can rouse him to protest" (Baldwin 1961, 25). Here Baldwin refers to the fact that the charge of communist infiltration had been applied liberally and used to discredit all manner of African American protest, most often in the South but in the rest of the country as well. In Baldwin's view, the African American activists demonstrating at the United Nations were "but a small echo of the black discontent now abroad in the world" (104). In light of this global reality, he urges his readers not to be deluded into accepting the narrative that these spectacular displays of discontent were the work of agent provocateurs. Instead, he locates the sources of that discontent in the ripple effects of Africa's entrance on the "stage of history," which "has proven to be a great antidote to the poison of self-hatred" and the "power of the white world to control [African American] identities" (104). Two weeks later, Hansberry echoed Baldwin's sentiments in a letter expressing her gratitude to the editor for printing Baldwin's article.

Hansberry's letter, which carried the title "Congolese Patriot," forcefully suggests that the mood of African Americans was one of righteous outrage and indignation. Like Baldwin, she takes offense at the attempt to link the demonstrations protesting Lumumba's death to Moscow or Mecca[7] and confesses that she, "a political and religious non-affiliate, 'intended,' like Mr. Baldwin, 'to be there myself'" (Hansberry 1961, 4). Of course, in asserting her political nonaffiliation, Hansberry was rehearsing a common gesture of the time, leftist disavowal. Recall that Hansberry began her literary career ten years earlier writing for *Freedom*, Paul Robeson's radical leftist newspaper, discussed in chapter 4, which immersed her in a "vibrant Black Left network that included Robeson, W. E. B. DuBois, Louis Burnham, Shirley Graham DuBois, and Alice Childress" (Higashida 2012, 57).[8] In expressing her willingness to protest alongside "Mustafa Bashire or Benjamin J. Davis[9] [the Communist Party leader and former New York City councilman] or any other Negro who had the passion and understanding to be there" (4), Hansberry reflected the spirit of the day, which privileged unity over sectarianism. As an indication of the contemporary African American mood, Hansberry's declaration suggests that impatience with the colonial and racist order had reached the point where African Americans ignored American antipathy to communism and Islam and embraced allies of different political and religious persuasions committed to African diaspora freedom struggles.

This embrace was not so capacious, however, to include those African Americans perceived as being apologists for Western imperialism, which explains the sharply worded rebuke of Ralph Bunche that concludes her letter. After the U.N. protest, Bunche issued a formal apology to senior officials of the United Nations in which he endorsed the NAACP's recognition of the "emotional link between Africans and black Americans," but expressed his disapproval of the "scandalous conduct of the demonstrators" who "were not representative of the thinking and standards of conduct held by the great majority" of African Americans (quoted in Halila 192). Counting herself among those "shocked and outraged at reports of Dr. Bunche's 'apologies' for the demonstrators" and "curious as to his *mandate* from our people to do so," Hansberry offers a public apology to "Mme. Pauline Lumumba and the Congolese people for our Dr. Bunche" (1961 4). Baldwin's essay also makes an oblique reference to Bunche when he mentions dismissively that it was not long "before prominent Negroes rushed forward to assure the Republic that the United Nations rioters did not represent the real feeling of the Negro community" (25). In the *Autobiography of LeRoi Jones*, Baraka follows Hansberry's lead in being explicit about his contempt for Bunche: "Ralph Bunche said he was ashamed and scandalized by such niggerism, while we were scandalized and ashamed of his negro-ass tom antics" (1984 181). In issuing his apology, Bunche was both performing his function as a leading racial liberal and coming to the support of his longtime friend Stevenson, the United States ambassador to the United Nations.[10]

In concluding her letter with a rebuke of Bunche, Hansberry left her readers with a critique of racial liberalism and those sections of the African American elite that aligned their interests with an ascendant U.S. global power. This interest-convergence was not without its consequence, particularly as revealed in the texts and events surrounding the Congo Crisis, which reverberated strongly throughout African diaspora political and cultural life. Indeed, according to James H. Meriwether, "African-American responses to the Congo Crisis and to Lumumba reveal how issues such as black nationalism, leftist thought, and militancy created fissures in black America" (2002, 209). If we extend the scale of Meriwether's assessment to the level of the diaspora, it raises pertinent questions about the costs and consequences of racial liberalism as the framework for African American inclusion in the United States. By decoupling racism from material conditions, racial liberalism has obscured the relationship between racial inequality and the global system of capitalist accumulation. The United States assumed direction over this system in the Cold War years, at the precise moment that African Americans were being included. This historical conjuncture has meant that African diaspora culture and its critics have had to contend with the seemingly contradictory situation of prosperity on one hand and dispossession on the other. In part, the institutions of the cultural Cold War have served a crucial function in helping to produce those subjectivities necessary for managing this fissure.

The intellectual consequences of this fissure can be considered if we look again at the diversity of activists at the United Nations that protested Lumumba's death. Besides the people already mentioned, the group included such individuals and groups as drummer Max Roach and Vouse Make,[11] deputy vice-chairman of the South African Pan-African Congress, as well as members of the Universal African Legion, the International Muslim Society, the Brooklyn-based United Sons and Daughters of Africa, and the Order of Damballah Ouedo.[12] Yet of all the individuals associated with this protest, the ones that have since garnered the most consideration in African American literary history and criticism are James Baldwin and Lorraine Hansberry, whose schedules or prior commitments prevented them from taking part in the protests. Maya Angelou is the exception to this characterization, but as Higashida argues "her remarkable popularity and cultural capital" were achieved in part by "emphasizing personal triumph and identity formation over sociohistorical narrative" and "the revolutionary politics she shared with comrades who have been exiled, persecuted, or otherwise banished from public memory" (2012, 28). The situation Higashida describes succinctly encapsulates the logic of racial liberalism and its attendant critical practices, which insist that we celebrate individual achievement at the expense of a more thoroughgoing structural critique of the prevailing conditions that make such achievement remarkable. Such conditions might demand a critical practice not overly concerned with the necessity of being either respectable or representative.

BRIEF FOR A SCANDALOUS CRITICISM

When Bunche issued an apology to the U.N. Assembly the day following the protests, he voiced his disapproval of the protesters' "scandalous conduct" (quoted in Halila 192). Here Bunche was clearly attempting to dissociate the protesters' method and message from the mainstream African American civil rights movement, which supported U.S. foreign policy in exchange for opening spaces in the American polity to "properly thinking and acting" African Americans. In their rejoinders to Bunche, both Hansberry and Baraka registered their sense of being scandalized at Bunche's presumption of the need to apologize and the authority to speak on behalf of African Americans. Other African Americans wrote to Bunche directly asking why he didn't "apologize for [his] own 'scandalous conduct,' the betrayal of [his] black fellowmen in helping the white man maintain his stronghold in the Congo" (quoted in Halila 192). What these writers found most scandalous in Bunche's conduct was his unabashed willingness to serve as an apologist for U.S. imperialism. Similarly, *Of Vagabonds and Fellow Travelers* locates the true scandal of the cultural Cold War not in those who defied the racial liberal consensus, but those who threw their support behind the U.S. project of anticommunism and global hegemony in exchange for the economic, political, and social advancement of elite African Americans.

Importantly, *Of Vagabonds and Fellow Travelers* seeks to move beyond simply locating an alternative site of scandal. It aims to further the conversation on the consequences for and lingering impact of this Cold War history on African diaspora literary and cultural criticism. For example, the African American literary and cultural critic Mary Helen Washington opens her important *The Other Blacklist* with personal reminiscences on her own Catholic school education in the 1950s, which prepared "even those . . . who benefited the most from civil rights militancy to be stand-up little anticommunists" (2014, 3). Her education in anticommunism, she avows, continued "in the 1960s and 1970s . . . at the universities where [she] was trained in literary criticism via the New Critical bibles of Brooks and Warren's *Understanding Poetry* and *Understanding Fiction*" (10). In these reminiscences Washington stops short of the conclusion that anticommunism was the price exacted not only from African American critics but also from the field of African American literary and cultural criticism itself for inclusion into the mainstream critical establishment. *Of Vagabonds and Fellow Travelers* seeks to raise such questions and to suggest a relationship between this concession and the class politics of the African American literary critical project, a politics raised to much controversy and extensive critical debate by Kenneth Warren's *What Was African American Literature?* (2011).[13] One suspects that Warren's book generated such scandal partly because of the impoverished conceptualization and understanding of class in American cultural criticism writ large, a possible lingering effect of the history traced in these pages. What seems to have been muddled in this discussion is the distinction between the function of particular critical approaches to enforce and reproduce certain class privilege and the class origins (and aspirations) of their practitioners. In this regard, what both Washington and Warren make visible is how the remnants of the cultural Cold War continue to exert an influence on contemporary critical practice.

The chill of the Cold War still exercised its influence, if in less evident ways, when I entered graduate school more than a quarter-century after Washington did. The graduate fellowship I was awarded from the University of Pennsylvania, which allowed me to begin the study that eventually became this book, was named in honor of William T. Fontaine. Fontaine, a professor of philosophy, had been the first fully affiliated African American faculty member and first African American to earn tenure at that institution. But more germane to the present discussion, Fontaine had been a member of the American delegation to the First Congress of Black Writers and Artists in Paris in 1956. You will recall that this delegation formed the leadership nucleus of AMSAC, the CIA cultural front organization formed the following year. In his biography of Fontaine, the historian and Penn professor Bruce Kuklick arrives at the conclusion that "Fontaine almost certainly did not know of the society's tainted origins and cash flow and had nothing to do with AMSAC's finances" (2008, 111). Perhaps this is the case, but it is inconceivable that someone Kuklick describes as a "Cold War liberal" that had "resolutely [written] off the Communists," (109) and who was the organization's secretary, was kept totally in the dark and never raised questions about the organization's finances. Surely, a scholar of Fontaine's stature would not have found it impossible to divine the source of the funds that allowed AMSAC's members to travel to international conferences and for the organization to maintain a well-appointed office in midtown Manhattan. The notion that somehow Fontaine was incapable of comprehending the stakes of the Cold War struggle and of his and other black intellectuals' place in that struggle reeks of dismissing African Americans as mere dupes.

To my knowledge, graduate students awarded the Fontaine fellowship were never encouraged to question who Fontaine was and the context for his rise. Of course, we were meant to celebrate his undeniable achievement and to emulate his trajectory by striking out in our respective fields, becoming if not the first, then one of a handful of African American faculty members on whatever campus the fortunes of the job market discharged us. It is not to diminish his accomplishments as a philosopher to suggest that his principled anticommunism made him an attractive candidate for the position at Penn, particularly given the Cold War practice of using such appointments to discredit Soviet propaganda about the persistence of racism in the United States. The implicit message for graduate students of my generation was, just as it had been for Fontaine, to not give much time to interrogating the conditions prevailing upon the production of knowledge in the mainstream academy, the assumed destination for most recipients of the Fontaine fellowship. This particular ideological enclosure deprived us of the opportunity to analyze the function of our own research and appointments within an academy that has increasingly become a crucial site in reproducing the scandalous poverty and income inequality in the United States, which has had devastating consequences on working-class African Americans in particular.

The specters of the Cold War haunt not only graduate education but also the pastoral scenes of elite undergraduate education in the United States. When I was in the final stages of completing the research for this book, I had the opportunity to share portions of it with the faculty and students at Williams College. As part of my visit, I was given a tour of the campus multicultural center, the Davis Center. The center is named after two of the college's black alumni, the brothers W. Allison Davis and John A. Davis. John A. Davis, readers will recall, was the executive director of AMSAC and the primary liaison with the covert funding infrastructure put in place by the CIA for this African American cultural front organization. During the course of my visit, the connection between my research and Davis went unmentioned. I can only presume, therefore, that AMSAC and Davis's role in the cultural Cold War does not figure in the multicultural education the institution imparts to its students. It is perhaps best that the lesson students take from John A. Davis's example be implied rather than made explicit, since one suspects many of them are being trained to occupy similar roles in elite economic, political, social, and intellectual circles in the United States.

Every day that I go to work on my own campus, the built environment reminds me that the supposedly past Cold War remains very much alive. The English Department at the University of Houston is housed in the Roy G. Cullen Building, named in honor of the son of Hugh Roy and Lillian Cullen. A self-made oil man and member of Houston's mid-twentieth-century elite, Cullen was (and the family continues to be) a major benefactor to the University of Houston. Hugh Cullen did not limit his philanthropy to educational causes, but extended it to support anticommunist causes. Cullen admired Sen. Joe McCarthy, and with that admiration came financial support, as "Cullen was the single largest contributor to McCarthy's Senate reelection campaign" in 1952 (Carleton 2014, 91). Of course, the university's past has not meant that professors are submitted to ideological tests, but neither has the university reckoned with the ghosts of its past and their weight on its future course. The buildings bearing Cullen's name, however, serve as a constant reminder that the right has not neglected the importance of culture in shaping the political direction of this country.

The present moment provides us with ample evidence that the radical right continues to invest in the cultural realm as a primary front in the battle against any vestige of "communism," by which it means pretty much any public good, including education. Having successfully ensconced an ideology of small government in state legislatures across the country, the radical right has successfully decimated funding for public research universities and institutions of higher learning. Into this void, the well-heeled supporters of the radical right have stepped in with their own institutions on those very same critically underfunded campuses. Academics associated with these institutions can then arrive on resource-deprived campus with external funds and be assured of an outsized impact, particularly in colleges of liberal arts and social sciences where even small amounts of funding, when compared to the money flowing into the STEM fields, can go a long way. With this support, agents of the contemporary radical right can quickly ascend to positions of power and act as sentinels over the production of knowledge. Here they are able to cause problems, when left unchecked, for those scholars who dare take a critical look at the consequences of American freedom for marginalized populations around the globe.

This description provides a picture of our contemporary intellectual and ideological enclosure and updates the picture that the literary and cultural critic Hortense Spillers provided, nearly twenty-five years ago now, of the "ground . . . on the site of the mainstream academy" (2003, 433) on which the black creative intellectual stands. It is from this site that I raise the call for a scandalous criticism that refuses to disconnect literature and *criticism* from its grounding in the economy. By refusing this disconnection, critics train their focus on the story not being told and accepts the scandal its telling invites. Such scandal, however, must be seen in its proper light, as merely a disciplinary tactic to dissuade the questioning of the truly scandalous operation and consequences of the present order. And finally, scandalous criticism as a mode sees itself not as a substitute for but as a complement to action. In that way, it insists that we add institution building on the ground of the contemporary academy to those tasks of "reader/writer/thinker/teacher" (457) that Spillers identifies as the specific domain of the black creative intellectual. On this ground, at this moment, it is critically important that we begin diverting some portion of our financial resources to establishing endowments to support our scandalous work. These endowments can be the seeds for the replanting of the intellectual commons. The blooming of such spaces across the contemporary academic landscape would well serve as sites of refuge and sustenance for vagabonds and fellow travelers on the weary road of intellectual struggle against present and future enclosures.

Notes

Introduction

1. Coincidentally Laurel, Mississippi, was the site of a major civil rights case involving Willie McGee, a black truck driver and yard man, convicted and executed on spurious charges of raping a white woman. While the initial trial began in late 1945, it was a focal point of activism and legal battles for the next five years up to the moment McGee was executed by the state of Mississippi in May 1951. When the trial began Price was already away at college in Ohio, but probably would have been aware of the case shining a spotlight on race relations in her hometown. One wonders if Chisholm's decision to fund Price's education at Juilliard was at least in part motivated by her concern to neutralize Robeson's support of the young singer. Chisholm might have known of Robeson's links to the Civil Rights Congress, the organization that took the lead in Willie McGee's legal defense and the political mobilization around his case. For more on the CRC's involvement in the case, see Horne (1988), particularly pgs. 74–98. Thank you to Gerald Horne for bringing this connection to my attention.

2. During her time at Juilliard, Price became a protégé of Nicolas Nabokov, who was elected the general secretary of CCF in 1951 and conceived of the Twentieth Century Masterpieces festival. When Nabokov and Albert Donnelley, an OPC officer who served as the festival's secretary, decided it would be politically expedient to have an all-black and *American* cast perform in the festival's production of *Four Saints in Three Acts*, Nabokov lobbied on Price's behalf, on at least three separate occasions to the opera's composer Virgil Thomson. According to Wilford, Donnelly started to work with the American Congress of Culture Freedom as part of the "extra security measures" adopted "when the ACCF began handing the large sums of money required to mount Nicolas Nabokov's 1952 Paris arts festival. On October 11, 1951, a first payment of $40,000 was deposited in an account opened at the Rockefeller Center branch of the Chase National Bank (Wilford 2008, 85).

3. According to her biographer, when she was a student at Juilliard, Price performed at a small private birthday party for Eisenhower, who was then president of Columbia University. The party had been organized by Clifford Roberts, a friend of the Chisholms (Lyon 1973, 57). When he became president, Eisenhower drew on his experience as a university president to dispense the $2.25 million allocated to his Emergency Fund for International Affairs, which supported tours by performing artists to "revitalize cultural diplomacy" and give "psychological warfare . . . a central place in the confrontation with the Soviet Union" (Barnhisel 2015, 72). A chief benefactor of this largesse was the Everyman Company production. Over a four-year relationship with the Department of State, the production toured twenty-two nations in Europe and Central and South America and benefited from more than $800,000 in direct subsidies from President Eisenhower's Emergency Fund for International Affairs and "an unspecified amount in USIA advertising and research and foreign mission time and entertainment" (Monod 2001, 284). Maya Angelou, another giant of African American cultural production in the twentieth century, also played the minor role of Ruby in this production of the opera.

4. Richard Delgado develops this connection in his 2002 review essay of Mary Dudziak's *Cold War Civil Rights*. See Delgado 2002.

5. Interestingly enough for my purposes Dawson traces the initial signs of this sundering back to 1947 and the outrage expressed by the NAACP leadership when, with Du Bois's backing, the organization presented a petition to the United Nations on the denial of human rights to African Americans. This outrage was a symptom of what he calls that organization's "growing dependence on and deference to Truman's Democratic Party" (78).

6. In the reprint of these lectures in *Against Racism*, Aptheker notes that Du Bois's trip was taken "at the invitation of the Haitian government and with the encouragement of the U.S. State Department" (229). This summary description overlooks the important role of the Cooks and ignores the "Good Neighbor" political context and how the government mobilized African American intellectuals in support of this policy. It is important for my argument that this history be sketched out more fully, as it provides an unremarked precursor to the CIA- and State Department–sponsored initiatives of the later cultural Cold War.

7. These two lectures are published under the title "Colonialism, Democracy, and Peace after the War (Summer 1944)" in Du Bois 1985a.

8. Aptheker's note on this lecture reveals that it was "among the papers left in [his] care, but there was no indication of date or the circumstances of its delivery" and he guessed "that this was a lecture, probably in 1944 or possibly at 1945, at a class in some local educational institution" (249). By comparing the English text to the French text, "La conception de l'éducation," which Aptheker published in the edited volume *Writings by W.E.B. Du Bois in Periodicals*, and consulting an article about the 1944 summer school for secondary teachers published in the September 1944 issue of *Cahiers d'Haiti*, I have reached the conclusion that Du Bois gave this lecture in Haiti.

9. In *Un-American* (2015), Bill Mullen offers a revolutionary reading of Du Bois's "Un-American" status that predates the U.S. Cold War state labeling him as such to mark his marginalization from the African American freedom struggle.

Chapter 1

1. For more on the importance of the Marshall Plan to U.S. global dominance in the postwar period, see Hunt 2007, 1661–72. Hitchcock provides an overview of the crises that shook France in 1947 and precipitated the emergency aid from the United States; see Hitchcock 1998, 828–87.

2. Christopher Miller, for one, notes the apparent gap between the "freedom of France" and the repressive environment in the colonies in his discussion of the confiscation of Lamine Senghor's *La Violation d'un pays* (1927) by French authorities in Africa. He writes, "The gap between, on the one hand, active and organized resistance to colonialism in France and, on the other, the effective suppression of dissent within the colonized territories during this period is dramatized by this failed attempt" (1998, 28).

3. As Wright stated in an interview with fellow European expatriate William Gardner Smith for *Ebony* magazine: "The break from the U.S. was more than a geographical change.... I was trying to grapple with the big problem—the problem and meaning of Western civilization as a whole and the relation of Negroes and other minority groups to it" (quoted in Gilroy 1993, 164). The original interview appeared in *Ebony* 8 (July 1953): 40.

4. The connection between the Malagasy nationalists and Ho Chi Minh is discussed in Little 1990, 536.

5. Miller illuminates the extent of Diop's "seduction" by the French system of colonial education. See Miller 1998, 62–63.

6. For a discussion of the inception of *Présence Africaine*, its "original hopes and the structural conditions that governed their realization," see Miller 1992.

7. In fact, Jacques Rabemananjara, one of the early collaborators on *Présence Africaine*, did not witness the launch of the journal because he had been detained and was facing the death penalty as a result of accusations that he was a lead organizer of the Malagasy revolt.

8. All translations from this work are Julie-Françoise Tolliver's and mine.

9. Equally, all translations from this work are Julie-Françoise Tolliver's and mine.

10. This is one of the central arguments of Césaire's *Discourse on Colonialism*. For a discussion of Arendt's thesis on this question see King 2004, 100-110.

11. For a discussion of FEANF see Ndiaye 2008, 327. For a larger discussion of the editing and anticolonial activities of François Maspero, see Maspero 2002.

12. For a fuller description of these efforts see Rosenberg 2006, chaps. 5 and 6.

13. It is interesting to note in passing that the translators Richard Wright and Thomas Diop elided the phrase "et dont la plupart ont tout oublié des moeurs africaines" [and who for the most part have forgotten everything of African mores].

14. All translations from this work are Julie-Françoise Tolliver's and mine.

15. The essay was subsequently published in his essay collection *Nobody Knows My Name* (1961).

16. Du Bois had also addressed the Bandung conference in a telegram. He also, according to historian Gerald Horne, "drafted a lengthy 'Memorandum on the Bandung Conference' which was unmistakeably [*sic*] directed at Adam Clayton Powell, Jr., Carl Rowan, and Richard Wright, and other Afro-Americans allowed to travel to Bandung for the purpose of refuting charges of United States racism" (1986, 287).

17. In a classic case of "one doth protest too much," Richard Wright opened the evening debate that followed the opening day's session with a reference to DuBois's letter: "We had a message today that hurt me and I think my role in this Conference will negate the implication of that message: that the Americans participating here were people who could not speak their minds freely. When my role [is] finished in this Conference[,] I would appreciate if you would tell me what governments paid me." See "Débats: 19 September, à 21h," *Presence Africaine*, no. 81–0 (Juin-Novembre 1956): 67.

18. For information on Davis's work at the State Department, see Krenn 1999, 624. For more background on his agitation within the government on behalf of African Americans, see Kilson 2007.

19. If he did not reflect on the sources behind his own organizations, he was suspicious of others. In his final report on the Congress, Bond wondered where the funds had come from to allow *Présence Africaine* to offer simultaneous translation. He, of course, suspected the communists as the source, which suggests that he was at least conscious of the stakes involved. See Wilford 2008, 203.

20. For more on this particular moment in Robeson's life and career and its wider implications, see Horne's biography of Robeson (2016) as well as his biographies of various figures on the Black left (Horne 1994; 2000; 2005; and 2013).

21. All translations from this work are Julie-Françoise Tolliver's and mine.

22. Davis, of course, was referring to the Black Belt thesis that emerged out of the Sixth World Congress of the Comintern, which argued that "blacks in the United States were an oppressed nation which had the right of self-determination in those parts of the South where they formed a majority of the population" (Naison 1983, 17).

23. See "Débats: 20 September, à 21h," *Presence Africaine*, no. 81–0 (Juin-Novembre 1956): 2062–26.

24. An anonymous postconference report refers to Blackman as "like a puppy dog," who "bowed and scraped to [Dorothy Brooks, the communist white woman who led the British delegation] her whenever he was in her presence" (Bond 1956).

25. In *The Eighteenth Brumaire of Louis Bonaparte*, Marx refers to these generals as "the heroes of Africa" (1852, 598). The editorial note states that "this refers to the generals distinguished for their savage deeds in Africa during the conquest of Algeria" (599 note 4).

26. For more on the nation-state skeptical but nevertheless anticolonial politics pursued by French West African leaders, see Cooper 2014.

27. For his part, Césaire was definitely familiar with Wright's work. In 1935, he had published a translation of Wright's long poem "I Have Seen Black Hands" in the recently discovered third issue of *l'Étudiant Noir* as "Mains noires." Indeed, the historian David Alliot has ventured that the translation served as material for the thesis that Césaire wrote to obtain his diploma from the prestigious l'École normal supérieure. The title of Césaire's thesis was "Le Thème du sud dans la poésie négro-américaine des États-unis" (The Theme of the South in Black American Poetry from the United States) (353–56). Coming from "the Other America," Césaire's title subtly draws our attention to the casual monopolization of the term "America" by the United States.

28. In an interview with Cedric Robinson, C.L.R. James makes the connection between ENS and Césaire's communism when he recalls a conversation with Césaire about his education: "[Aime] Cesaire and I were talking one day, and I asked him: 'Where do you come from?' He said, 'Well I grew up in Martinique [and went to] the Victor Shoelscher school.' . . . So I said: 'What did you do there?' He told me: 'Latin and Greek and French literature.' And I said: 'What next?' He said, 'I went to France, and went to the Ecole Normale Superiore [*sic*].' I said, 'Yes I know that school. It is famous for producing scholars and Communists.' (Cesaire was one of the first in each department: he was one of the finest scholars and he was a notable communist.)" (2000, 183).

29. The article was reproduced as a facsimile in Christopher Filostrat's 2008 book *Negritude Agonistes: Assimilation against Nationalism in the French-Speaking Caribbean and Guyane.* The article is notable for being the first time that Césaire uses the neologism *négritude.* Prior to that the critical consensus had been that negritude was born in Césaire's celebrated long poem "Cahier d'un retour au pays natal" (Notebook of a Return to the Native Land).

30. Césaire's insistence on the necessity of African diaspora writers to develop an independent political aesthetic not beholden to the party's dictates was reinforced the year prior to his resignation. In a debate on the form and content of poetry sponsored by *Présence Africaine,* he encouraged the Haitian poet René Depestre to embrace marronage as the proper relationship to the party's aesthetic dictates. See Hale and Véron 2009, 49–50.

31. Regarding autonomous political organization, it is worth noting that the twelve-year period from 1945 to 1957, when the FCM was formally tied to the PCF, represents a departure from the norm. From its inception in 1919 up until 1945, "the Martinican communist movement did not have any link, either juridical or electoral, with the Party of Maurice Thorez . . . and was in complete control of his destiny" (Alliot 2013, 104).

32. The turn of phrase "racism at capitalism's dawn" is meant to echo Peter James Hudson's review essay, "The Racist Dawn of Capitalism" published in the Boston Review. Accessed online on March 21, 2016.

33. Contemporary examples of attempts to correct this misreading are Young 2004 and Kevin Anderson's *Marx at the Margins* (2010).

Chapter 2

1. The discussion in chapter 1 elaborates on the Cold War context of Du Bois's message.

2. Translations of this work are mine.

3. Today, America retains control over this vital waterway with the U.S. naval facilities at Guantanamo Bay, Cuba, standing guard over the southern approach.

4. As discussed in chapter 3, upon his return from a series of concerts in Panama, Paul Robeson joined forces with W.E.B. Du Bois and the black newspaper owner and radical activist Charlotta Bass in the Committee to End the Jim Crow 'Silver-Gold' System in the Panama Canal Zone. It was these activities on behalf of black workers in key nodal points of American imperialism that made Robeson a target of the Cold War security state, not his apparent fealty to Stalin and Stalinism.

5. U.S. Navy, Lt. Cdr. Ephraim R. McLean Jr. provides a detailed description of this process from the perspective of a World War II military officer in his "The Caribbean— An American Lake" (1941).

6. It is deeply ironic that a year prior to the publication of In the Castle of My Skin, the McCarran-Walter Act of 1952 severely restricted the Caribbean immigration that someone like Trumper would have benefited from. Lamming makes note of this in The Pleasures of Exile: "[Many West Indians] asked to enter America for the simplest and most acceptable reasons, a request that should never be refused. It was Caliban's request: 'I must eat my dinner.' And many hungry West Indians, could have had their dinner if MacCarran [sic] could have based the emigration act on our example of living a way through the world's different races" (154). The coauthor of the 1952 immigration act was the Pennsylvania congressman in charge of the HUAC committee that compelled Paul Robeson's testimony discussed in chapter 4.

7. On how the social context of its wearing made the zoot suit a political statement, see Kelley 1996.

8. Trumper's political awakening here parallels Marcus Garvey's in that he too comes to what Michelle Stephens describes as "global" as opposed to national consciousness, largely owing to his experience of travel and encounter with other black workers in the circum-Caribbean regions of Central America under U.S. influence, if not domination, prior to his travel to the British metropole.

9. In The Pleasures of Exile, Lamming makes a similar comment on the difference between the United States and the Caribbean: "The West Indian, however black and dispossessed, could never have felt the experience of being in a minority.... [T]he West Indian has learned, by sheer habit, to take that white presence for granted. Which is, precisely, his trouble.... To be black, in the West Indies, is to be poor; whereas to be black (rich or poor) in an American context is to be a traditional target for specific punishments" (33).

10. Robeson's ordeal is the subject of chapter 4.

11. This British tour was "a replacement for eighty-five concert dates within the United States that had been cancelled" as consequence of "the quick dive to the right" in the entertainment industry following the presidential election and the indictment of the "Hollywood Ten" (Duberman 1989, 338). And for more on the racial and political context of Robeson's tour of the British Isles, see Marc Matera's *Black London*.

12. Matthew Smith also notes the FBI monitoring of leftist radicals in Haiti, particularly those who maintained contacts with their counterparts in neighboring Cuba (87 note 69).

13. Roumel is a character based on Jacques Roumain. In early August 1934, Roumain was arrested and tried before a military tribunal on a charge of communist conspiracy and later sentenced to three years in prison (Fowler 1980, 152–55). Alexis met Roumain in September 1942, who accompanied the Cuban poet Nicolás Guillén on a tour of poetry recitals (Coates 1999, x). In October, Roumain was despatched to Mexico to be the chargé d'affaires by the Lescot regime (Fowler 1980, 223). Despite the brevity of Roumain's time in Haiti following their meeting, Alexis adopted him as an artistic and political mentor, as did other radical students who participated in the small reading group, "Les amis de Jacques Roumain," cofounded by Gérald Bloncourt (Smith 74).

14. According to Kate Ramsey, "as the largest American-owned enterprise and foremost icon of the agribusiness that was steadily displacing peasant sharecroppers across these regions by means of lands appropriations, HASCO was ... a highly likely object of sorcery discourse in early-occupation Cul-de-Sac and Léogâne" (2011, 173).

15. According to Kaussen, thousands of peasants were driven from their lands to build the HASCO plantations and sugar refineries, and thousands more to make way for the Haitian *chemin de fer* constructed beginning in 1905 by the Haitian American Corporation that controlled HASCO, the Haitian electric company, the Port-au-Prince wharf, and the Compagnie des Chemins de fer. The HASCO plantation and *chemin de fer* were favorite targets of the Caco insurgents (Kaussen 2008, 42).

16. Borno "was an avowed admirer of Mussolini and an advocate of complete American domination as the fastest way to modernize Haiti and reconstruct viable economic and efficient governmental institutions" (Schmidt 15).

17. On the experience of Haitian and other West Indian workers in the Cuban sugar industry during the boom years, see Carr 1998.

18. On U.S.-owned United Fruit Company's dominance of the agricultural export economy of Central America, see Colby 2011.

19. Piquion mentions in his article a list of organizations that includes la Mission Sanitaire Américaine, la Mission des professeurs d'Anglais pour la préparation des lycées nationaux, le Comité de Rapprochement Haïtiano-Américain, l'Institut Haïtiano-Américaile Comité des Relations Artistique et Intellectuelles entre les Amériques, and le Comité Haïtiano-Américain d'Education and the Inter-American Educational Foundation (6). Piquion dedicates his article to Mme Mercer Cook (Vashti Smith Cook) as a testament of his respectful admiration ("en témoignage de respecteuse admiration").

20. In *Represent and Destroy* Melamed argues that these very same foundations nurtured the careers of African Americans called upon to represent and manage the transition in the United States from economic inequality justified by white supremacist ideology to an official racial liberalism that disconnected persistent material inequalities from matters of race.

21. Their letters to Du Bois in the *W.E.B. Du Bois papers* frequently mention their access to figures in the Haitian government such as Stephen Alexis, Dantès Bellegarde, and Jean-Price Mars, among others.

22. While Cook was circumspect in his letter to Du Bois about his reasons for resigning, Vashti Cook confided more details in a letter to Ellen Irene Diggs, a friend who had been Du Bois's research assistant at Atlanta University and who traveled with Du Bois to Haiti. Vashti Cook begins her letter, "as you know we have had a most interesting affair with Dr. Bond." Although the Cooks had first attempted to resign in September, the day after Diggs and Du Bois left Haiti, Bond only accepted their resignation in November. He failed, however, to inform Washington of their resignation, and "three weeks later the big boss arrived and announced that the D.D. office had not accepted the resignation and that Mercer must stay until the end of the school year." While she does not elaborate on their relationship with Bond, she provides a glimpse of "the Bond setup": "He has made the Mission into a huge government agency with six or seven Haitian employees and two chauffeurs. Everyone has a fine-sounding title, and Dr. Bond is the last judgment on all matters" (Vashti Smith Cook 1945). The online note incorrectly identifies Horace M. Bond as the subject of Mercer and Vashti Cook's letters to Du Bois and Diggs, respectively.

23. Given the difficulties with Bond, Cook was undoubtedly relieved to not return to Atlanta University, whose long-serving president Rufus was Ruth Clement Bond's brother.

24. As discussed in chapter 4, Paul Robeson would articulate a similar utopian vision in an article he published the following year.

25. In an interview in *Jeune Afrique*, Léon Damas suggested that when Césaire was a student at the École Normale Supérieure, "he was . . . a great fan of Alain. As a matter of fact, he had written an editorial (entitled "Négritude") which sounded ever so much like Alain at that period" (14). See Keith Q. Warner, *Critical Perspectives on Léon Gontran Damas* (Three Continents Press, 1988).

26. It is worth noting that the English title of the conference, The First Inter-American Congress of Philosophy, betrays its association with the Good Neighbor policy. Indeed, according to Cornelius Kruse, "there would not have been any actual representation of [the American Philosophical Association] at this Congress" without "the stimulus and help" of the U.S. State Department's Division of Cultural Cooperation (1945, 30). He also noted that daytime meetings of the conference were held in the Haitian-North American Institute, "a cultural center of the type established and maintained in all capi-

tals of Latin America partly through local initiative and partly through assistance from the Division of Cultural Coöperation of our State Department" (38).

27. In contrast to my argument that locates Césaire's concern with the relation between poetic creativity and science solidly within the "colonial and postcolonial thematics and rhetoric" of Euro-American political domination in the Caribbean, Cailler seeks to "liberate" (417) Césaire and comparative literature from such an approach by comparing Césaire with the French-Romanian poet Lorand Gaspar.

28. Mabille was a French cultural attaché who settled in Haiti during the occupation of France in 1941 and who "was instrumental in strengthening cultural links with France through the formation of the Institut Français, and the founding of an important cultural and literary journal in January 1946, *Conjonction*." (Smith 2009, 73).

Chapter 3

1. Recall that Hughes traveled to Spain in July 1937 to serve as a political correspondent for the Baltimore *Afro-American*. Many of the African Americans who volunteered to fight on the side of the Loyalists during the Spanish Civil War as part of the Abraham Lincoln Brigades did so as a substitute for Ethiopia, where they were prevented from fighting.

2. Hughes's analysis here follows a black radical line on China articulated more than twenty years earlier in A. Phillip Randolph and Chandler Owen's *The Messenger*. In 1927, the magazine featured several pieces on Chinese independence, which, according to Rosenberg, "the editors identified [as] the dawn of a new historical epoch, 'the beginning of the end of the unchallenged control and supremacy of the white race over the darker races'" (2006, 96).

3. Plummer writes, "few Afro-Americans thought that communism was a major domestic problem. Black were less susceptible to anticommunist appeals as a rationale maintaining the social and political status quo" (1996, 184).

4. Fowler notes that Hughes published "Free Jacques Roumain: A letter from Langston Hughes" in the May–June 1935 issue of *Dynamo: A Journal of Revolutionary Poetry* and that the same or similar letter had been published in *Commune* (Paris) in January of that year (156 note 19). Dash suggests that a similar letter was published in the February 1935 issue of *The Crisis* (1997, 54).

5. The poem is found in the the the Langston Hughes Papers, JWJ MSS 26, box 383, folder 6827, James Weldon Johnson Collection in the Yale Collection of American Literature, Beinecke Rare Book and Manuscript Library. According to a handwritten note in the margins, copies of the poem were sent to Cook, René Piquion, *New Masses*, Arna Bontemps, and Nancy Cunard, among others. I thank Sarah Ehlers for providing me with a copy of the poem.

6. It is worth noting that the statement "je suis communiste" appears to quote the let-

ter that Roumain addressed to Tristan Rémy, which was discovered in a police raid on his home and was presented as evidence of his subversive activities against the Haitian state when he was arrested and detained in early 1933. For a discussion of the letter, see Fowler 1980, 154.

7. Senator Pat McCarran, it is worth noting, joined forces with Mississippi senator James Eastland in calling for the resignation of secretary of state Dean Acheson. In appreciation of his support, McCarran extended Eastland membership on his Senate Internal Security Subcommittee. McCarran was also the cosponsor with Rep. Walter Francis of the Immigration and Nationality Act of 1952, which Robeson criticized in his appearance before the HUAC. See Chapter 4.

8. A copy of the handbill is included in the Childress Papers, box 38, folder 6, Schomburg Research Center.

9. The typescript of the play found in the Alice Childress Papers at the Schomburg Center has the title *All is Simple*. For consistency, I have kept the titled used to advertise the play.

10. A clipping of the column can be found in the Childress Papers, box 38, folder 6, Schomburg Research Center. Brian Dolinar mistakenly identifies the club's owner as Herman Baron, a "white leftist sympathizer." Baron was the director and owner of the ACA gallery, which featured the work of CNA-affiliated artists like Charles White, who had his first exhibition there (for more on Charles White, see Washington 2014). This misattribution of ownership is probably a result of wanting to situate the theater within the context of the interracial alliances that were a feature of the left at this moment. Allying with Baron would clearly have brought even more scrutiny to Childress's activities, as he had recently been condemned by Michigan representative George Dondero, a McCarthy sympathizer, as "un-American."

11. The newspaper's close relationship to the Communist Party is suggested in a prospectus for the newspaper found in the James and Esther Cooper Jackson Papers. The prospectus calls for a two-month advanced subscription drive preceding the first issue. According to this document, the success of this drive "will require that every Party branch in the Negro concentration communities throughout the nation be alerted, politically prepared, and organized to secure the maximum number of subscriptions." See box 21, folder 38.

12. A transcript of the interview can be found in the Childress Papers, box 11, folder 13.

13. Robeson makes the comparison in an unpublished sketch possibly meant to serve as an introduction to the first edition of *Like One of the Family*, which can be found in the Childress Papers, box 11, folder 2.

14. All of my citations will be from that version of Childress's work.

15. Washington cites the original version of this column as having appeared in the February 1955 issue of *Freedom*, which would have been one of the final issues before the paper was shuttered in the summer of that year (Washington 2003, 192). According to

Lamphere, the newspaper opened 1955, after having been suspended for technical and financial reasons, with an acknowledgment that "the paper's prospects were not good" (2003, 241). One of the first mentions of Robeson in the *Freedom* column is titled "In Walks Paul Robeson," which was the seventh of her columns, published in the May 1952. Ironically, the subject of this column is the dire financial situation of the newspaper. In the column, Mildred visits with her friend Marge and relates her story of having gone to *Freedom's* 125th street office to find out what use has been made of her $1.00 subscription payment. After having a conversation with the editor, Louis Burnham, about the paper's financial difficulties, Mildred is on her way out when Robeson walks in. After hearing Mildred's story, Robeson shakes her hand and expresses his thanks and understanding. The encounter renews her commitment to increase the newspaper's subscribers and happens to be the reason for her visit with Marge.

16. Washington writes that she believes "that when Childress invented Mildred Johnson for her *Freedom* columns and her novel *Like One of the Family*, she was attempting to answer Jones's concerns about the way Popular Front literature ignored black women" (Washington 2003, 195). McDonald argues that "many of [Childress's] columns can be traced directly to Jones's article, especially in regards to black women's triple oppression, black women's labor history, and the need to challenge stereotypical representations of black women" (McDonald 2012, 57).

17. Washington usefully notes that the original version of this column appeared in an issue that featured "columns by Robeson and DuBois, pictorial maps illustrating colonial domination, a summary of U.S. companies reaping profits all over the continent, and a series of pictures juxtaposing apartheid signs in South Africa and Jim Crow signs in the United States" (Washington 2003, 189–90).

Chapter 4

1. This appellation refers to an article by C.L.R. James that was published in the *Black World* (James 1970).

2. According to Žižek, "the duty of the critical intellectual ... is precisely *to occupy all the time*, even when the new order (the 'new harmony') stabilizes itself and again renders invisible the hole as such, *the place of this hole*, i.e. to maintain a distance toward every reigning Master-Signifier (1993, 2).

3. For an astute reading of Robeson's concert in the Panama Canal Zone, see Zien 2013.

4. In her testimony at the *Hearings Regarding Communism in Labor Unions in the United States*, Ann Mathews estimated that the union had 8,000 members and that there were about 150 communists in Winston-Salem (U.S. Congress 1947, 65, 71).

5. For more information on the CAA's organized opposition to the Smuts annexation plan, see Von Eschen 1997, 87–95.

6. Jacques Stephen Alexis, the Haitian communist writer whose novel *General Sun*

My Brother is discussed in chapter 2, attended both this conference and *Présence Africaine*'s 1956 conference. See Coates 1999, xii.

7. For more on Ferdinand Smith, see Horne (2005).

8. The fund would gain notoriety in the 1990s because of its connection to Charles Murray's *The Bell Curve*. Many of the sources supporting Murray's thesis had been published in the *Mankind Quarterly*, a journal of scientific racism funded by the Pioneer Fund.

9. Mr. Arens lost his congressional job four years later when it was disclosed that he was "a paid consultant to Draper-financed committees" (Lichtenstein 1977, 76).

10. When the committee voted to recommend that Robeson be held in contempt of Congress, Chairman Francis cited Robeson's disparaging remarks about Senator Eastland as one of the major offenses motivating the decision; see Dunnigan 1956.

11. The present discussion of Senator Eastland seems the most appropriate place to address the question of Robeson's Stalinism. It is indisputable that he took indefensible positions such as support of the Smith Act convictions of Trotskyists and silence about the disappearance of Jews in the Soviet Union (see Arnesen 2012, 24–25). It seems to me, however, that the obligatory denunciations of the Stalinism of CP-affiliated leftists should be accompanied by an account of the historical situation and the strength of the opposition that those like Robeson faced. In this regard, Judith Stein's review of Duberman's biography of Robeson is instructive. In that review, Stein suggests that Robeson's stubbornness "precluded giving his enemies satisfaction, especially when they assumed the form of reactionary congressmen like James Eastland and Francis Walter" (Stein 1989, 575). Despite pretensions in the United States to making significant progress since the days when Eastland and Walter held court, it is surely telling that there remains relatively few detailed analyses of the "white resistance" these congressmen authorized. The state of the scholarship leads one to wonder how much black lives matter in a scholarly sense.

12. At one point during the hearing, when he was being questioned about his association and friendship with the black communist leader Benjamin Davis, Robeson charged that the committee members were "the nonpatriots, and you are the un-Americans and you ought to be ashamed of yourselves" (U.S. Congress 1956, 4509).

13. The United Freedom Fund was formed shortly after Robeson was denied entry into Canada in February of 1952. The organization's purpose was to "encourage and support through financial grants in aid, organizations, projects, and activities, as may contribute substantially to full and equal citizenship status for Negro people in the United States and the exercise of their maximum role in the progress of all humanity" ("United Freedom Fund constitution," *Paul Robeson Collection*, microform, reel 7). At least two of the organizations supported by the fund—CAA and NNLC—were charged with failing to register with the U.S. Attorney General's Subversive Activities Control Board. Ultimately, the cost and time associated with mounting a legal defense against the charge of being communist-front organizations and the harassment of their leaders crippled both

organizations and forced them to disband. See Von Eschen (1997) for more information on the CAA.

14. Lamphere writes that in an interview with African American communists Esther Cooper and James Jackson, Jackson "suggested that Robeson had little to do with putting the columns together." After this revelation, Esther Cooper interjected to remind her husband that "[he] was not supposed to tell [Lamphere] that" (2003, 130).

15. On the first page of the prospectus there is a handwritten note indicating that the prospectus was prepared "by Louis E. Burnham, C J E J & Ed Strong" in 1949. See James and Esther Cooper Jackson Papers, box 21, folder 38, "Louis Burnham," Tamiment Library and Robert F. Wagner Labor Archives, New York University.

16. For more information on Lorraine Hansberry, see Higashida 2012; on Vicki Garvin, see Gore 2011.

17. Two years later Yergan journeyed to Berlin under the auspices of the Congress of Cultural Freedom and eventually established a new identity for himself as leading black cold warrior.

18. The text of Robeson's address is printed in the NNLC convention program found in the *Paul Robeson Collection*, microform, reel 8, slides #602–.

19. For more information on the history of the NNLC, see Fullilove 1978 and Lang 2009.

20. For an in-depth consideration of Charles White's work and his engagement with the African American cultural left, see Washington 2014, specifically pages 69–122.

21. Eslanda Robeson responded to White's charges with a detailed defense of her husband's positions, which *Ebony* refused to print. In her response, Robeson targets the propaganda initiatives of the Truman administration. She contrasts the appointment of African American ambassadors to the United Nations and to Liberia and the millions allocated for the Voice of America program with the correspondingly little progress toward "improv[ing] the condition of the Negro People here, [and] Colored people anywhere" and the failure to "grant the Negro People and other Minorities their democratic rights" (Robeson 1951, 5). The article was subsequently published in the *California Eagle*, a Los Angeles black newspaper run by the Robesons' friend and fellow black radical Charlotta Bass. See Eslanda Robeson 1951.

22. For a carefully and persuasively argued treatment of this thesis, see Dudziak 2000 and Borstelmann 2001.

23. For an insightful discussion of the gendered implications of this insistence on African American loyalty as expressed through military service, see Friedman 2007, particularly pages 455–56.

24. *The Pittsburgh Courier* launched the "Double V" campaign in February of 1942. For a discussion of how the campaign extended to other black newspapers and into other areas of daily life, see Kimberley L. Phillips's *War! What Is Good For?: Black Freedom Struggles and the U.S. Military*, particularly pages 20–63.

25. The trade unionist A. Phillip Randolph repeats many of the charges that Wilkins's

editorial lodged against Robeson in a letter to the editor of the *New York Times*, published October 9, 1949, in response to the Peekskill concert riot. In this letter Randolph first rebuts the claim that racism motivated the American Legion and Veterans of Foreign Wars to disrupt Robeson's concert and imputes their action to fervid anticommunism. Randolph's primary objection, however, is to Robeson presuming to speak for African Americans in Paris at the World Peace Conference. Robeson, according to Randolph, "had no warrant to speak as the voice of the Negro people of America," particularly since "he has been chiefly associated with left-wing movements, with little, if any contact with the Negro masses." See Randolph 1949.

26. Other African American anticommunists, Richard Wright, Ralph Ellison, and Harold Cruse, to name the most obvious examples, also promoted this characterization.

27. A copy of the pamphlet can be found at the New York University's Tamiment Library, PAM 685. Unfortunately, the animosity generated by Paul Robeson Jr.'s selection of Martin Duberman to write the authorized biography of his father's life, despite a prior arrangement with Brown, means that not much is known about the extent of their collaboration. In an interview with Alice Childress, Duberman acknowledges that "Lloyd [Brown] did ghost-write *Here I Stand*, and Lloyd was close to him" (1984, 4). The interview can be found in the Alice Childress Papers, box 11, folder 13, Interview w/ Martin Duberman 10/9/84. Schomburg Manuscript and Archive Division.

28. The 1988 reissue of the text by Beacon Press also includes an introduction by the historian Sterling Stuckey and a 1971 preface by Lloyd Brown, Robeson's collaborator in the writing of the text.

29. What I am calling the black left position bears close affinities with the "autonomous" black radicalism that Brent Hayes Edwards maps in his introductory article for a special issue of *Social Text*. Like Edwards's black radicalism, Robeson's current of black leftism stakes out a "position and a praxis that [attends] to both class *and* race in promoting social transformation" (2001a, 2).

30. Writing of the post-1830 boom in slave narratives sponsored by antislavery societies, Sekora writes that "not black storytelling but white authentication made for usable narratives. . . . Letters testifying to . . . moral and intellectual character avowed that [the slave narrator] was reporting events as he knew them. . . . If the story of a former slave was thus sandwiched between white abolitionist documents, the story did carry the aegis of a movement preaching historical veracity." See Sekora 1987, 497.

31. Apparently his great-great-grandfather, Cyrus Bustill, a Quaker and owner of a profitable bakery, baked bread for Washington's troops during the 1777–1778 winter ordeal at Valley Forge; see Wright 2007, 122.

32. For a recent discussion of Mrs. Shipley's storied career in the State Department and the enormous power she wielded in deciding which U.S. citizens would be granted the legal authorization to travel outside the country, see Kahn 2013, particularly pages 97–124. It should also be noted that Shipley was the sister of the Bureau of Investigation (the precursor to the FBI) director A. Bruce Bielaski, who oversaw the first Red

Scare in the United States during World War I; see Fischer 2016, particularly pages 40-44.

33. Indeed, it was only in 1958 (the year *Here I Stand* was published) that the Eisenhower administration's policy toward Africa was not filtered through "the priority of America's NATO allies" or Africans' incapacity for self-government (Borstelmann 2001, 123).

34. For information on Sampson's career in government service, see Laville and Lucas 1996. In an epigraph to this article, the authors incorrectly attribute as Robeson's words in *Here I Stand* disparaging remarks about the individuals who participated. In the text, these words are quoted as the "rather unflattering comment about these individuals . . . recently made by a columnist in the New York *Amsterdam News.*" See Robeson 1958, 81. J. Saunders Redding wrote about his experience in India in a memoir titled *An American in India* (1954). The columns Carl Rowan wrote from India, Pakistan, and Southeast Asia were collected and published in a volume titled *The Pitiful and the Proud* (1956).

35. For an insightful discussion of the diplomatic maneuvering surrounding the submission of the *We Charge Genocide* petition by the Civil Rights Congress, see Anderson 2003, specifically pages 166–209, as well as Horne (1988) and Horne (2013). The other petitions were *A Petition to the United Nations on Behalf of 13 Million Oppressed Negro Citizens of the United States of America* submitted by the National Negro Congress in 1946 and *An Appeal to the World* submitted by the NAACP in 1947. See Borstelmann 2001, 299 note 149.

36. Robeson never mentions these people by name in *Here I Stand*, perhaps reflecting his principled refusal to engage in the kinds of ad hominem attacks of which he was most often on the receiving end during this period. This stance is in keeping with the text's overall tone of reconciliation and promotion of black solidarity above all differences. He was far more combative in a speech he gave to the first convention of the NNLC held in Cincinnati in 1951. In his address to the convention, Robeson stated, "The people know what's going on. It won't do for the Sampsons, the Grangers, and the Schuylers to be shouting about how good it is for Negroes in the United States today. No, they won't get away with that." Robeson Collection, microform, reel 8, slide #62.

37. The first concert was held in 1952, but the concerts would be held annually for the next three years. For an in-depth discussion of the concerts from the Canadian perspective, please see MacDowell 2003.

38. For a compelling argument on the liberal, as opposed to conservative, character of anticommunism, see Delton 2013. The insufficiency of liberalism to address the consequences of the systemic subjugation of African Americans is, however, made painfully obvious when Delton trumpets the fact "that beginning in the 1950s white people in positions of power devised and supported various measures, including legislation, to end racial discrimination and segregation in employment, education, housing, and public facilities" (2013, 3), but remains curiously silent on the fact that these same measures

provoked a violent reaction directed at African Americans from powerful and not so powerful whites.

39. The stance Robeson takes here, particularly the emphasis on independence, bears some resemblance to one taken by the West Indian Trotskyist (and sworn enemy of the CP) C.L.R. James in his "The Revolutionary Answer to the Negro Problem in the United States," a widely anthologized address from 1948 given to the Socialist Workers Party. In this address James declares that the "independent Negro movement . . . is in itself a constituent part of the struggle for socialism. In this was way we challenge directly any attempt to subordinate or to push to the rear the social and political significance of the independent Negro struggle for democratic rights" (James 1996, 139).

40. As early as 1971, Jack O'Dell offered a similar assessment of the place of organized labor in the black freedom movement, writing that "by the time the Second World War had ended, it was the industrial working class of the black community whose organizational strength was making the most profound impact on the outlook and style of the Freedom Movement" (2010, 200).

41. Richard Delgado (2002) develops this connection in his review of Mary Dudziak's *Cold War Civil Rights*.

Chapter 5

1. For more information on members of the American delegation and the reports they produced for "official and quasi-official consumption," see Gaines 2006, 91–103.

2. Aimé Césaire puts these pressures front and center of his consideration of Bunche's role in his representation of the events surrounding the Congo Crisis in *A Season in the Congo*. The play first mentions Bunche in the context of a conversation between Lumumba and Secretary-General Hammarskjöld, in which the secretary-general explains the organization's decision to not send troops into Katanga for fear of violent resistance from the local population. Upon hearing this explanation, Lumumba suggests that the leaders of the secession had made a fool of Bunche with their suggestion of possible resistance: "Katangese resistance? Tzumbi et M'siri may well laugh. . . . Your Bunche has allowed himself to be abused like a child." After considering the possibility that Bunche's decision was the result of his naivety, he reconsiders and suggests more sinister motives behind his actions: "Bunche made a mistake! Unless. . . . After all, Bunche is American." (Césaire 2010, 75–76). The reference to his nationality suggests that Bunche reached his decision to not move against the secessionist Katanga province because his goal "after all" was safeguarding the United States' interests in the province. In writing the scene this way, Césaire endorses the view held by Lumumba and others (and subsequently validated by the historical record) that Western powers supported the Katanga secessionists to further their own interests in the mineral-rich province.

3. Cynthia Young identifies Watts as On Guard's leader and spokesman (2006, 50).

4. In his article, Baldwin implies that it was when "Stevenson stated . . . that the

United States was 'against' colonialism" that the African Americans in the gallery visibly expressed their outrage (1961, 25). The distinction is important. By suggesting that it was disapproval of Hammarskjöld that was at issue, the *Times* report subtly implicates the Soviet Union. In the General Assembly's 1960 session the preceding year, the Soviets had made repeated calls for his resignation over U.N. actions in the Congo (Henry 1999, 202). Baldwin's account obviously highlights American duplicity in support of European colonial powers as the source of indignation: he mentions the recent U.S. abstention when the General Assembly voted on Algeria in December 1960 (1961, 25).

5. *The Omni-Americans* was the title of Albert Murray's collection of essays published in 1970. Murray along with Ellison became the most visible articulators of this position during the Black Power era, a time when its influence seems to have been waning.

6. For more on Mallory's history in the black freedom struggle, including her fight against school segregation in New York City and her work with Robert Williams in Monroe, North Carolina, see Foong (2010) and Farmer (2017).

7. The reference to Mecca appears to refer to the *Times* article of February 16, 1961, "Riot," which describes "a man in white Arab headdress," identified as "Mustafa Bashir," leading demonstrators in a march toward Time Square ("Riot," 10).

8. Robeson and *Freedom* are discussed in chapter 4 of the present work. For more on Shirley Graham Du Bois's role at *Freedom* and in these Black left circles more generally, see Horne (2000).

9. For more on Davis's role in the event and the general rapprochement between communists and nationalists, see Horne (1994).

10. According to Henry, the two had begun a lifelong friendship in the fall of 1945 when they traveled to London together. Stevenson was Edward R. Stettinius's deputy, whom Bunche was sent to advise at the Preparatory Commission of the United Nations. See Henry 1999, 138–39.

11. Make was an intimate associate of Maya Angelou's. Thanks to Ira Dworkin for bringing this to my attention.

12. This list of participants is found in Plummer 1996, 302.

13. This debate raged across the pages of several publications, among them a symposium in the *LA Review of Books*, June 13, 2011, the theories and methodologies section of PMLA 128, no. 2 (March 2013), 386–408, and a review, author response, and reviewer response in *Diacritics* 42, no. 4 (2014), 26–52.

Bibliography

Acheson, Dean. 1947. "The Requirements of Reconstruction." *Department of State Bulletin* 60, no. 411 (May 18): 991–94. *Hein Online*. Web. Sept. 3, 2015.

Aldridge, Daniel W. 2003. "A Militant Liberalism: Anti-Communism and the African American Intelligentsia, 1939–1955." December 2003 Conference Paper American Historical Association. Aug. 14, 2008. http://www.hartford-hwp.com/archives/45a/689.html.

Alliot, David. 2013. *"Le communisme est à l'ordre du jour": Aimé Césaire et le P.C.F., de l'engagement à la rupture (1935–1957): essai.* Paris: Pierre-Guillaume de Roux.

Alexis, Jacques Stephen. 1999 [1955]. *General Sun, My Brother.* Translated by Carrol F. Coates. Charlottesville: University Press of Virginia.

Althusser, Louis. 1971. *Lenin and Philosophy and Other Essays.* Translated by Ben Brewster. New York: Monthly Review Press.

Anderson, Carol. 2003. *Eyes Off the Prize: The United Nations and the African American Struggle for Human Rights, 1944–1955.* New York: Cambridge University Press.

Anderson, Kevin. 2010. *Marx at the Margins: On Nationalism, Ethnicity, and Non-Western Societies.* Chicago: University of Chicago Press.

Anthony, David Henry. 2006. *Max Yergan: Race Man, Internationalist, Cold Warrior.* New York: New York University Press.

Aptheker, Herbert. 1985. Editor. *Against Racism: Unpublished Essays, Papers, Addresses, 1887–1961.* Amherst: University of Massachusetts Press.

Arnesen, Eric. 2012. "Civil Rights and the Cold War at Home: Postwar Activism, Anticommunism, and the Decline of the Left." *American Communist History* 11, no. 1: 5–44. *Academic Search Complete.* Web. July 23, 2015.

Baldwin, James. 1961. "A Negro Assays the Negro Mood." *The New York Times.* 12 March 1961, SM25, 103-4. Web. *ProQuest Historical Newspapers.* 4 April 2014.

Baldwin, James. 1998a. "Alas, Poor Richard." In *Collected Essays*, edited by Toni Morrison, 247–68. New York: Library of America.

Baldwin, James. 1998b. "Princes and Powers." In *Collected Essays*, edited by Toni Morrison, 143–69. New York: Library of America.

Baraka, Amiri. 1984. *The Autobiography of LeRoi Jones*. New York: Freundlich Books.

Barnhisel, Greg. 2015. *Cold War Modernists: Art, Literature, and American Cultural Diplomacy*. New York: Columbia University Press.

Bell, Derrick. 1980. "*Brown v. Board of Education* and the Interest-Convergence Dilemma." *Harvard Law Review* 93, no. 3: 518–533. *JSTOR*. April 4, 2012.

Bell, Kevin. 2007. *Ashes Taken for Fire: Aesthetic Modernism and the Critique of Identity*. Minneapolis: University of Minnesota Press.

Belletto, Steven. 2012. *No Accident, Comrade: Chance and Design in Cold War American Narratives*. New York: Oxford University Press.

Berghahn, Volker R. 2001. *America and the Intellectual Cold Wars in Europe*. Princeton, NJ: Princeton University Press.

Berman, Marshall. 1988. *All That Is Solid Melts Into Air: The Experience of Modernity*. 2nd. ed. New York: Penguin.

Biondi, Martha. 2003. *To Stand and Fight: The Struggle for Civil Rights in Postwar New York City*. Cambridge, MA: Harvard University Press.

Boggs, James. 1970. "Liberalism, Marxism, and Black Political Power." In *Racism and the Class Struggle: Further Pages from a Black Worker's Notebook*, 26–32. New York: Monthly Review Press.

Bond, Horace Mann. 1956. "Report on the First Congress of Negro Writers and Artists Held in Paris, France, The Sorbonne, September 19–22, 1956." Horace Mann Bond, Council on Race and Caste in World Affairs, August 13, 1956—October 23, 1956. Horace Mann Bond Papers (MS 411). Special Collections and University Archives, University of Massachusetts Amherst Libraries. mums411 -b034-f016.

Bond, Ruth Clement. 1992. Interview. By Jewell Fenzi. November 12, 1992. The Association for Diplomatic Studies and Training Foreign Affairs Oral History Program Foreign Service Spouse Series. Frontline Diplomacy, Manuscript Division, Library of Congress, Washington, D.C.

Borstelmann, Thomas. 2001. *The Cold War and the Color Line: American Race Relations in the Global Arena*. Cambridge, MA: Harvard University Press.

Brogi, Alessandro. 2011. *Confronting America: The Cold War Between the United States and the Communists in France and Italy*. Chapel Hill: University of North Carolina Press.

Brown, J. Dillon. 2006. "Exile and Cunning: The Tactical Difficulties of George Lamming." *Contemporary Literature* 47, no. 4: 669–94. *Project Muse*. Web. March 14, 2008.

Brown, Lloyd L. 1988 [1971]. Preface. In *Here I Stand*, by Paul Robeson, xxv–xxxvi. Boston: Beacon Press.

Buck-Morss, Susan. 2000. "Hegel and Haiti." *Critical Inquiry* 26, no. 4: 821–65. *JSTOR*. Web. June 11, 2008.

Burnham, Louis. 1949. "Freedom—Paul Robeson's Paper: A Prospectus." James and Esther Cooper Jackson Papers, Tamiment Library and Robert F. Wagner Labor Archives, New York University.

Cailler, Bernadette. 2013. "Interface: Aimé Césaire's "Poésie et connaissance" and Lorand Gasper's *Approche de la parole* Revisited." *Comparative Literature Studies* 50, no. 3: 415–29. JSTOR. Web. April 3, 2015.

Campbell, James. 1995. *Exiled in Paris: Richard Wright, James Baldwin, Samuel Beckett, and Others on the Left Bank.* New York: Scribner.

Carleton, Don. 2014 [1985]. *Red Scare: Right-Wing Hysteria, Fifties Fanaticism, and Their Legacy in Texas.* Austin: University of Texas Press.

Carr, Barry. 1998. "Identity, Class, and Nation: Black Immigrant Workers, Cuban Communism, and the Sugar Insurgency, 1925–1934." *The Hispanic American Historical Review* 78 no. 1: 83–116. JSTOR. Web. November 20, 2014.

Casanova, Pascale. 2004. *The World Republic of Letters.* Translated by M. B. DeBevoise. Cambridge, MA: Harvard University Press.

"The Case of Paul Robeson." *The New York Times*, April 25, 1949, 22. *ProQuest Historical Newspapers.* Web. January 16, 2011.

Césaire, Aimé. 1956a. "Culture and Colonization." Translated by Brent Hayes Edwards. *Social Text* 103 28, no. 2 (Summer 2010): 127–44. *Duke University Press Journals ONLINE.* Web. July 13, 2015. "Culture et Colonisation." *Présence Africaine* (June–Nov. 1956): 190–205. Print.

Césaire, Aimé. 1956b. *Letter to Maurice Thorez.* Translated by Chike Jeffers. *Social Text. Social Text* 103 28, no. 2 (Summer 2010): 145–52. *Duke University Press Journals ONLINE.* Web. July 13, 2015. *Une Lettre à Maurice Thorez.* Paris: Présence Africaine, 1956.

Césaire, Aimé. 1990. "Poetry and Knowledge." Translated by Clayton Eshleman and Annette Smith. In *Lyric and Dramatic Poetry, 1946–82.* Charlottesville: University Press of Virginia.

Césaire, Aimé. 2010 [1966]. *A Season in the Congo.* Translated by Gayatri Chakravorty Spivak. London: Seagull Books.

Césaire, Suzanne. 2012. "Alain and Esthetics." In *The Great Camouflage: Writings of Dissent (1941–1945)*, 11–18. Edited by Daniel Maximin. Translated by Keith L. Walker. Middletown, CT: Wesleyan University Press.

Chakrabarty, Dipesh. 2000. *Provincializing Europe: Postcolonial Thought and Historical Difference.* Princeton, NJ: Princeton University Press, 2000. Print.

Childress, Alice. 1950. "Just a Little Simple." Alice Childress Papers, box 38, folder 5. New York Public Library, Schomburg Center for Research in Black Culture.

Childress, Alice. 1954. "Old Master Said to Jim: 'You Got Your Faults and I Got Mine.'" *Freedom* 4, no. 5 (August): 8. Web. Tamiment Library & Robert F. Wagner Labor Archives at New York University. Feb. 8, 2019.

Childress, Alice. 1983. Interview with Martin Duberman (typescript). Alice Childress

Papers, Box 9, folder 13. New York Public Library, Schomburg Center for Research in Black Culture.

Childress, Alice. 1986 [1956]. *Like One of the Family*. Boston: Beacon Press.

Coates, Carrol F. 1999. Introduction. In *General Sun, My Brother*, by Jacques Stephen Alexis, ix–xxxviii. Translated by Carrol F. Coates. Charlottesville: University Press of Virginia.

Coats, Geoffrey. 1997. "From Whence We Come: Alioune Diop and Saint-Louis, Senegal." *Research in African Literature* 28, no. 4: 206–19.

Colby, Jason M. *The Business of Empire: United Fruit, Race, and U.S. Expansion in Central America*. Ithaca: Cornell University Press, 2011. Print.

Coleman, Peter. *The Liberal Conspiracy: The Congress for Cultural Freedom and the Struggle for the Mind of Postwar Europe*. New York: The Free Press, 1989.

Cook, Mercer. 1945. Letter to W.E.B. Du Bois. January 9. *W.E.B. Du Bois Papers* (MS 312). Special Collections and University Archives, University of Massachusetts, Amherst Libraries. *Credo*. Web. Oct. 23, 2015.

Cook, Mercer. 1948. "Education in Haiti." Bulletin 1948, no. 1. Washington, DC: U.S. Office of Education.

Cook, Mercer, trans. 1957. "A Distinguished Martinican Leaves the Communists." Translation of Césaire's *Une Lettre à Maurice Thorez*. *The Crisis* (March): 154–56.

Cook, Vashti Smith. 1945. Letter to Ellen Irene Diggs. February 8, 1945. W. E. B. Du Bois Papers (MS 312). Special Collections and University Archives, University of Massachusetts, Amherst Libraries. *Credo*. Web. 23 Oct. 2015.

Cooper, Frederick. 2014. *Citizenship Between Empire and Nation: Remaking France and French Africa, 1945–1960*. Princeton, NJ: Princeton University Press.

Crawford, Neta C. 2010. "Decolonization through Trusteeship: The Legacy of Ralph Bunche." In *Trustee for the Human Community: Ralph J. Bunche, the United Nations, and the Decolonization of Africa*, edited by Robert A. Hill and Edmond J. Keller, 93–115. Athens, OH: Ohio University Press.

Crossman, Richard, ed. 1965 [1950]. Introduction. In *The God That Failed*, 1–10. New York: Bantam Books.

Dalleo, Raphael. 2011. *Caribbean Literature and the Public Sphere: From the Plantation to the Postcolonial*. Charlottesville: University of Virginia Press.

Dash, J. Michael. 1978 [1947]. Introduction. In *Masters of the Dew*, by Jacques Roumain, 5–21. Translated by Langston Hughes and Mercer Cook. Portsmouth, NH: Heinemann.

Dash, J. Michael. 1981. *Literature and Ideology in Haiti, 1915–1961*. Totowa, NJ: Barnes & Noble Books.

Dash, J. Michael. 1997. *Haiti and the United States: National Stereotypes and the Literary Imagination*. New York: St. Martin's Press.

Dash, J. Michael. 1998. *The Other America: Caribbean Literature in a New World Context*. Charlottesville: University Press of Virginia.

Dash, J. Michael. 2013. "Afterword: Neither France nor Senegal: Bovarysme and Haiti's Hemispheric Identity." In Haiti and the Americas, 219–30. Edited by Carla Calargé, Raphael Dalleo, Luis Duno-Gottberg, and Cleavis Headley. Jackson: University Press of Mississippi.

Davies, Carole Boyce. 2001. "Deportable Subjects: U.S. Immigration Laws and the Criminalizing of Communism." South Atlantic Quarterly 100, no. 4 (Fall): 949–66. Duke University Press Online. Web. July 2, 2014.

Dawson, Michael C. 2013. Blacks in and out of the Left. Cambridge, MA: Harvard University Press.

"Debats." 1956. Présence Africaine 8–10 (June–Nov.): 66–83.

Delgado, Richard. 2002. "Explaining the Rise and Fall of African American Fortunes— Interest Convergence and Civil Rights Gains." Harvard Civil Rights-Civil Liberties Law Review 37: 369–87. LexisNexis Academic. March 18, 2012.

Delton, Jennifer A. 2013. Rethinking the 1950s: How Anticommunism and the Cold War Made America Liberal. New York: Cambridge University Press.

Denning, Michael. 1996. The Cultural Front: The Laboring of American Culture in the Twentieth-Century. New York: Verso.

Denning, Michael. 2004. Culture in the Age of Three Worlds. New York: Verso.

De Santis, Christopher, ed. 1995. Langston Hughes and the Chicago Defender: Essays on Race, Politics, and Culture, 1942–1962. Urbana: University of Illinois Press.

Diawara, Manthia. 1998. In Search of Africa. Cambridge, MA: Harvard University Press.

Diop, Alioune. 1947. "Niam n'goura or Présence Africaine's raison d'être." Translated by Richard Wright and Thomas Diop. Présence Africaine 1 (Oct.–Nov.): 185–92. The French original appears in the same issue, 7–14.

Diop, Alioune. 1956. "Opening Remarks" [Discours d'Ouverture]. Présence Africaine 8-10 (June–Nov.): 9–18.

"A Distinguished Martinican Leaves the Communists." 1957. Translated by Mercer Cook. The Crisis 64, no. 3 (March): 154–56.

Dolinar, Brian. 2012. The Black Cultural Front: Black Writers and Artists of the Depression Generation. Jackson: University Press of Mississippi.

Duberman, Martin B. 1989. Paul Robeson. New York: Knopf.

Duberman, Martin B. 1984. Interview with Alice Childress. Alice Childress Papers, box 11, folder 13, Interview w/Martin Duberman 10/9/84. Side 2, page 4. Schomburg Manuscript and Archive Division.

Du Bois, W.E.B. 1943. "Reconstruction, Seventy-Five Years After." Phylon 4, no. 3: 205–12. JSTOR. Web Oct. 28, 2015.

Du Bois, W.E.B. 1944. Letter to Camille Lhérisson September 14, 1944. Travaux du Congrès International de Philosophie. Port-au-Prince: Imprimerie de l'Etat.

Du Bois, W.E.B. 1945. Color and Democracy: Colonies and Peace. New York: Harcourt, Brace and Co.

Du Bois, W.E.B. 1985a. "Colonialism, Democracy, and Peace after the War." In Against

Racism: Unpublished Essays, Papers, Addresses, 1887–1961, edited by Herbert Aptheker, 229–43. Amherst: University of Massachusetts Press.

Du Bois, W.E.B. 1985b. "The Meaning of Education." In *Against Racism: Unpublished
Essays, Papers, Addresses, 1887–1961,* edited by Herbert Aptheker, 249–52. Amherst:
University of Massachusetts Press.

Du Bois, W.E.B. 1989 [1903]. *Souls of Black Folks.* New York: Bantam.

Du Bois, W.E.B. 1998 [1935]. *Black Reconstruction in America.* New York: Free Press.

Dudziak, Mary L. 2000. *Cold War Civil Rights: Race and the Image of American Democracy.* Princeton, NJ: Princeton University Press.

Dunham, Katherine. 1969. *Island Possessed.* Chicago: University of Chicago Press.

Dunnigan, Alice. 1956. "U.S. Needs to Clean Up Mississippi, Alabama!" *Pittsburgh Courier,* 23 June, p. 27. *ProQuest Historical Newspapers.* Web. July 4, 2014.

Dworkin, Ira. 2017. *Congo Love Song: African American Culture and the Crisis of the Colonial State.* Chapel Hill: University of North Carolina Press.

Eagleton, Terry. 2000. *The Idea of Culture.* Oxford: Blackwell Publishers.

Eastland, James O. 1955. "We've reached era of judicial tyranny." December 1, 1955. Uni-
versity of Southern Mississippi. McCain Library and Archives, M393 McCain
(William D.) Pamphlet Collection. Civil Rights in Mississippi Digital Archive.
Web. July 3, 2014.

Edwards, Brent Hayes. 2001a. "Introduction: The Autonomy of Black Radicalism." *Social Text* 19, no. 2 (Summer): 1–13. *Project Muse.* Web. December 7, 2008.

Edwards, Brent Hayes. 2001b. "The Uses of Diaspora." *Social Text* 19, no. 1 (Spring): 45–
73. *Project Muse.* Web. December 7, 2008.

Edwards, Brent Hayes. 2003. *The Practice of Diaspora: Literature, Translation, and the
Rise of Black Internationalism.* Cambridge, MA: Harvard University Press.

Edwards, Brent Hayes. 2010. "Introduction: *Césaire in 1956.*" *Social Text* 28, no. 2 (Summer): 115–25. *Duke University Press Journals ONLINE.* Web. July 13, 2015.

Esty, Jed. 2004. *A Shrinking Island: Modernism and National Culture in England.* Princeton, NJ: Princeton University Press.

Espinosa, J. Manuel. 1976. *Inter-American beginnings of U. S. cultural diplomacy, 1936–
1948.* Washington, D. C.: Bureau of Educational and Cultural Affairs, U. S. Dept. of
State, U. S. Govt. Print. Off.

Evans, Martin, and John Phillips. 2007. *Algeria: Anger of the Dispossessed.* New Haven,
CT: Yale University Press.

Fabre, Michel. 1993. *The Unfinished Quest of Richard Wright.* 2nd ed. Translated by Isabel
Barzun. Urbana: University of Illinois Press.

Farmer, Ashley. 2017. *Remaking Black Power: How Black Women Transformed an Era.*
Chapel Hill: University of North Carolina Press.

Fejzula, Merve. 2016. "Women and the 1956 Congress of Black Writers and Artists in
Paris." *Black Perspectives.* Nov. 3, 2016. Web. Accessed Nov. 7, 2016.

Filostrat, Christopher. 2008. *Negritude Agonistes: Assimilation against Nationalism in the
French-Speaking Caribbean and Guyane.* Cherry Hill. Africana Homestead Legacy.

Fischer, Nick. 2016. *Spider Web: The Birth of American Anticommunism*. Urbana: University of Illinois Press.

Foong, Yie. 2010. "Frame Up in Monroe: The Mae Mallory Story." Masters Thesis. Sarah Lawrence College. Dissertation and Theses Databases (ProQuest Only). Web. 15 October 2015.

Foray, Philippe. 1993. "Alain (1868–1951)." *Prospects: The Quarterly Review of Comparative Education* 23, no. 1–2: 21–37.

Fowler, Carolyn. 1980. *A Knot in the Thread: The Life and Work of Jacques Roumain*. Washington, D.C.: Howard University Press.

Frederick, Rhonda. 2005. *"Colón Man a Come": Mythographies of Panama Canal Migration*. Lanham, MD: Lexington Books.

Friedman, Andrea. 2007. "The Strange Career of Annie Lee Moss: Rethinking Race, Gender, and McCarthyism." *Journal of American History*, September: 445–68. *Oxford Journals Online*. Web. July 26, 2012.

Frioux-Salgas, Sarah. 2009. "*Présence Africaine*: une tribune, un movement, un réseau." *Gradhiva* 10: 4–21. https://gradhiva.revues.org/1475. Web. June 4, 2011.

Fullilove, Mindy Thompson. 1978. "The National Negro Labor Council: A History." Occasional Paper No. 27. New York: American Institute for Marxist Studies.

Gaines, Kevin. 2006. *American Africans in Ghana: Black Expatriates and the Civil Rights Era*. Chapel Hill: University of North Carolina Press.

Gaines, Kevin. 2009. "Revisiting Richard Wright in Ghana." *Social Text* 67 19, no. 2 (Summer): 75–101. *Project Muse*. Web. January 11, 2009.

Gates, Henry Louis, Jr. and K. A. Appiah. 1993. *Richard Wright: Critical Perspectives Past and Present*. New York: Amistad.

Gikandi, Simon. 1992. *Writing in Limbo: Modernism and Caribbean Literature*. Ithaca, NY: Cornell University Press.

Gikandi, Simon. 2004a. "Poststructuralism and Postcolonial Discourse." In *The Cambridge Companion to Postcolonial Literary Studies*, edited by Neil Lazarus, 97–119. Cambridge: Cambridge University Press.

Gikandi, Simon. 2004b. "Race and Cosmopolitanism." *American Literary History* 14, no. 3: 593–615. *Project Muse*. Web. November 25, 2004.

Gildea, Robert. 2002. *France since 1945*. 2nd ed. Oxford: Oxford University Press.

Gilroy, Paul. 1993. *The Black Atlantic: Modernity and Double Consciousness*. Cambridge, MA: Harvard University Press.

Giroud, Vincent. 2015. *Nicolas Nabokov: A Life in Freedom and Music*. New York: Oxford University Press.

Goodman, Jordan. 2013. *Paul Robeson: A Watched Man*. New York: Verso.

Gordon, Avery F. 2008. *Ghostly Matters: Haunting and the Sociological Imagination*. New ed. Minneapolis: University of Minnesota Press.

Gore, Dayo F. 2011. *Radicalism at the Crossroads*. New York: New York University Press.

Goluboff, Risa. 2007. *The Lost Promise of Civil Rights*. Cambridge, MA: Harvard University Press.

Gramsci, Antonio. 1971. *Selections from the Prison Notebooks*. Edited and translated by Quintin Hoare and Geoffrey Nowell Smith. New York: International Publishers.

Guinier, Lani. 2004. "From Racial Liberalism to Racial Literacy: *Brown v. Board of Education* and the Interest-Divergence Dilemma." *Journal of American History* 91, no. 1: 92–118. *JSTOR*. Web. June 19, 2011.

Hale Thomas A., and Kora Véron. 2009. "Aimé Césaire's Break From the Parti Communiste Français: Nouveaux élans, nouveaux défis." *French Politics, Culture & Society* 27, no. 3: 47–62. *Academic Search Complete*. Web. March 17, 2016.

Halila, Souad. 1988. "The Intellectual Development and Diplomatic Career of Ralph J. Bunche: The Afro-American, Africanist, and Internationalist." PhD dissertation, University of Southern California. *Dissertation and Theses Databases (ProQuest Only)*. Web. 18 October 2015.

Hall, James C. 2001. *Mercy, Mercy Me: African-American Culture and the American Sixties*. Oxford: Oxford University Press.

Halpern, Martin. 1997. "'I'm Fighting for Freedom': Coleman Young, HUAC, and the Detroit African American Community." *Journal of American Ethnic History* 17, no. 1: 19–38. *JSTOR*. Web. November 19, 2010.

Hansberry, Lorraine. 1961. "Congolese Patriot." *The New York Times*. 26 March 1961, SM4. Web. *ProQuest Historical Newspapers*. 11 April 2014

Harper, Donna Akiba Sullivan, ed. 1994. *Langston Hughes: The Return of Simple*. New York: Hill and Wang.

Harper, Donna Akiba Sullivan. 1995. *Not So Simple: The "Simple" Stories by Langston Hughes*. Columbia: University of Missouri Press.

Harris, Trudier. 1986. Introduction. In *Like One of the Family by Alice Childress, xi–xxxiv*. Boston: Beacon Press.

Harvey, David. 2003. *Paris, Capital of Modernity*. New York: Routledge.

Hassan, Salah D. 1999. "Inaugural Issues: The Cultural Politics of the Early *Présence Africaine*, 1947–1955." *Research in African Literature* 30, no. 2: 194–221. *Project Muse*. Web. March 24, 2008.

Henry, Charles. 1999. *Ralph Bunche: Model Negro or American Other*. New York: New York University Press.

Hickman, Nollie W. 1986. "Black Labor in the Forest Industries of the Piney Woods, 1840–1933. In *Mississippi's Piney Woods*, edited by Noel Polk. Jackson: University Press of Mississippi.

Higashida, Cheryl. 2012. *Black Internationalist Feminism: Women Writers of the Black Left, 1945–1995*. Urbana: University of Illinois Press.

Himes, Chester. 1972. *The Quality of Hurt: The Autobiography of Chester Himes, vol. 1*. Garden City, NY: Doubleday.

Hitchcock, William I. *France Restored: Cold War Diplomacy and the Quest for Leadership in Europe, 1944–1954*. Chapel Hill: The University of North Carolina Press, 1998. Print.

Holder, Daniel. 2012. "I Got a Home in That Rock": Paul Robeson's *Here I Stand* and Cold War Resistance to McCarthyism." *a/b: Auto/Biography Studies* 27, no. 1: 67–100. *Project Muse*. Web. October 21, 2013.

Holloway, Jonathan Scott. 2002. *Confronting the Veil: Abram Harris, Jr. E. Franklin Frazier, and Ralph Bunche, 1919-1941*. Chapel Hill: University of North Carolina Press.

Hook, Sidney. 1949. "Report on the International Day Against Dictatorship and War." *Partisan Review* 16, no. 7: 722–32.

Hook, Sidney. 1950. "The Berlin Congress for Cultural Freedom." *Partisan Review* 17, no. 7: 715–22.

Horne, Gerald. 1986. *Black and Red: W. E. B. DuBois and the Afro-American Response to the Cold War 1944–1963*. Albany: State University of New York Press.

Horne, Gerald. 1988. *Communist Front?: The Civil Rights Congress, 1946–1956*. Rutherford, NJ: Fairleigh Dickinson University Press.

Horne, Gerald. 1994. *Black Liberation/Red Scare: Ben Davis and the Communist Party*. Newark, Del.: University of Delaware Press.

Horne, Gerald. 2000. *Race Woman: The Lives of Shirley Graham Du Bois*. New York: New York University Press.

Horne, Gerald. 2005. *Red Seas: Ferdinand Smith and radical black sailors in the United States and Jamaica*. New York: New York University Press.

Horne, Gerald. 2013. *Black Revolutionary: William Patterson and the Globalization of the African American Freedom Struggle*. Urbana: University of Illinois Press.

Horne, Gerald. 2016. *Paul Robeson: The Artist as Revolutionary*. London: Pluto Press.

Horton, Carol A. 2005. *Race and the Making of American Liberalism*. Oxford: Oxford University Press.

Howlett, Jacques. 1958. "Présence Africaine 1947–1958." *Journal of Negro History* 43, no. 2: 140–50. *JSTOR*. Web. April 5, 2007.

Hunt, Michael H. 2007. *The American Ascendancy: How the United States Gained and Wielded Global Dominance*. Chapel Hill: University of North Carolina Press.

Iton, Richard. 2000. *Solidarity Blues: Race, Culture, and the American Left*. Chapel Hill: University of North Carolina Press.

Iton, Richard. 2008. *In Search of the Black Fantastic*. New York: Oxford University Press.

Jackson, Lawrence. 2000. "Birth of the Critic: The Literary Friendship of Ralph Ellison and Richard Wright." *American Literature* 72, no. 2: 321–55. *Project Muse*. Web. Jan. 26, 2016.

Jackson, Lawrence. 2011. *The Indignant Generation: A Narrative History of African American Writers and Critics, 1934–1960*. Princeton, NJ: Princeton University Press.

James, C.L.R. 1970. "Paul Robeson: Black Star." *Black World*, November: 106–15.

James, C.L.R. 1992. *The C.L.R. James Reader*. Edited by Anna Grimshaw. Malden, MA: Blackwell Publishers.

James, C.L.R. 1996. "The Revolutionary Answer to the Negro Problem in the United States." In *C.L.R. James on the 'Negro Question,'* edited by Scott McLemee, 138–47. Jackson: University Press of Mississippi.

James, C.L.R., and Constance Webb. 1996. *Special Delivery: The Letters of C.L.R. to Constance Webb, 1939–1948*. Edited by Anna Grimshaw. Malden, MA: Blackwell Publishers.

James, Winston. 1998. *Holding Aloft the Banner: Caribbean Radicalism in Early Twentieth-Century America*. New York: Verso.

Janken, Kenneth R. 1998. "From Colonial Liberation to Cold War Liberalism: Walter White, the NAACP, and Foreign Affairs, 1941–1955." *Ethnic and Racial Studies* 21: 1074–95. *JSTOR*. Web. Sept. 15, 2008.

Jones, Clauda. 1949. "An End to the Neglect of the Problems of the Negro Woman!" *Political Affairs* 28, no. 6: 51–67.

Jones, William P. 2005. *The Tribe of Black Ulysses: African American Lumber Workers in the Jim Crow South*. Urbana: University of Illinois Press.

Joseph, Miranda. 2002. *Against the Romance of Community*. Minneapolis: University of Minnesota Press.

Jules-Rosette, Bennetta. 1992. "Conjugating Cultural Realities: *Présence Africaine*." In *The Surreptitious Speech*, edited by V. Y. Mudimbe, 14–44. Chicago: University of Chicago Press.

Jules-Rosette, Bennetta. 1998. *Black Paris: The African Writers' Landscape*. Urbana: University of Illinois Press.

Kahn, Jeffrey. 2013. *Mrs. Shipley's Ghost: The Right to Travel and Terrorist Watchlists*. Ann Arbor: University of Michigan Press.

Kanza, Thomas. 1979. *The Rise and Fall of Patrice Lumumba: Conflict in the Congo*. Boston: G. K. Hall.

Kaussen, Valerie. 2008. *Migrant Revolutions: Haitian Literature, Globalization, and U. S. Imperialism*. Lanham, MD: Lexington Books.

Keith, Joseph. 2013. *Unbecoming Americans: Writing Race and Nation from the Shadows of Citizenship, 1945–1960*. New Brunswick, NJ: Rutgers University Press.

Kelley, Robin D. G. 1996. "The Riddle of the Zoot: Malcolm Little and Black Cultural Politics during World War II." In *Race Rebels: Culture, Politics, and the Black Working Class*, 161–82. New York: Free Press.

Kemedjio, Cilas. 2010. "Aimé Césaire's *Letter to Maurice Thorez*: The Practice of Decolonization." Translated by R. H. Mitch. *Research in African Literatures* 41, no. 1: 87–108. *Project Muse*. Web. March 3, 2016.

Kennan, George. 1947. "The Sources of Soviet Conduct." *Foreign Affairs* 25, no. 4: 566–82. *JSTOR*. Web. October 14, 2011.

Kilson, Martin. 2007. "Political Scientists and the Activist-Technocrat Dichotomy: The Case of John Aubrey Davis." In *African American Perspectives on Political Science*, edited by Wilbur Rich. Philadelphia: Temple University Press. *ProQuest ebrary*. Web. April 21, 2015.

King, Richard. 2004. *Race, Culture, and the Intellectuals: 1940–1970*. Baltimore: Johns Hopkins University Press.

Korstad, Robert Rodgers. 2003. *Civil Rights Unionism: Tobacco Workers and the Struggle for Democracy in the Mid-Twentieth-Century South*. Chapel Hill: University of North Carolina Press. *Ebrary*. Web. July 24, 2014.

Krenn, Michael. 1999. *Black Diplomacy: African Americans and the State Department, 1945–69*. Armonk, NY: M. E. Sharpe.

Kristmanson, Mark. 2003. *Plateaus of Freedom: Nationality, Culture and State Security in Canada, 1940–1960*. Oxford: Oxford University Press.

Kruse, Cornelius. 1945. "International Congress in Haiti." *The Journal of Philosophy* 42, no. 2: 29–39. *JSTOR*. Web. Nov. 1, 2015.

Kruse, Kevin M., and Stephen Tuck, ed. 2012. "Introduction: The Second World War and the Civil Rights Movement." In *Fog of War: The Second World War and the Civil Rights Movement*. New York: Oxford University Press.

Kuklick, Bruce. 2008. *Black Philosopher, White Academy: The Career of William Fontaine*. Philadelphia: University of Pennsylvania Press.

Lamming, George. 1972. Interview. In *Kas-Kas: Interviews with Three Caribbean Writers in Texas, 5-21*. Edited by Ian Munro and Reinhard Sander. Austin, TX: African and Afro-American Research Institute, University of Texas at Austin.

Lamming, George. 1991 [1953]. *In the Castle of My Skin*. Ann Arbor: University of Michigan Press.

Lamming, George. 1992 [1960]. *The Pleasures of Exile*. Ann Arbor: University of Michigan Press.

Lamphere, Lawrence. 2003. "Paul Robeson, *Freedom* Newspaper, and the Black Press." PhD dissertation, Boston College. *Dissertation and Theses Databases (ProQuest Only)*. Web. September 10, 2014.

Lang, Clarence. 2009. "Freedom Train Derailed: The National Negro Labor Council and the Nadir of Black Radicalism." In *Anticommunism and the African American Freedom Movement: "Another Side of the Story,"* edited by Robbie Lieberman and Clarence Lang. New York: Palgrave Macmillan.

Laville, Helen, and Scott Lucas. 1996. "The American Way: Edith Sampson, the NAACP, and African American Identity in the Cold War. *Diplomatic History* 20, no. 4: 565–90. *Academic Search Complete*. Web. July 24, 2014.

Leffler, Melvyn P. 1992. *A Preponderance of Power: National Security, the Truman Administration, and the Cold War*. Stanford, CA: Stanford University Press.

Leiner, Jacqueline. 1993. Entretien avec Aimé Césaire, Paris 1975. In *Aimé Césaire: Le Terreau Primordial*, 111–128. Tübingen: Gunter Nar Verlag.

Lewis-Colman, David M. 2008. *Race against Liberalism: Black Workers and the UAW in Detroit*. Urbana-Champaign: University of Illinois Press.

Lichtenstein, Grace. 1977. "Fund Backs Controversial Study of 'Racial Betterment.'" *New York Times*, Dec. 11, p. 76. *ProQuest Historical Newspapers*. Web. February 21, 2014.

Lipman, Jana K. 2009. *Guantánamo: A Working-Class History between Empire and Revolution*. Berkeley: University of California Press.

Little, Douglas. 1990. "Cold War and Colonialism in Africa: The United States, France, and the Madagascar Revolt of 1947." *Pacific Historical Review* 59, no. 4: 527–52. *JSTOR*. October 7, 2012.

Logan, Rayford. 1943. Letter to W.E.B. Du Bois. October 18, 1943. W.E.B. Du Bois Papers (MS 312). Special Collections and University Archives, University of Massachusetts, Amherst Libraries. *Credo*. Web. Oct. 23, 2015.

Lyon, Hugh Lee. 1973. *Leontyne Price: Highlights of a Prima Donna*. New York: Vantage Press.

MacDowell, Laurel Sefton. 2003. "Paul Robeson in Canada: A Border Story." *Labour / Le Travail* 51 (Spring): 177–221. *JSTOR* Web. Sept. 16, 2003.

Major, John. 1993. *Prize Possession: The United States and the Panama Canal, 1903–1979*. New York: Cambridge University Press.

Marable, Manning. 1991. *Race, Reform, and Rebellion: The Second Reconstruction in Black America, 1945–1990*. 2nd ed. Jackson: University Press of Mississippi.

Martin, Waldo E., Jr. 2005. *No Coward Soldiers: Black Cultural Politics and Postwar America*. Cambridge, MA: Harvard University Press.

Marx, Karl. 1978a [1852]. *The Eighteenth Brumaire of Louis Bonaparte*. *The Marx-Engels Reader*. Edited by Robert C. Tucker, 2nd ed., 594–617 New York: Norton.

Marx, Karl. 1978b. "Manifesto of the Communist Party." In *The Marx-Engels Reader*. 2nd ed. Edited by Robert C. Tucker. New York: W. W. Norton.

Marx, Karl. 1990. *Capital, Vol. I*. Translated by Ben Fowkes. New York: Penguin Classics.

Marx, Karl. 1992a [1975]. "A Contribution to the Critique of Hegel's *Philosophy of Right*. Introduction." In *Early Writings*. Translated by Rodney Livingstone and Gregor Benton, 243–58. New York: Penguin.

Marx, Karl. 1992b [1975]. "On the Jewish Question." In *Early Writings*. Translated by Rodney Livingstone and Gregor Benton, 211–42. New York: Penguin.

Maspero, Francois. 2002. *Les abeilles & la guêpe*, Paris: Éditions du Seuil.

Maxwell, William J. 2015. *F. B. Eyes: How J. Edgar Hoover's Ghostreaders Framed African American Literature*. Princeton, NJ: Princeton University Press.

McCarthy, Patrick. 1985. "Sartre, Nizan and the Dilemmas of Political Commitment." *Yale French Studies* 68: 191–205. *JSTOR*. Web. March 15, 2016.

McDonald, Kathlene. 2012. *Feminism, the Left, and Postwar Literary Culture*. Jackson: University Press of Mississippi.

McDuffie, Erik S. 2011. *Sojourning for Freedom: Black Women, American Communism, and the Making of Black Left Feminism*. Durham, NC: Duke University Press.

McLean, Jr, Lieutenant Commander Ephraim R. 1941. "The Caribbean-An American Lake." *Proceedings of the United States Naval Institute*. July 1941: 947–52.

Melamed, Jodi. 2011. *Represent and Destroy: Rationalizing Violence in the New Racial Capitalism*. Minneapolis: University of Minnesota Press.

"Mercer Cook." 1943. *Cahiers d'Haïti*, October: 6.

Meriwether, James H. 2002. *Proudly We Can Be Africans: Black Americans and Africa, 1935–1961*. Chapel Hill: University of North Carolina Press.

Miller, Christopher. 1992. "Alioune Diop and the Unfinished Temple of Knowledge." In *The Surreptitious Speech*, edited by V. Y. Mudimbe, 427–34. Chicago: University of Chicago Press.

Miller, Christopher. 1998. *Nationalists and Nomads: Essays on Francophone African Literature and Culture*. Chicago: University of Chicago Press.

Miller, Christopher. 2010. "The (Revised) Birth of Negritude: Communist Revolution and 'the Immanent Negro' in 1935." *PMLA* 125, no. 3: 743–49. *JSTOR*. March 8, 2016.

"Modern Culture and Our Destiny" [La culture moderne et notre destin]. 1956. *Présence Africaine* 1 (June.–Nov.): 3–6.

Monod, David. 2001. "Disguise, Containment, and the *Porgy and Bess* Revival of 1952–1956." *Journal of American Studies* 35, no. 2: 275-312. JSTOR. May 19, 2016.

Morisseau-Leroy, Félix. 1944. "Les cours d'Eté des Instituteurs des Lycées." *Cahiers d'Haïti*, September: 2–3, 13.

Mostern, Kenneth. 1999. *Autobiography and Black Identity Politics: Racialization in Twentieth-Century America*. New York: Cambridge University Press.

Mouralis, Bernard. 1992. "*Présence Africaine*: Geography of an 'Ideology.'" *The Surreptitious Speech*, edited by V. Y. Mudimbe, 3–13. Chicago: University of Chicago Press, 1992.

Mullen, Bill V. 2015. *Un-American: W.E.B. Du Bois and the Century of World Revolution*. Philadelphia: Temple University Press.

Myrdal, Gunnar. 1962 [1944]. *An American Dilemma: the Negro Problem and Modern Democracy*. New York: Harper & Row.

Naison, Mark. 1983. *Communists in Harlem during the Depression*. Urbana: University of Illinois Press.

Ndiaye, Pap. 2008. *La Condition Noire: Essai sure une minorité française*. Paris: Calmann-Lévy.

Neptune, Harvey R. 2007. *Caliban and the Yankees: Trinidad and the United States Occupation*. Chapel Hill: University of North Carolina Press.

Nielsen, Aldon Lynn. 2005. "The Future of an Allusion: The Color of Modernity." In *Geomodernisms: Race, Modernism, Modernity*, edited by Laura Doyle and Laura Winkiel. Bloomington: Indiana University Press.

Nolan, Teodore. 1947. "Paul Robeson Thrills Panamanians." Special to *The People's Voice*. Paul Robeson Collection, Microfilm, reel #7, slide #264.

"Notre politique de la culture". 1959. *Présence Africaine* N.S. 24–5 (Fév.-Mai): 5–7.

O'Dell, Jack. 2020 [1971]. "A Rock in a Weary Lan': Paul Robeson's Leadership and 'The Movement" in the Decade before Montgomery." In *Climbin' Jacob's Ladder: The Black Freedom Movement Writings of Jack O'Dell*, edited by Nikhil Pal Singh, 199–214. Berkeley: University of California Press. Original published in *Freedomways* 11, no. 1: 34–49.

Padmore, George. 1971 [1931]. *The Life and Struggles of Negro Toilers*. Hollywood, CA: Sun Dance Press.

Paquet, Sandra Pouchet. 1982. *The Novels of George Lamming*. London: Heinemann.

Perucci, Tony. 2012. *Paul Robeson and the Cold War Performance Complex: Race, Madness, Activism*. Ann Arbor: University of Michigan Press.

Phillips, Kimberley. 2012. *War! What Is It Good For?: Black Freedom Struggles and the U.S. Military From World War II to Iraq*. Chapel Hill: University of North Carolina Press.

Pike, Fredrick B. 1995. *FDR's Good Neighbor Policy: Sixty Years of Generally Gentle Chaos*. Austin: University of Texas Press.

Piquion, René. 1944. "Qu'est-ce que le Nègre Américain." *Cahiers d'Haiti*, August: 6–11, 36.

Plummer, Brenda Gayle. 1988. *Haiti and the Great Powers, 1902–1915*. Baton Rouge: Louisiana State University Press.

Plummer, Brenda Gayle. 1996. *Rising Wind: Black Americans and U.S. Foreign Affairs, 1935–1960*. Chapel Hill: University of North Carolina Press.

Plummer, Brenda Gayle. 2013. *In Search of Power: African Americans in the Era of Decolonization, 1956–1974*. New York: Cambridge University Press.

Price-Mars, Jean. 2001 [1919]. *La Vocation de l'Élite*. Port-au-Prince, Haiti: Editions des Presses Nationales d'Haïti.

Price-Mars, Jean. 1943. "Trois Mois aux Etas-Unis en Guerre." *Cahiers d'Haiti*, October: 14–16.

Putnam, Lara. 2013. *Radical Moves: Caribbean Migrants and the Politics of Race in the Jazz Age*. Chapel Hill: University of North Carolina Press.

Rabemananjara, Jacques. 1977. "Alioune Diop, le cenobite de la culture noire." In *Hommage à Alioune Diop, Fondateur de Présence Africaine*, 17–36. Rome: Éditions des amis italiens de présence africaine.

Rampersad, Arnold. 1994. Introduction. In *Langston Hughes: The Return of Simple*, edited by Akiba Sullivan Harper, xv–xxii. New York: Hill and Wang.

Rampersad, Arnold. 2002. *The Life of Langston Hughes: Volume II: 1941–1967. I Dream A World*. 2nd ed. New York: Oxford University Press.

Ramsey, Kate. 2011. *The Spirits and the Law: Vodou and Power in Haiti*. Chicago: University of Chicago Press.

Randolph, A. Phillip. 1949. Letter. *New York Times*, October 9, 1949, p. E10. *ProQuest Historical Newspapers*. Web. February 7, 2014.

Ransby, Barbara. 2013. *Eslanda: The Large and Unconventional Life of Mrs. Paul Robeson*. New Haven, CT: Yale University Press.

Read, Jason. 2003. *The Micro-politics of Capital: Marx and the Prehistory of the Present*. Albany: State University of New York Press.

Redding, Arthur F. 2008. *Turncoats, Traitors, and Fellow Travelers: Culture and Politics of the Early Cold War*. Jackson: University Press of Mississippi.

Reid-Pharr, Robert. 2007. *Once You Go Black: Choice, Desire, and the Black American Intellectual*. New York: New York University Press.

Renda, Mary A. 2001. *Taking Haiti: Military Occupation and the Culture of U.S. Imperialism, 1915–1940*. Chapel Hill: University of North Carolina Press.

"Riot in Gallery Halts U.N. Debate." New York Times. 16 Feb. 1961. *ProQuest Historical Newspapers*. Web. April 4, 2014.

Rioux, Jean-Pierre. 1987. *The Fourth Republic, 1944–1958*. Translated by Godfrey Rogers. Cambridge: Cambridge University Press.

Robeson, Eslanda. 1951. "The Not So Strange Case of Paul Robeson." *California Eagle*, April 5, 1951, 1, 5.

Robeson, Paul. 1945. "Some Reflections on *Othello* and the Nature of Our Time." *The American Scholar* 14, no. 4: 391–92.

Robeson, Paul. 1952. "Here's My Story." *Freedom* 2, no. 3: 1. *NYU Libraries*. Web. February 12, 2019.

Robeson, Paul. 1988 [1958]. *Here I Stand*. Boston: Beacon Press.

Robinson, Cedric J. 2000 [1983]. *Black Marxism: The Making of the Black Radical Tradition*. Chapel Hill: University of North Carolina Press.

Robinson, William I. 1996. *Promoting Polyarchy: Globalization, U.S. Intervention, and Hegemony*. New York: Cambridge University Press.

Roediger, David. 1999. *The Wages of Whiteness: Race and the Making of the American Working Class*. Rev. ed. New York: Verso.

Rogers, Alan. 1985. "Passports and Politics: The Courts and the Cold War." *The Historian* 47, no. 4: 497–511. *ProQuest Periodicals Archive Online*. Web. January 23, 2014.

Rosenberg, Clifford. 2006. *Policing Paris: The Origins of Modern Immigration Control between the Wars*. Ithaca, NY: Cornell University Press.

Rosenberg, Jonathan. 2006. *How Far the Promised Land?: World Affairs and the American Civil Rights Movement from the First World War to Vietnam*. Princeton, NJ: Princeton University Press.

Rowley, Hazel. 2001. *Richard Wright: The Life and Times*. New York: Henry Holt.

Sallis, James. 2000. *Chester Himes: A Life*. New York: Walker.

Saunders, Frances Stonor. 1999. *The Cultural Cold War: The CIA and the World of Arts and Letters*. New York: The New Press.

Savage, Barbara D. 1999. *Broadcasting Freedom: Radio, War, and the Politics of Race, 1938–1948*. Chapel Hill: University of North Carolina Press.

Scharfman, Ronnie. 2010. "Aimé Césaire: Poetry Is/and Knowledge." *Research in African Literatures* 41, no. 1: 109–20. *Project Muse*. Web. Oct. 22, 2015.

Schmidt, Hans. 1995 [1971]. *The United States Occupation of Haiti, 1915–1934*. New Brunswick, NJ: Rutgers University Press.

Schreiber, Rebecca M. 2008. *Cold War Exiles in Mexico: U.S. Dissidents and the Culture of Critical Resistance*. Minneapolis: University of Minnesota Press.

Scott, David. 2004. *Conscripts of Modernity: The Tragedy of Colonial Enlightenment.* Durham, NC: Duke University Press.

Scott-Smith, Giles. 2000. "The 'Masterpieces of the Twentieth Century' Festival and the Congress for Cultural Freedom: Origins and Consolidation." *Intelligence and National Security* 15, no. 1: 121–43. *Humanities International Complete.* Web. May 18, 2016.

Sekora, John. 1987. "Black Message/White Envelope: Genre, Authenticity, and Authority in the Antebellum Slave Narrative." *Callaloo* 32 (Summer): 482–515. *JSTOR.* Web. June 24, 2014.

Shandell, Jonathan. 2007. "The American Negro Theatre: Staging Inter-racialism in Harlem, 1940-49." PhD dissertation, Yale School of Drama. *Dissertation and Theses Databases (ProQuest Only).* Web. 2 December 2015.

Shannon, Magdaline W. 1996. *Jean Price-Mars, the Haitian Elite, and the American Occupation, 1915–1935.* New York: St. Martin's Press.

Sharpley-Whiting, T. Denean. 2002. *Negritude Women.* Minneapolis: University of Minnesota Press.

Singh, Nikhil. 2004. *Black Is a Country: Race and the Unfinished Struggle for Democracy.* Cambridge, MA: Harvard University Press.

Singh, Nikhil Pal. 2010. "'Learn Your Horn': Jack O'Dell and the Long Civil Rights Movement." In *Climbin' Jacob's Ladder: The Black Freedom Movement Writings of Jack O'Dell,* edited by Nikhil Pal Singh, 1–68. Berkeley: University of California Press.

"6 Teen-Agers Seized as 350 Police Guard Against Racial Clash." *Chicago Daily Tribune,* July 27, 1949, 3. *ProQuest Historical Newspapers.* Web. February 9, 2011.

Smethurst, James. 2002. "'Don't Say Goodbye to the Porkpie Hat': Langston Hughes, the Left, and the Black Arts Movement." *Callaloo* 25, no. 4: 1–14. *Project Muse.* Web. Accessed March 5, 2016.

Smith, Matthew. 2009. *Red and Black in Haiti: Radicalism, Conflict, and Political Change, 1934–1957.* Chapel Hill: University of North Carolina Press.

Smith, Neil. 2003. *American Empire: Roosevelt's Geographer and the Prelude to Globalization.* Berkeley: University of California Press.

Smith, Preston H. 2012. *Racial Democracy and the Black Metropolis: Housing Policy in Postwar Chicago.* Minneapolis: University of Minnesota Press.

Spencer, Theodore. 1966 [1942]. *Shakespeare and the Nature of Man.* New York: Collier.

Spillers, Hortense. 2003. "The Crisis of the Negro Intellectual: A Post-Date." In *Black, White, and in Color: Essays on American Literature and Culture,* 428–70. Chicago: University of Chicago Press.

Städtler, Katharina. 1998. "Genèse de la literature afro-francophone en France entre les années 1940 et 1950." *Mots Pluriels* 8. Web. June 17, 2011.

Stein, Judith. "The Robeson Story." *Dissent* 36, no. 4: 573–75.

Stephanson, Anders. 2000. "Liberty or Death: The Cold War as U.S. Ideology." In *Re-*

viewing the Cold War: Approaches, Interpretations, Theory, edited by Odd Arne Westad, 81–100. Portland, OR: Frank Cass.

Stephens, Michelle. 2005. *Black Empire: The Masculine Global Imaginary of Caribbean Intellectuals in the United States, 1914–1962.* Durham, NC: Duke University Press.

Storrs, Landon R. Y. 2013. *The Second Red Scare and the Unmaking of the New Deal Left.* Princeton: Princeton University Press.

Stovall, Tyler. 1996. *Paris Noir: African Americans in the City of Light.* New York: Houghton Mifflin.

Stuckey, Sterling. 1988 [1958]. Introduction. In *Here I Stand,* by Paul Robeson, ix–xxiv. Boston: Beacon Press.

Swindall, Lindsey R. 2011. *The Politics of Paul Robeson's Othello.* Jackson: University Press of Mississippi.

Tinson, Christopher. 2017. *Radical Intellect: Liberator Magazine and Black Activism in the 1960s.* Chapel Hill: University of North Carolina Press.

Torpey, John C. 2000. *The Invention of the Passport: Surveillance, Citizenship, and the State.* New York: Cambridge University Press.

Trotsky, Leon. 1960 [1924]. *Literature and Revolution.* Ann Arbor: University of Michigan Press.

Tucker, William H. 2002. *The Funding of Scientific Racism: Wickliffe Draper and the Pioneer Fund.* Urbana: University of Illinois Press.

Urban, Wayne T. 1992. *Black Scholar: Horace Mann Bond, 1904–1972.* Athens: University of Georgia Press.

U.S. Congress, House of Representatives, Committee on Un-American Activities. 1947. *Hearings Regarding Communism in Labor Unions in the United States.* 80 Cong., 1 sess., February 27; July 23, 24, 25.

U.S. Congress, House of Representatives, Committee on Un-American Activities. 1956. *Investigation of the Unauthorized Use of United States Passports—Part 3.* 84 Cong., 2 sess., June 12, 13. *Internet Archive.* Web. October 23, 2013.

Véron, Kora. 2013. "Césaire at the Crossroads in Haiti: Correspondence with Henri Seyrig." *Comparative Literature Studies* 50, no. 3: 430–44. *JSTOR.* Web. March 4, 2015.

Von Eschen, Penny M. 1997. *Race Against Empire: Black Americans and Anticolonialism, 1937–1957.* Ithaca, NY: Cornell University Press.

Von Eschen, Penny M. 2000. "Who's the Real Ambassador? Exploding Cold War Racial Ideology." In *Cold War Constructions: The Political Culture of United States Imperialism, 1945–1966,* edited by Christian G. Appy, 110–31. Amherst: University of Massachusetts Press.

Von Eschen, Penny M. 2006. *Satchmo Blows Up the World: Jazz Ambassadors Play the Cold War.* Cambridge, MA: Harvard University Press.

Wald, Alan. 2002. *Exiles from a Future Time: The Forging of the Mid-Twentieth-Century Literary Left.* Chapel Hill: University of North Carolina Press.

Wald, Alan. 1994. "Lloyd Brown and the African American Literary Left." In *Writing from the Left: New Essays on Radical Culture and Politics*, 212–32. New York: Verso.

Walsh, John Patrick. 2013. *Free and French in the Caribbean: Toussaint Louverture, Aimé Césaire, and Narratives of Loyal Opposition*. Bloomington: Indiana University Press.

Warner, Keith Q. 1988. *Critical Perspectives on Léon Gontran Damas*. Washington, D.C.: Three Continents Press.

Warren, Kenneth W. 2003. *So Black and Blue: Ralph Ellison and the Occasion of Criticism*. Chicago: University of Chicago Press.

Warren, Kenneth W. 2011. *What Was African American Literature?* Cambridge, MA: Harvard University Press.

Washington, Mary Helen. 2003. "Alice Childress, Lorraine Hansberry, and Claudia Jones: Black Women Write the Popular Front." In *Left of the Color Line: Race, Radicalism and Twentieth-Century Literature of the United States*, edited by Bill V. Mullen and James Smethurst, 183–204. Chapel Hill: University of North Carolina Press.

Washington, Mary Helen. 2014. *The Other Blacklist: The African American Literary and Cultural Left of the 1950s*. New York: Columbia University Press.

Wenzel, Jennifer. 2006. "Remembering the Past's Future: Anti-Imperialist Nostalgia and Some Versions of the Third World." *Cultural Critique* 62 (Winter): 1–32. *Project Muse*. Web. August 19, 2008.

White, Walter. 1951. "The Strange Case of Paul Robeson." *Ebony* 6, no. 4 (Feb.): 78–84. *MasterFile Premier*. Web. March 3, 2014.

Whitfield, Stephen J. 1996. *The Culture of the Cold War*. 2nd ed. Baltimore: Johns Hopkins University Press.

Wilder, Gary. 2005. *The French Imperial Nation State: Negritude and Colonial Humanism Between the Two World Wars*. Chicago: University of Chicago Press.

Wilder, Gary. 2015. *Freedom Time: Negritude, Decolonization, and the Future of the World*. Durham, NC: Duke University Press.

Wilford, Hugh. 2008. *The Mighty Wurlitzer: How the CIA Played America*. Cambridge, MA: Harvard University Press.

Wilkins, Roy. 1949. "Robeson Speaks for Robeson." Editorials. *Crisis* 56 (May): 137.

Williams, Raymond. 1977. *Marxism and Literature*. Oxford: Oxford University Press.

Woods, Jeff. 2003. *Black Struggle, Red Scare: Segregation and Anti-Communism in the South, 1948–1968*. Baton Rouge: Louisiana State University Press.

Worthy, William, Jr. 1954. "Our Disgrace in Indo-China." *Crisis* 61 (February): 77–83.

Wright, Charles H. 1975. *Robeson, Labor's Forgotten Champion*. Detroit: Balamp Publishing.

Wright, Giles R. 2007. "Moving Toward Breaking the Chains: Black New Jerseyans and the American Revolution." In *New Jersey in the American Revolution*, edited by Barbara J. Mitnick, 113–38.

Wright, Richard. 1954a. *Black Power: A Record of Reactions in a Land of Pathos*. New York: Harper & Bros.

Wright, Richard. 1954b [1953]. Introduction. In *In the Castle of My Skin*, by George Lamming, v–viii. New York: McGraw-Hill.

Wright, Richard. 1956. "Tradition and Industrialization." *Présence Africaine* 8–10 (June–Nov.): 347–60.

Wright, Richard. 1965 [1950]. "I Tried to Be a Communist." In *The God That Failed*, edited by Richard Crossman, 103–46. New York: Bantam Books.

Wynter, Sylvia, and Katherine McKittrick. 2015. "Unparalleled Catastrophe for Our Species? Or, to Give Humanness a Different Future: Conversations." In *Sylvia Wynter: On Being Human as Praxis*, edited by Katherine McKittrick, 9–89. Durham, NC: Duke University Press.

Young, Crawford. 2010. "Ralph Bunche and Patrice Lumumba: The Fatal Encounter." In *Trustee for the Human Community: Ralph J. Bunche, the United Nations, and the Decolonization of Africa*, edited by Robert A. Hill and Edmond J. Keller, 128–47. Athens, OH: Ohio University Press.

Young, Cynthia A. 2006. *Soul Power: Culture, Radicalism, and the Making of the U.S. Third World Left*. Durham, NC: Duke University Press.

Young, Robert J. C. 2004. *White Mythologies: Writing History and the West*. 2nd ed. New York: Routledge.

Zien, Katherine. 2013. "Race and Politics in Concert: Paul Robeson and William Warfield in Panama, 1947–1953." In *Interoceanic Diasporas and The Panama Canal's Centennial*, edited by Claudia Milia and Ifeoma Kiddoe Nwankwo. Special issue of *Global South* 6, no. 2: 107–29. *Project Muse*. Web. August 8, 2014.

Žižek, Slavoj. 1993. *Tarrying with the Negative: Kant, Hegel, and the Critique of Ideology*. Durham, NC: Duke University Press.

Index